THE ECLIPSE OF 'ELEGANT ECONOMY'

The Eclipse of 'Elegant Economy'

The Impact of the Second World War on Attitudes to Personal Finance in Britain

MARTIN COHEN
Queen Mary University of London, UK

Routledge
Taylor & Francis Group

LONDON AND NEW YORK

First published 2012 by Ashgate Publishing

2 Park Square, Milton Park, Abingdon, Oxon OX14 4RN
711 Third Avenue, New York, NY 10017, USA

Routledge is an imprint of the Taylor & Francis Group, an informa business

First issued in paperback 2016

British Library Cataloguing in Publication Data
Cohen, Martin.
  The eclipse of 'elegant economy' : the impact of the Second
  World War on attitudes to personal finance in Britain. --
  (Modern economic and social history)
  1. Finance, Personal--Great Britain--History--20th
  century. 2. Consumption (Economics)--Great Britain--
  History--20th century. 3. Debt--Great Britain--Public
  opinion--History--20th century. 4. Public opinion--Great
  Britain--History--20th century. 5. World War, 1939-1945--
  Economic aspects--Great Britain. 6. World War, 1939-1945--
  Social aspects--Great Britain.
  I. Title II. Series
  306.3'0941'0904-dc23

Library of Congress Cataloging-in-Publication Data
Cohen, Martin.
  The eclipse of 'elegant economy' : the impact of the Second World War on
attitudes to personal finance in Britain / Martin Cohen.
      p. cm. -- (Modern economic and social history)
  Includes bibliographical references and index.
  ISBN 978-1-4094-3972-1 (hardcover) -- ISBN 978-1-4094-3973-8 (ebook)
  1. Great Britain--Economic conditions--1945-1964. 2. Finance,
Personal--Great Britain--History. 3. World War, 1939-1945. 4. Consumption
(Economics)--Great Britain. I. Title.
  HC256.5.C526 2012
  330.941'0855--dc23

                                                                        2011036627

ISBN 978-1-4094-3972-1 (hbk)
ISBN 978-1-138-24990-5 (pbk)

To Diana and the worshipped ground she walks on

Figure f.1   Prudential Group Assurance, Poster Publicity *c.* 1947–50
Note: Reproduced with kind permission of Prudential Group Archives.

Contents

Contents

List of Figures

Foreword

From the moment I read the early chapters of Martin Cohen's doctoral thesis my special curiosity was aroused. For his was a new approach to the post-war Britain into which I was born and whose assumptions I imbibed with my welfare-state provided cod liver oil and concentrated orange juice. I am so pleased that he has converted his research into a book which will have a percussive resonance for his own age group and fascinating vibrations for the current generation in an era of debt, recession and deficit reduction.

I grew up in a household whose family warmth was not matched by the balm of a rich flow of financial lubricant. I suspect both Martin and I carry within us what Richard Hoggart calls a 'siege economy of the mind' and share a horror of spending or borrowing beyond our means. This is why the early bloom of the first mass-consumption society ever to people these islands is such a vivid phenomenon caught on the Velcro of our memories.

But, for Martin, this world is a thing of hard facts and measurements, too. He has a passion for precision and *The Eclipse of 'Elegant Economy'* shows him to be a natural cartographer of spreading affluence, a gifted calibrator of financial flows and a careful analyst of the shifting states of mind they induced. His book is a hugely welcome addition to the economic, social and psychological histories of post-1945 Britain.

Lord Hennessy of Nympsfield, FBA.
Attlee Professor of Contemporary British History,
School of History,
Queen Mary University of London, UK

Acknowledgements

First and foremost I must repeat my sincerest thanks and acknowledge my great indebtedness to Dr Peter Catterall, Dr James Ellison, Professor Peter Hennessy, (especially for his wonderful foreword), Dr Dan Todman, and the late Professor John Ramsden of Queen Mary University of London for their constant help and counsel when writing my PhD thesis and for encouraging me to publish it in the much revised form of this book. I am equally grateful for the patience of others I tormented with earlier drafts, including Michael Heller, John Hubbard, James Obelkevich (for his particularly incisive criticism), Ross McKibbin, Alycen Mitchell, and Frank Trentmann, all of whom contributed invaluable comments and suggestions, time and again refocusing my ideas, enabling me to make improvements and, I trust, produce a lucid and interesting result.

The Mass-Observation archivists at the University of Sussex deserve my pre-eminent appreciation for their invariably courteous and helpful assistance on the numerous occasions they provided access to their unique collection. In particular, I must acknowledge their guidance in identifying documents in which observers, in defiance of contemporary convention, directly question the sensitive theme of personal finance and occasionally record their own comments on the response and thus provided my most productive primary source.

The archivists of the Prudential Group similarly deserve special commendation and thanks for their unfailing assistance and permitting the reproduction of the 'Ambassador of Thrift' poster. The group records shed invaluable light on the rarely acknowledged economic and social historical significance of personal financial security. I am similarly grateful to the staff of the Co-operative National Archives, whose indispensible advice on my visits to Manchester provided the source of my chapter on the movement, its members, and their attitudes to austerity. My grateful thanks are also due to Ken Culley CBE, the former chairman of the Building Society Association, for giving up his valuable time to enlighten me on building society history.

The perspectives on the era of true customer–manager relationship expounded through this book were made possible by researching the records of Britain's leading banks. The archivists of Lloyds Banking Group in particular have earned my special thanks for the many occasions on which they allowed me access to their files and for permission to publish advertisements. I am similarly appreciative of the co-operation of RBS (National Provincial, Westminster, William Deacons), HSBC (Midland), and Barclays (Woolwich Equitable Building Society). Other fruitful sources include the Bank of England Archive and Museum, British Library Newspaper Collection, Building Society Association, Institute of Chartered

Accountants library and archives, Maughan Library Institute of Taxation Collection, Museum of London sound archives, National Archives, National Savings and Investment, Post Office Archive, and Salvation Army Heritage Centre, all of whose archivists and assistants should be aware of my enormous gratitude for the edifying experience of researching their collections.

Finally, no words are adequate to express my gratitude to my wife, Diana, whose patience I have tried beyond reasonable endurance throughout the protracted gestation of this book.

List of Abbreviations

BB/WEBS	Barclays Bank/Woolwich Equitable Building Society Group Archive
BSA	Building Society Association
HSBCGA	HSBC Group Archive
LTSB	Lloyds TSB – Lloyds Banking Archive
MO	Mass-Observation Archive
NA, PRO	National Archives, Public Record Office
NCA	National Co-operative Archive
NSI	National Savings and Investments Archive
PGA	Prudential Group Archive
RBSGA	Royal Bank of Scotland Group Archive
RM	Royal Mail Archive
SAHC	Salvation Army Heritage Centre Archive

Modern Economic and Social History Series
General Editor's Preface

Economic and social history has been a flourishing subject of scholarly study during recent decades. Not only has the volume of literature increased enormously but the range of interest in time, space and subject matter has broadened considerably so that today there are many sub-branches of the subject which have developed considerable status in their own right.

One of the aims of this series is to encourage the publication of scholarly monographs on any aspect of modern economic and social history. The geographical coverage is world-wide and contributions on the non-British themes will be especially welcome. While emphasis will be placed on works embodying original research, it is also intended that the series should provide the opportunity to publish studies of a more general thematic nature which offer a reappraisal or critical analysis of major issues of debate.

Derek H. Aldcroft
University of Leicester

Prologue

In 1941 a bomb fell on our London home and my parents and I were evacuated to the garrison town of Colchester about fifty miles to the north east. I was then just eighteen months old. While my mind still harbours a few disjointed pictures of our life during the Second World War, my recollections of the ensuing years are naturally more vivid. Among them, one recurring scenario has haunted me through six decades because its prosaic detail invites so many questions about the unique spirit of the times to which history has hitherto failed to provide satisfactory answers.

***

Mr Springwell knocks at our front door. There is no bell. Before she lets him in, my mother hastily hides our modest bowl of fruit in the cupboard of our large ornate sideboard. She does that every Monday evening. Mr Springwell is as rich as Croesus, possibly richer, or that is how it sounds to me at the age of six or seven from the talk at home. He must never be allowed to see that we too are so rich that we indulge in the apples and pears from our garden and maybe a few plums or tangerines. He removes his bicycle clips and hangs his pork-pie hat on the hallstand; a melange of hooks, mirrors, drawers, cupboards and a tall empty wooden frame over a metal tray that I later learn is meant for umbrellas. We have no umbrellas. Even they are luxuries in the age of austerity. I never cease to be fascinated by the intricacies of my parents' furniture. It was built for them by a private cabinet maker when they married in 1936, some as reproduction antique and some in art deco style. They are very proud of it. It is valuable and, in a sense, heroic. It survived Hitler's attempt to destroy their pre-war home.

My mother offers Mr Springwell a cup of tea – not coffee, that is an expensive scarcity. He politely refuses, as he does every week. We are his last call of the day and he has drunk enough tea. My mother is secretly relieved. She would have felt compelled to put out a biscuit or two – another sign of our opulent lifestyle. Mr Springwell represents the London and Manchester Insurance Company, long since sucked into a maelstrom of mergers and takeovers, and he has come to collect the weekly payments for the simple policies into which my father pours his faith for our future security. I understand little of the conversation about mysterious things like endowments, life cover, bonuses and premiums, but soon the subject changes. 'There will be another war before long'. 'Britain is a conquered country; why else do we still have American bases on our doorstep?' '*They* (the American forces) don't have to worry about rationing'. 'We used to buy sweets for a farthing'.

'Conservative! What do we have to conserve?' Mr Springwell makes what for me is a particularly bewildering statement – I will hear it again more than once in my formative years: 'All *they* (unidentified) want is to get as much as possible out of life'. The conversation drones on. 'England is finished': it has lost another test match, whatever that is.

Eventually my mother hands over the precise premium in shilling and penny coins counted out in advance. No other money can be allowed to pass Mr Springwell's sensitive eyes. He makes his neat entries in our passbooks, bids us farewell and cycles off to his house a few doors away. My mother retrieves the fruit bowl, permitting me to steal a glimpse of the back of the cupboard that conceals the most guarded of her possessions: three or four dark-blue paper bags of plain white sugar.

Was this, or something like it, happening in millions of family homes throughout the country? Why did it matter if Mr Springwell saw our fruit? Would it really have made him think we were as rich as he and why did that matter? What riches lay within his semi-detached house, identical to ours in every detail including the peeling paintwork? Why did he ride a bicycle and not have a motor car? Why did he dress much like my father and not as I imagined a rich man? If my parents owned fine furniture had they too once been rich? Why did my mother lock away a few bags of sugar, surely not worth very much? Would there really be another war? I had been to a street party and seen a victory parade so I knew England (never Britain) had won the war – so why was it a conquered country? Why did we still have rationing and the Americans not? Why could I not buy sweets at all, let alone for a farthing? What did Conservative and conserve mean? Why would *they* (unidentified) want anything other than to get as much as possible out of life? Was my father really talking about sport when he said England was finished? He had given me an illustrated children's history book that showed it ruled a great empire, its kings and queens had defeated tyrants and invaders, it had produced the greatest writers and inventors and the character of its people was supreme among the nations. Was none of this true?

This book does not attempt to definitively answer all these questions but to explore the economic and social history that caused me to ask them.

Chapter 1

Introduction

There, economy was always 'elegant' and money-spending always 'vulgar and ostentatious;' a sort of sour-grapeism, which made us very peaceful and satisfied.

Elizabeth Gaskell, *Cranford*

Consumption has been shown to be central to discussions of gender, to cultural critiques of luxury, the rise of the bourgeoisie, the development of the modern nation state, the emergence of political economy and the commercialised market place, the end of both aristocratic clientage and the moral economy and the development of modern subjectivities through the categorisation of individuals as consumers ...

Consumption, consumerism, consuming, price and material culture are all crucial to our understandings of twentieth-century history.

Matthew Hilton[1]

The study of 'consumption, consumerism and consuming' that has come to prominence in recent years does not sit easily with the study of economic and social history. History is by definition retrospective, while consumption, from the viewpoint of the consumer, is anticipatory. The most perceptive of consumerist historians, including Hilton cited above, ignore or give small prominence to a basic tenet, familiar in one form or another to every student of commerce or marketing. *Nobody buys the physical thing they receive in exchange for a payment: they buy only an expectancy of benefit or pleasure to be derived from its consumption, ownership or practical use.* This rule is applicable not only to sustenance and material objects but to everything and anything that involves the disbursement of money. Consumption, consumerism and consuming must therefore embrace expenditure on culture, education, healthcare, security, travel and entertainment, as well as gambling, voluntary donation, obligatory taxation, savings, investment and more, where nothing tangible is expected or received in return for a payment. As personal financial situations improve, as they did in Britain in the 1940s and 1950s, the proportion of income and capital disbursed for such ethereal purposes inevitably grows much faster than for the acquisition of tangible commodities. Intangible consumption, consumerism and consuming, especially of money itself, must therefore be seen as of much greater historical significance.

This book explores the impact of the Second World War on the attitudes of the British people to their money and its usage. It combines a review of essential background history from 1939 until the end of the 1950s with comment on the cultural and political events which helped prompt a transformation from imperfect affluence, to imperfect austerity, and back to imperfect affluence. It also attempts to negate the allegation that during and as a result of this evolution, producers and entrepreneurs, through aggressive publicity or resourceful marketing techniques, in some way beguiled people into spending their money on that which they neither wanted nor needed. The leading proponent of that thesis, John Kenneth Galbraith proclaimed in *The Affluent Society*:

> Integrating outlay on advertising with the theory of consumer demand ... recognising that wants are dependent on production ... accords to the producer the function of both making the goods and making the desires for them. It recognises that production, not only passively through emulation, but actively through advertising and related activities creates the wants it seeks to satisfy ... The point is indeed obvious.[2]

Nothing could be less obvious. Galbraith and his defenders, notably fellow American Vance Packard in his anti-advertising thesis *The Hidden Persuaders*, fail to accept that no producer can successfully satisfy a 'want' unless it has been pre-created by natural human desire or nurtured by the culture of the society in which the end consumer lives. Commercial publicity in any form can never influence attitudes to expenditure, since in isolation it can neither create nor destroy the want and desire at the root of all markets. The economic and social history of Britain's age of austerity provides a particularly poignant illustration of how, in both material and ethereal markets, consumer expectancies of benefit and pleasure invariably evolve through forces beyond the control of commerce.

It must be explained at the outset that in preference to 'expectation' I mainly employ the term 'expectancy' for its air of greater uncertainty when applied to the attitudes of individuals as consumers. How often do we hear or say: 'I don't know what I want, but I'll know it the moment I see it'? However uncertain their nature, expectancies are present wherever there is demand and although they cannot always be precisely identified, they can at least be loosely categorised. For the purposes of this book I have designated three categories: *emotional* expectancies, stimulated for example by fear, hope, nostalgia, ambition or desperation; *conventional* expectancies, stimulated by peer pressure, class, rank, religious or national tradition; and *romantic* expectancies, stimulated by culture and every manifestation of the arts, most potently by the oral legends, myths and fairy tales we all learn in childhood. One or more of these expectancies is involved in every decision to spend or to save.

It would not only be close to impossible but fruitless to attempt to explore the countless avenues through which the entire population employed their money and I am aware of many omissions. There is no reference, for example, to expenditure on prostitution, narcotics and other vices, while investment in marriage for money is mentioned only briefly, partly because there can be no reliable evidence and partly because it can be safely deduced that these were of small significance in the financial affairs of the overwhelming majority. Food and drink, although intrinsic to every personal budget and not ignored, are given small prominence since they have been more than adequately dealt with by others, notably by Ina Zweiniger-Bargielowska in her brilliantly researched *Austerity in Britain* (2004). Also, with the exception of housing and motor cars, this book has little to add to the wide historiography of 'material' consumerism. Regional attitude variations too are deliberately sidestepped: not only are they complex and hard to clearly define but would contribute nothing of value to this already multifaceted study. Comparisons with other countries are avoided for similar reasons. I do, however, include considerable analysis of the national Budgets and their impact on personal finance. The individual taxpayer's reaction to legislative change has never featured prominently in historical literature: Martin Daunton's unique work *Just Taxes*, for example, provides an incisive discourse on the cause and effect of tax measures from the government's point of view. But before the advent of so-called 'money' columns, only on budget days did the press find issues of personal finance newsworthy from the individual's point of view. Contemporary commentary on the chancellors and their budget proposals thus provides some of the most reliable evidence of prevailing attitudes to personal finance.

During the Second World War the chancellors and their budget proposals impacted especially profoundly on prevailing attitudes to personal finance. For the first time, income tax became a factor in the lives of the majority – so did thoughts of tax avoidance and, in some cases, evasion. The innovative hire-purchase and term-payment schemes that had realised so much interwar consumer expectancy vanished, and with them personal debt and insolvency. The brutal curtailment of consumer choice by rationing and production controls also added a new dimension to consumerist decisions – a conflict between national and self-interest.

At the end of the war most British people were demonstrably left in a stronger personal financial position than at its outbreak but, like all wars, it also bequeathed pain and bereavement. Neither would be relieved nor comforted through the long aftermath of deep austerity, when their new-found wealth could not buy the British people the pleasures and benefits they most craved. While attitudes to these disorientating circumstances were inconsistent, they can be generally divided between those of the abject spenders who yielded to 'conspicuous consumption' and those of the initially greater numbers who stoically resisted it through the practice of 'elegant economy'. The definitions and significance of these diametrically opposed epithets will be explained and expounded through the following chapters.

Endnotes

1   Hilton, Matthew, *Consumerism in 20th Century Britain: The Search for an Historical Movement* (2003), 6, 9.
2   Galbraith, John Kenneth, *The Affluent Society*, 1958 (1999), 128.

Chapter 2
Fleeting Crescent
(*1918 to 1939 and Before*)

I have never accepted the view that war, post-war and pre-war are separate things.
War may be an intensification in the development of our lives, but there is no
definite break. Everything you do before a war determines largely what will happen
in the war, while everything you do in the war will largely determine what will
happen after the war.

Ernest Bevin, October 1942

There still lingers a sense of loss of respectability. We feel that the opportunity to
buy with cash would be better and more straightforward. We never talk to anybody
about our dealing with these clubs. Collectors call, and neighbours notice things
like that, still we keep it to ourselves as much as possible.

Mass-Observation survey respondent, January 1939[1]

Within a decade of the ending of both the First and Second World Wars talk
of gloom and despair gave way to talk of consumer boom. On both occasions
the transition was no whim of fate. On both occasions the British people were
given no financial reward for their sacrifice and victory but with resolve and
determination pulled themselves back from economic abyss. On both occasions
the needs and desires of ordinary people became more demanding in parallel with
regeneration and the development of mass-communication and mass-production.
On both occasions the revitalisation of commercial enterprise proved constructive
and of unequivocal benefit to both the individual and to the national economy. Yet
on both occasions overt money-spending was frowned upon by all sectors of the
community, just as it had been through a millennium of moral and legal censure.
Twentieth-century Britain remained unable to exonerate consumption – a natural
desire, which when fulfilled, has invariably made a constructive contribution to
every sphere of human activity.

The intuitive abhorrence of perceived extravagance in both religious and
secular tradition can be traced back beyond the advent of money itself. From the
prophets and scribes of the Old Testament to the orators of ancient Rome, luxury,
seemingly embracing the acquisition or use of anything beyond the demands of
primitive survival, has time and again been disparaged. In his work, *Consumption*,
sociologist Alan Aldridge records the condemnation of such indulgence in ancient
Greece, but like most commentators fails to provide a clear definition of the
wrong condemned by the fathers of philosophy or explain the motive of their

condemnation. He cites philosopher Roger Scruton's interpretation of Aristotle's argument that there is a profound distinction between happiness and pleasure:

> Pleasure is precarious because it depends on good luck but happiness is robust because it flows from virtue. Consumption delivers only pleasure, not happiness. But happiness, not pleasure, is the final goal of human life and only virtuous people can be happy.[2]

If this is true, then those who buy or attempt to buy pleasure or benefit for themselves can be neither virtuous nor happy. Whether or not this was the impression Aristotle intended, it is improbable that he would have been aware of the concept of consumption in any all-embracing sense. Aldridge himself writes that the term 'consume' was not used until the fourteenth century when, inevitably, it was given a series of derogatory meanings: 'to use up, destroy, devour, waste, squander or exhaust', while in the sixteenth century similar critical connotations were attributed to the word 'consumer'.[3] These definitions suggest that consumption meant no more than superfluous self-satisfaction. Even food, clothing and shelter, it was thought, were destructive and wasteful if greater than the absolute minimum necessary to sustain life, or worse, if associated with pleasure.

Peter N. Stearns, in the introduction to his study *Consumerism in World History*, was not the first to attempt a definitive interpretation but like all others it is flawed. Stearns applies no limits to consumerism but his reference to 'goods' would seem to exclude ethereal commodities:

> Consumerism describes a society in which many people formulate their goals in life partly through acquiring goods that they clearly do not need for subsistence or for traditional display.[4]

However desirable an alternative society, it has never existed in reality and probably could never exist. Mankind has acquired unneeded ornamentation and bodily adornment since primitive times, well before the advent of 'traditional display'. Nor can the needs of many people be said to be clear. Examples of one man's meat being another man's poison are legion. Christopher Berry devotes his perceptive *The Idea of Luxury* to a thoroughly researched but inconclusive attempt to differentiate between luxury and necessity. In particular he cites the complex anomalies that governments have always encountered in selecting luxuries for their many endeavours to tax private indulgence.[5] Stearns's definition is a paradox. Taken to its logical conclusion, everyone in a society free of the totally negative consumerism he describes would constantly vary his or her diet to equal the 'need' to replace expenditure of energy, and would change clothing with the 'need' dictated by every variation in temperature. This surely would promote greater 'need' and hence consumerism by any definition. Stearns appears to make the common error of confusing his innate moral distaste for self-indulgence, waste, and greed with evidence of human behaviour. To him and those of similar mind, a consumerist society is one prone to their own engendered perception of extravagance. The mid-twentieth century British attitude to personal finance can therefore only be fully appreciated by consideration of some of the long history of its evolution.

Probably the earliest recorded denunciation of the display of wealth in Britain was in the thirteenth century when zealous Franciscan brothers first arrived from Italy and preached and its message of the virtue of poverty to the barbaric natives. Converts and their descendants for centuries thereafter adopted this lesson as their edict to condemn consumption in all its concepts. Alan Hunt writes of 'perennial [religious] criticism of preoccupation with personal appearance and with fashion that is evidence of the sin of pride', citing Phillip Stubbes who in 1583 attacked 'the sinne of pride and excesse in apparel that induceth man to wickedness and sinne'.[6] Like so many followers of Christianity, before and since, Stubbes found in its creed the right to call down the wrath of the Lord upon those who spend their own money as they themselves see fit – a supposed sin not only to be condemned by the religious.

The first secular laws to regulate what might be recognisable as conspicuous consumption date from 1336. These banned anyone beneath the rank of 'knight and his lady' from wearing furs and limited their meals to '[no] more than two courses and each mess of two sorts of victuals at the utmost – except on the three principal feasts of the year'.[7] It was, however, widely held that the fabric of society could only be sustained if the echelons of the aristocracy and ruling classes were distinguishable from their vassals by appearance (an attitude not entirely exorcised by the mid-twentieth century). The twenty Sumptuary Acts decreed through the reigns of Henry VIII and Elizabeth I thus endeavoured to legally restrain forms of dress, dining and banqueting to designated standards in accord with social status. These unenforceable obligations, it was claimed, were imposed out of 'fear for the impoverishment of the landed classes and loss of patrimony through extravagant consumption'. Tudor nobles and courtiers were still expected to always publicly display the costly insignia of rank, which determined not only their privileges but their level of taxation.[8]

Also in the first Elizabethan era, Puritans arrived in Britain bringing with them a brand of Christianity synonymous with disproportionate abstinence. Their hosts regarded these pious newcomers as little more than troublemakers who believed it their duty to stand in judgement of their fellow Christians and publicly condemn them for the mildest profanity. In 1591 the citizens of Rye became alarmed at the appearance of a 'smale sect of Purytanes, more holy in shewe than in dede', the descendants of whom, for the next two centuries were to make an outstanding contribution to the economic prosperity of the Kentish port and simultaneously create a prodigious trail of misery.[9] The uncompromising precepts and ruthless business practices of the Puritans of Rye enabled them to make great personal fortunes, but according to local historian Paul Monod, having done so 'after the cultural revolution of the eighteenth century … left the austerity and self-denial of small-town Puritanism behind'.[10] Consumerist historian Robert

Bocock, considered such Puritan businessmen had held sufficient sway to enable them to operate:

> A system of production which employed a legally free wage labour force (as distinct from slaves or serfs) and which pursued the peaceful, systematic rational generation of profits through the sale of commodities produced for a free market … [It] also aided the growth of businesses because they reinvested the profits which they made, rather than spending them on a luxurious lifestyle.[11]

Although religious fundamentalism did not always prove so lucrative, British Christians remained faithful to the doctrine that frugality and self-denial will reap their own reward, especially at times of austerity. In Bocock's apt words:

> These cultural values were not determined by economic factors, even if they were affected by shortages both in periods of economic depression and during the Second World War. In other societies with less Protestant, puritanical cultural values, such as France, Italy and Spain, [they] have had values which have encouraged spending on what the British have traditionally defined as extravagant items – such as fashionable clothing, jewellery, eating and drinking well at home and in restaurants. These differences go back to the Reformation of the sixteenth century, and to the [Puritan] Cromwellian government of the seventeenth century.[12]

The joylessness and irrationality of unnecessary self-denial did not escape early intellectual recognition. Spending on extravagant items involved neither religious nor moral inhibitions for the pioneer economist, banker and reputed ruthless entrepreneur, Nicholas Barbon (1637–1698). To him it was:

> The wants of the mind, fashion and desire of Novelties and Things scarce that causeth trade. Trade in its turn has manifold advantages – it provides employment, improves the natural stock of the country, raises rent and improves yield, occasions peace, increases revenue, enlarges defensive capabilities and can help in the Inlarging [sic] of Empire.

This in essence was the thesis of Barbon's *A Discourse of Trade* (1690) which deeply influenced the Dutch born political philosopher, poet and satirist, Bernard de Mandeville (1670–1733) who, accepting his mentor's belief in the 'universality of desire', questioned the extent to which yielding to 'the wants of the mind' was inherently sinful. He was among the first bold enough to publish open criticism of those who proclaimed contempt for extravagance, whether on religious or moral grounds. In the face of contemporary Christian teaching, he bravely pronounced overt abstinence and needless frugality: 'virtues of dubious benefit to mankind' and wrote that 'the contempt of riches is seldom sincere'. He was also among the first after Barbon to argue that wealth generated by the sinful pursuit of pleasure brings great benefits to mankind.[13] In his epic poem which opens *The Fable of the Bees: or, Private Vices, Publick Benefits* (1705) he illustrates this dilemma with such lines as:

> The root of all evil, Avarice,
> That damn'd ill-natured baneful Vice,
> Was slave to Prodigality,
> That Noble Sin; whilst Luxury
> Employ'd a Million of the Poor,
> And odious Pride a Million more
> Envy in itself, and Vanity
> Were Ministers of Industry;

John Maynard Keynes, Britain's most respected economist of the mid-twentieth century still could find no definitive answer. Instilled in childhood with the ethics of the Victorian Anglican Church, even so clear a thinker as Keynes could not quite bring himself to fully condone the unrestrained disbursement of private money. Unable to decide if saving and spending were advantageous to the individual or to the economy in equal measure, he could do no better than to simply re-designate De Mandeville's conundrum 'The Paradox of Thrift'.

In the nineteenth century endeavours to establish middle-class superiority through overt abstinence and needless frugality had again become sufficiently practised for Elizabeth Gaskell to mock them in her satirical novel *Cranford*. The genteel ladies of this fictitious English village made a great show of economising down to those necessities they imagined essential to the maintenance of their social position, while fruitlessly trying to resist what they believed to be the iniquitous temptations of money spending. Their practice of 'elegant economy' exposed not only its own futility but that of its precise antithesis, 'conspicuous consumption'.

This most emotive of terms was coined by the Norwegian-American pioneer economist Thorstein Veblen in his celebrated work *The Theory of the Leisure Class* (1899). Despite lengthy commentary on its merits, and greater demerits, his definition is obscure but implies that consumption is conspicuous only when its satisfaction 'derives from audience reaction'. Veblen alleges that conspicuous consumption 'in order to be reputable must be wasteful, that is, not a "necessity"' and is the prerogative of the 'leisure class', but admits that in his *fin de siècle* America others were not exempt.[14] Conspicuous consumption was then, he writes:

> an essential way to establish reputation and respectability (and perhaps breeding) ... One's neighbours, mechanically speaking, often are socially not one's neighbours, or even acquaintances; and still their transient good opinion has a high degree of utility. The only practical means of impressing pecuniary ability on these unsympathetic observers of one's everyday life is an unremitting demonstration of ability to pay.[15]

Veblen's opinion of conspicuous consumption is barely more charitable than that of the prime guardian of Victorian morality, Samuel Smiles, who commended to those who had drawn life's short straw that abstinence be their constant companion on the road to 'self-help'. In common with almost all of similar persuasion, before and since, Smiles came from a wealthy supportive family and his advocacy of high but unaffordable principles would later be subjected to much ridicule. *Self Help*, *Thrift*, *Duty*, *Character* and his other works extolling the frugal lifestyle as the surest route to Heaven, nonetheless, for decades remained indispensible manuals for every aspiring social reformer. Like his contemporary Rochdale pioneers, (see Chapter 6) he too advocated the enigmatic concept of 'self-employment'. This term was not intended to commend to the equally indefinable 'deserving poor' that, with the least access to capital, they set up in trade on their own account. To Smiles, working-class self-employers were evidently those capable of earning an adequate living without resorting to outside help, while retaining constant control of their own financial affairs. Given the plight of the average Victorian worker, it is hardly surprising that the Smilesian school of well-intentioned social reform made so little inroad into the relief of poverty.

Although generally beyond the reach of the very poorest classes, Smiles was heartened by the expansion (*c.*1848–1875) of the 'friendly societies' he described as exemplifying 'a healthy spirit of independence amongst the working people … inculcating the values of respectability'. Rooted in freemasonry and aping its ritual, splendidly named bodies like The Independent Order of Oddfellows, The Ancient Order of Foresters, The Independent Order Reshabiles and The Hearts of Oak pursued the objectives of 'friendship, conviviality and benevolence'.[16] They attracted large numbers of mainly relatively prosperous working and lower-middle-class members[i] with free accessible reading rooms, ceremonial meetings and social events that added a pleasurable dimension to the mutually beneficial financial activity underlying their existence. Funded by subscriptions and donations, the societies offered assistance in the event of misfortune, poverty in old age, sickness, accident, death and funeral expenses; supposedly on a non-commercial basis. Principally due to the abysmal inadequacy of state welfare, by 1939 they had collectively achieved a reputed following of some fourteen million. During the war most of the cultural and ritual pursuits had to be curtailed, causing the friendly societies to emerge indistinguishable from commercial insurance companies. The post-war advent of universal state welfare had rendered their original *raison d'être* redundant. Some doggedly defended their cultural facade to the last, but their survival had become immutably dependent on competing in the commercial markets. It should not be forgotten, however, that the friendly society had been the most financially beneficial friend of the Victorian self-helping worker, when Victorian society provided him with very few financially beneficial friends.

---

[i]   By 1900 the Oddfellows had about one million members and the Foresters about 800,000 (Cordery, 2003, 160).

Not everyone agrees. 'One of the many myths about [English] Victorianism is that it was ruthlessly materialistic, acquisitive, and self-centred, [is demonstrated by] the enormous surge in social consciousness and philanthropic activity on the part of the middle and upper classes', writes American anglophile historian, Gertrude Himmelfarb. This is indeed a rose-tinted image of a Victorian era where materialism, acquisitiveness and self-centredness were certainly no myths. Himmelfarb herself cites the American writer Ralph Waldo Emerson who after a stay in England concluded that 'there is no country in which so absolute homage is paid to wealth', and French critic and historian, Hippolyte Taine, who was 'appalled by the ruthless money-worship'.[17] Such observations by occasional visitors leave little doubt that moneyed Victorians saw no virtue in concealing their wealth from their guests and peers. Their opulent homes, adorned with furnishings excessive in quantity and quality, were in stark contrast to the meagre belongings of the servants who slept beneath the same roof. 'Social consciousness and philanthropic activity' more commonly involved conspicuous charitable donation or undemanding voluntary work as a means of private exculpation or display of deference to the Church. Legislative reforms intended to ease the lot of the Victorian working classes generally proved unpoliceable and were widely violated, not least by industrial and commercial employers, themselves often overt philanthropists. Samuel Butler derides this social paradox in his satire *Erewhon*, where the worthy of this bizarre utopia, a parody of England, go to endless lengths to be seen depositing brightly decorated but worthless notes in 'musical banks' (churches), while their practical transactions are effected surreptitiously using a nondescript currency of genuine monetary value.

By the turn of the twentieth century the show of frugality had lost most of its social significance. The infamous prodigality of Edward VII inspired a minor rebellion against the sombre 'not amused' character of his mother's long widowhood. The display of wealth became a shield to protect middle- and upper-class cultures from the threat of financially ascendant inferiors. This imagined assault could be resisted, it was believed, only by a social infrastructure underpinned by money and distinguished, when not by aesthetic material possessions, at least by sartorial elegance. The working classes continued to take studious pride in their 'decent' dress and preserve their unpretentious collar and tie and 'Sunday best' for special occasions. The low-born aspirant to gentility would need exceptional good fortune, the strongest of wills, or both, to challenge his or her 'betters' by rejecting such deeply entrenched convention. The few who had the courage or acquired the money to do so were derided rather than admired; the antagonism meted out more by their peers than by those they tried to emulate. Laurie Lee's poetic observation of English rural life, *Cider with Rosie*, describes the brutal murder of an émigré returning from 'the Colonies' soon after the First World War. Apparently based on a true incident, the victim's only offence is to boast of the fortune he has made abroad and show some small contempt for his village contemporaries who still 'slogged for the squire … for a miserable twelve bob a week'. While it is improbable that ostentation *per se* was often the cause of gratuitous violence, working-class animosity to social and financial ambition, concurrent with admiration for those born rich and privileged, is indisputable and not entirely extinct today.

For the duration of the Great War the prestigious department store Harrods invented the slogan 'Business as Usual'. It was not quite business as usual. Gentlemen now ordered the fine-tailored uniforms of military rank, instead of City suits or country sportswear of social rank. And when the war was over, gentlemen again ordered the fine-tailored uniforms of social rank that no more protected them from awareness of the social devastation of the 1920s and 1930s than the fine-tailored military uniforms had protected their fellow officers who did not return. It would seemingly have required extraordinary insensitivity to ignore the bereaved, severely wounded, shell-shocked, *nouveaux pauvres* and the vast numbers of unemployed and resume the pursuits of privilege and wealth, but as the society columns of Britain's grand newspapers and the gossip columns of its rising tabloids testify, there were some who did just that. The press afforded little space to complimenting the often more than generous and, in most cases, anonymous donations of wealthy philanthropists when there were upper-class and *nouveaux riche* spendthrifts indulging in high jinks to write about in less complimentary terms. Even liberal journals contending that the 'bright young things' and the jazz lovers of the 'roaring twenties' brought desperately needed colour to a despairing nation, censured upper-class indulgence, on the flimsiest of pretext. Simultaneously other journals lauded images of the glamorous modern highlife and conveyed the impression that it was within the reach of their beguiled readers, on the flimsiest of pretext. For all its hypocrisy and distance from reality, this impression was to have a profound and enduring effect on attitudes to both personal finance and social mobility.

By the mid-1930s the nightmares of the First World War had tentatively begun to recede and, while an end to unemployment remained at best a daydream, the worst of the economic depression had passed. The National Savings movement, the building societies and the insurance companies were all expanding with the growing inclination to save and invest for an increasingly uncertain future. At the same time a growing proportion of the working and aspiring middle classes were experiencing their first taste of financial security and softening their approach to spending. Exciting new shops and department stores were opening, offering wider and more affordable choice. Mortgages and credit facilities were becoming more readily accessible. Conspicuous consumption was becoming less indictable. Families investing in their own home and taking pride in their new possessions were becoming less in awe of the judgement of their similarly placed neighbours, and making no secret of their Austin 10, art-deco furniture, 'New World' cooker, ready-to-wear fashionable clothes, well-filled larder, seaside holiday and domestic servant.

Harry Hopkins later wrote: 'Social equality was a potent idea, but it was technology, through mass-production and mass-distribution that had clothed it. It was Science that, at a dozen points, had broken the old class structure, throwing it into confusion'.[18] Hopkins was referring to the 1950s but his words are equally applicable to the late 1930s. The advance of technology, the foremost catalyst to cultural change, was also the foremost catalyst to resentment of cultural change. Contemporaries were convinced that the film *Modern Times* (1936) authentically predicted the individual spirit irreparably broken by mechanisation and electrification. Charlie Chaplin's imaginary chimera could be no more destructive while, in the real world, mass-production and mass-distribution could be no more constructive. They inspired rather than destroyed individuality. They relieved the monotony of the manual process. They created opportunities for personal fulfilment. They galvanised every branch of the arts. They aided the dissemination of culture and education. They improved health and healthcare. Above all, they satisfied consumer expectancy.

After the war the Labour Party, aiming to encourage support for socialism, lost no time in evoking working-class dread of a return to the anguishes of pre-war financial deficiency. Its organ, the *Daily Herald*, criticising the publication of a twelve-part Conservative policy plan, informed its readers:

> But under these headings nothing is suggested that departs from the traditional methods, which between the wars gave us mass unemployment and widespread malnutrition;which enabled a minority to profit from the exercise of 'individual initiative' at the expense of the community ... The Conservative policy is 'as you were' – and we will remember how we were.[19]

'We', presumably meaning committed socialists, were reminded of the excesses of the notorious means test, the great depression, the general strike, inflation, unemployment, unaffordable doctors, hospitals and medicines, slum dwellings, grasping landlords and oppressive employers. Historically indisputable and often terrible, none of these were universal realities. Asked in 1945 why people turned against Churchill, their supposed wartime hero, the new Prime Minister, Clement Attlee famously retorted: 'They did not turn against him; they turned against the Tories. They remembered what happened in the thirties'.[20] This too was no universal reality. Many people who voted Labour did so forgetting the social and political inequities and remembering the commercial innovations that to a greater or lesser degree had benefited every British citizen. They had hoped to elect a modern government which would both revive the best of their pre-war memories and fulfil the best of their post-war expectancies.

Yet when support for Labour began to wane in 1948, the party instigated a publicity campaign advising the post-war generation to 'Ask Your Dad'. A letter to the *Daily Telegraph* suggested that the origin of the slogan was the Book of Deuteronomy, where the wise are exhorted to 'ask thy father' about the blessings, not the evils, of times past.[21] Misguided propaganda commending the latter unsurprisingly backfired. As the now defunct right-wing *Recorder* put it:

The three wise men [Michael Foot, Herbert Morrison and Morgan Phillips]
should not have created a slogan which made people think. Above all they
should not have stirred memories into action. ... 'Bad old days be blowed',
roars Dad. 'When you earned money you had it to spend. What's more it bought
something. Now we just get it and hand it over to Stafford Cripps'.[22]

The *Daily Mail* in equally scathing mode painted an embellished picture of a
Britain where 'a working man could have his own car in the 1930s – but not
now' and where his wages went 'twice or four times as far'.[23] As the *Mail* surely
knew, few people had relinquished their yearnings for the benefits and pleasures
of pre-war innovation. No matter how ominous or oft repeated, forebodings of a
resumption of past atrocities would not alter the fact that personal expectancies
had risen, were rising, and would continue to rise. In the 1930s the normalities of
life had undergone a face lift at the hands of commerce, science and art, and to
be denied their progeny was as abhorrent to the war's survivors as a return to its
torments.

Not quite everyone welcomed interwar modernity with open arms. Before
paying for automated servants, possibly not up to the job, many consumers had
remained circumspect in their judgement of machines of questionable quality,
which might require regular and expensive maintenance. Labour-saving 'gadgets'
(as all forms of unfamiliar technology were disparagingly called, especially if of
American origin) were dismissed by working-class housewives as only for the
lazy, uncaring or those with more money than sense. Domestic machinery with the
power to vanquish the Smilesian virtues and the Protestant work ethic was similarly
shunned by the upper and middle classes, not for reasons of Luddism or economy,
but to maintain their inherent obligation to provide work for the servant classes.

Although this function was progressively being assumed by commercial
employers, notably the distributive and catering trades, the demise of the servant
classes would prove a more protracted process than is often imagined. The number
of domestic servants actually increased between the wars, principally due to high
levels of unemployment forcing those with jobs to remain with their private
employers and those without to accept domestic work as a last resort. There
were also more subtle reasons. The upper classes were reluctant to dispense with
retainers employed not simply for practical purposes but as a form of conspicuous
consumption intended to impress social status upon visitors to their homes.
Regardless of available time or the efficiency of domestic appliances, those
who regarded themselves as socially superior could hardly be seen to do their
own housework. In 1931 almost every family with an annual income exceeding
£400 employed one or more servants, of whom as many as half a million were
residential.[24] The new owner-occupiers of the 1930s building boom similarly
regarded the employment of domestic servants as a mark of social prestige,
although more often on a part-time or casual basis. Towards the end of the decade,
growing affluence as well as war preparation began to create large numbers of jobs
more rewarding than domestic service in both pay and conditions. As the supply

of housekeepers, maids, cooks and gardeners dried up, their former employers were left with little choice but to turn on the gas and electricity and to yield to the domestic manifestations of modernity.

The domestic manifestations of modernity were for some a major upheaval but were really a minor factor in the interwar evolution of consumerism. Printing technology had advanced in parallel with mass literacy and spread affordable access to the written word on a scale previously unknown. Roads, railways and passenger ferries had improved in parallel with enlightened employers providing holidays with pay and brought seaside excursions, tourism and travel to within the reach of millions. Typewriters, adding machines, punched-card collators, telephones and other office machinery had developed in parallel with savings banks, building societies, insurance and professional services, and offered financial facilities to unprecedented numbers. The new media of broadcasting and cinema had developed in parallel with the performing and graphic arts, and exposed the masses to culture, science, the world and its peoples, to diverse opinions and ideas – and to *instant* mass communication.

On 14th November 1922, the hitherto creators of consumer expectancy found themselves with an unwitting challenger, soon to become more influential than any in their wildest dreams. At first only a handful of enthusiasts listened to the weak signals transmitted by the British Broadcasting Company, but by 1927, when it was renamed The British Broadcasting Corporation (BBC), there were queues at post offices across the country to pay ten shillings for an annual licence[ii] to receive a daily diet of beautifully enunciated news, talks, reports, 'live' sporting events, music, drama and religion, all censored to the 'moral vision' of an uncompromising former engineer.[25] Andrew Crisell did not exaggerate when he described the BBC's first director-general, John (later Lord) Reith as an 'austere Calvinist Scot'.[26] Among Reith's immutable decrees was that the BBC shall never broadcast the most banal hint of profligate commerciality and no broadcaster shall speak the name of a business or branded product. Trade and the profit motive, like sex and vice, shall be regarded as if they did not exist.

As early as 1923 the BBC reassured the directors of *The Times*: 'We want to act in such a way that broadcasting may become an incentive to the public to buy more newspapers'.[27] As leaders of an industry dependent upon advertising revenue the directors undoubtedly would have welcomed this assurance, but as businessmen they might have soon realised that if non-commercial broadcasting can be an incentive to the public to buy more newspapers it can be an incentive to the public to buy more of anything else. Reith himself wrote: 'The BBC must lead, not follow its listeners'. In that it never wavered, but it did not always lead its listeners in the directions its director-general intended or approved. It became and remained as effective as any other media in creating consumer demand. To remain commercially viable *The Times* and its press competitors would have no option

---

[ii]   The radio licence fee remained 10s from 1922 until June 1946 when it was raised to £1.

but to compete with the BBC to retain the interest of their readers, who were also its listeners.

In its early days financial considerations tended to limit the number of BBC listeners. The first valve wireless which replaced the primitive crystal set and its crackly headphones, and enabled BBC broadcasting to be heard clearly was inordinately expensive (starting at £17 10s). The audience thus remained select and generally middle-class until about 1930 when the first mass-produced radios appeared at £5 to £6. Although still a fortnight's wages for an average worker the entertainment value, even of Reith's staid offerings, proved so enthralling that even the poorest somehow managed to raise the money. Whereas in 1923 just 125,000 broadcasting licences had been issued, by 1939 over nine million per annum were being bought by listeners of all classes.[28]

Class was included in Reith's policy of total impartiality but given the cost of listening and the edifying nature of the programmes early broadcasters could be forgiven for presuming to address a middle-class audience, adhering to middle-class values, and following middle-class conventions. The BBC, never to be led by its listeners, evoked the exemplary English lifestyle and code of behaviour it (or its director-general) considered appropriate to audience aspiration, and emerged as the most effective leader of taste and fashion. Concurrently but not coincidently, Marks and Spencer expanded dramatically to become Britain's most successful chain store without placing a single advertisement. It had no need to advertise. Reith's middle-England paradigms, invariably endorsed by his rival media, disseminated sufficient publicity at no cost. To meet the expectancies of the British mass market the directors and executives of Marks and Spencer need only listen to the BBC and match affordable merchandise to what they heard. They were not alone. Broadcasting inspired every type of producer, retailer and service provider to empower consumers, rich and poor, to emulate its ethereal product. Reith might have been surprised and no doubt displeased to discover, if he ever did, that his BBC so ably promoted the very commercialism he so studiously disdained.

Even less would he have appreciated its leading role in nurturing the 'cult of celebrity', which has never failed to galvanise commerce. It did not take radio commentators long to learn the art of painting seductive word pictures. Society journalists and fashion experts were engaged to articulate detailed descriptions of well-known personalities, well-dressed spectators and, above all, royalty attending public occasions and sporting events like Ascot, Henley and Wimbledon. Eloquent portrayal conveyed a sense of intimate acquaintance as inspirational as encountering the celebrities in photographs, film appearances or even in the flesh. Regardless of how obviously embellished, such seemingly unblemished portraits could motivate listeners to buy, or attempt to buy, the lifestyle trappings of role models they had neither seen nor heard.

Romantic consumerist expectancy was also the greatest by-product of the cinema's progression from silence to sound. Images of infinite diversity with dialogue and music captivated audience fascination in a way that no author, journalist, photographer or even radio broadcaster could match. Films mainly shot in black and white were coloured by the cinemagoer's imagination which could effortlessly romanticise every feature of a star's screen appearance, clothing, voice, behaviour, home and possessions, exotic or familiar. American films and their actors, despite an enduring image to the contrary, adhered to much the same conservative conventions as their British counterparts. The cowboys of the Wild West and the desperate New York gangsters always managed to be neatly groomed, well dressed, clearly spoken and avoid vulgar expletives. Contemporary scenes and protagonists reflected the styles and tastes presumed acceptable to their audience. The theatre and its directors too took the attitudes of their comparatively small but overwhelmingly middle-class audience for granted. Even the music halls mocked their working-class audience for its inability to adhere to middle-class convention.

The more media creativity motivated conventional, emotional and romantic expectancies, the further the distributive trades pushed new bounds. The doors of their department and chain stores were opened for all to enter uninhibited by obligation to buy, class consciousness or lack of money – in theory. Fervent retail competition spawned special promotions, discounts and seasonable sales permitting, if not the poorest, at least those of modest means, access to a new world of consumption. Simultaneously service providers mushroomed, promoting non-material expenditure as never before. Commercial expansion demanded workers. Unemployment, in some areas, was showing signs of abatement and personal financial situations were showing signs of improvement.

Among those whose financial situations showed signs of improvement was a younger working-class generation able and inclined to spend its wages on benefits and pleasures over and above basic necessities. For the first time 'youth' become a market in its own right. David Fowler explores this phenomenon in depth in *The First Teenagers*, commenting that young people acquired a taste for 'invariably enjoying a standard of living higher than that of the rest of the family'.[29] Fowler is right to go no further than to attribute to them nothing other than the enjoyment of a higher standard of living. Changes in young people's attitudes were not extraordinary. British youth was not yet ready to confront British convention head on. Not until the late 1950s would a clearly identifiable 'youth culture' openly affront social uniformity and attempt to buy distinctiveness as an end in itself. Modernity had nonetheless begun the transformation in young people's expectancies destined to resurface reinvigorated by the waning of post-war austerity. In the 1930s radical dissent remained a rarity, but a new spirit of curiosity and adventure had been aroused.

Usually due to financial necessity more than 80 per cent of interwar working-class youth had left school by their fourteenth birthday with few opportunities for further education or vocational training.[30] But most were at least literate. The ability to read and the rapidly changing environment together generated growing demand for information and literature. Development in printing and distributive technology met this demand and publications could now be circulated in their millions rather than tens of thousands. By the mid-1930s the *Daily Express* was selling more than two million copies a day and the *Daily Mail* one and a half million. Alongside the national and local newspapers a plethora of modestly priced journals, especially women's magazines, rapidly enlarged their circulations. For the outlay of a few coppers, everyone could reap a harvest of enlightenment, advice, opinions and practical information.[31]

Even schoolchildren could be encouraged to spend their pocket money to augment their education. Arthur Mee published his *Children's Newspaper* aimed, to say the least over-optimistically, at 'educating the next generation to save the world from the sins and follies and blunders of this'. With the attributes of a quality newspaper this unsurpassed weekly continued to inform and entertain children and many adults too until 1965. Mee's equally outstanding *Children's Encyclopaedia*, with complete clarity and never yielding to condescension, inspired children not only to read and seek knowledge, but introduced them to poetry, music, sports and other leisure and cultural pursuits. Originally published in affordable monthly instalments, bought by or for children of all classes, the collated ten-volume encyclopaedia was distributed through many editions before and after the war.

The interwar working and expanding middle classes took every opportunity to buy reading matter of every kind. Special editions of reference works, classical and popular novels, offered in collectable series as newspaper and periodical promotions sold in their tens of thousands and more. According to Richard Hoggart, self-educators bought two million copies of H.G. Wells' *Outline of History* and his *Science of Life* and *Work, Wealth and Happiness of Mankind*. The Watts Thinker's Library one-shilling editions of the works of philosophical and political luminaries, as well as specialist publications like those of Gollancz's Left Book Club, all similarly enjoyed a wide following across the social divide.[32] Rooted in the eighteenth century, when small groups of literary enthusiasts pooled their limited resources to acquire private libraries, the circulation of mail-order book clubs escalated.[33] Each month publisher or bookseller proprietors sent a copy of a recent novel to their fixed-rate subscribers throughout the land. They offered no choice, did not accept books back when read, and were expensive compared to the public or subscription libraries, and yet retained their popularity for many years. The book club was a respectable form of conspicuous consumption: collections of its uniform volumes took pride of place on the bookshelves of its mainly middle-class members, while the 'book of the month' proved their most dependable conversation piece.

The proliferation of the printed word produced a concurrent burgeoning of advertising and associated industries. Ubiquitous press advertisements, posters, leaflets and creative promotional material demanded a moment of attention and perhaps of thought – not necessarily shallow thought. The role of commercial publicity in the advance of popular education remains almost totally unacknowledged. No qualifications were required for admittance to the open university of the cigarette card that provided free illustrated lectures on every conceivable subject, condensed into two inches by one. Press advertisements often afforded detailed and thought-provoking, if not always entirely accurate, discourses on the research, raw materials, processes and design work in promoted products, often throwing in enlightening irrelevancies. Even though advertisers had yet to appreciate the advantages of minimal wording, reading created knowledge, knowledge created money, and money created expectancy of a more fulfilled personal or family lifestyle.

By far the strongest evidence of interwar intensification of personal expectancy can be found in the streets of surviving houses and terraces in the towns and cities of Britain, to this day sought after as fashionable homes. The annual average of 334,405 houses completed between 1935 and 1938 exceeded all records.[34] Private sector homes, in marked contrast to many of their predecessors and post-war successors, were designed to meet both the practical needs and the conventional and romantic expectancies of their owners. Architects responded resourcefully and creatively to the challenge of the first generation to be inspired by mass communication. Indoor toilets, bathrooms, water heaters, gas points, electric wiring and lighting became standard fittings, although central heating was as yet no substitute for the romantic appeal of the open fireplace with its familiar hearth and mantelpiece. The British home was no place for the bulky iron radiators that had long defaced the nation's distinctly unromantic factories, schools and public buildings. On the other hand, the British homeowner needed a place to keep the motor car he would buy at the first opportunity. Many new houses now featured integral or detached garages, while the comparatively few urban blocks of flats now provided parking spaces or garages for their residents. Only the benefits and pleasures of owning a motor car equalled and, in some minds, exceeded those of a owning a home. Motoring 'became a central factor in the lifestyle of approximately one in five families': from just 109,000 in 1919, by 1939 over two million cars were on the roads of Britain.[35] These unmistakeable marks of an embryonic affluent society were everywhere to be seen.

And everywhere to be seen were the marks of another society where there was no embryonic affluence, no prospect of owning a car, or even of raising the money to buy one of Britain's millions of near-derelict worker's dwellings. Still the smoke from the chimneys of the notorious barely habitable back-to-back terraces blackened the landscape of the industrial north. No tears were shed for the 342,940 such homes demolished between 1930 and 1939 in slum clearance programmes, except perhaps by their former landlords compensated only with basic land values for compulsory requisition. Local authorities used the land to build new houses for working-class families to be leased at heavily subsidised rents, varying from place to place but always kept within the budget of a low-paid worker. In 1932, for example, a fortunate tenant paid 10s 9d per week for a new three-bedroomed council house in Sheffield or 12s 11d for four bedrooms. That was more than double the average rent of their former slum accommodation, but never more than a third of the income of all but 7.3 per cent of the new occupiers.[36]

The working-class population was growing fast and the 1,112,000 council dwellings constructed between the wars fell far short of demand. The small minority of applicants who secured a tenancy generally appreciated their good fortune and delighted in the modern amenities, often beyond anything in their previous experience. Most took a pride in maintaining their new homes and buying the best furnishings and decorations they could afford. Contrary to popular legend, they found no difficulty in adapting to comparatively luxurious surroundings. John Burnett dismisses as a myth, the celebrated stories of former slum dwellers using their unfamiliar bath to store coal, but cites reports of large families found huddled in a single room apprehensive of the cost of lighting and heating an entire house.[37] Certainly another myth romanticised over time is the existence of a widespread yearning for the lost community spirit and traditional cultures of working-class life. A degree of nostalgia was natural enough and the council estates had more than their share of faults and failings, but few, if any, of their tenants would have returned by choice to a squalid nineteenth-century industrial ghetto.

It involved the largest single disbursement of personal finance in a lifetime, but owning a home in preference to renting became the foremost aspiration of anyone believing themselves in a position to buy. By 1938 owner-occupation escalated to 32 per cent.[iii] Of the four million domestic properties built between the wars, 72 per cent were to private order or sold on the open market, mostly to first-time buyers.[38] Architects blended features evocative of a picture-book English country life with the demands of urban and, increasingly, suburban life. 'Stockbroker Tudor' with its exposed mock beams and plasterwork was not a style to be derided: it answered the romanticism of the first 'upwardly mobile' generation who, like the 'first teenagers', wanted to enjoy a higher standard of living than their parents. As John Benson puts it, 'Every Englishman was, or felt he was, a disinherited country gentleman'.[39] While an inspired architect and a skilled builder could realise that illusion, they could not realise the illusory lost inheritance – the finance had to be realised elsewhere.

New building societies appeared throughout the land to meet the accelerating demands of would-be buyers. At the end of the First World War private mortgage debt had amounted to no more than £60 million, by 1930 it had reached £316.3 million, and by 1937 that had more than doubled to £636.1 million.[40] Interwar building society advances totalled £1,600 million, when a comfortable three-bedroomed house could be bought for between £400 and £600.[41] Buyers had begun to appreciate that their new home was a vehicle to a better lifestyle and their mortgage a vehicle to financial independence. Ironically, at the outbreak of the Second World War, British people enjoying the novel experience of home equity had never felt more secure.

One route by which that equity and security might be acquired was known as the 'builder's pool': an arrangement employed when mortgage demand overwhelmed supply, as it often did in the 1930s housing-boom years. Without this simple scheme many successful buyers, especially first-time buyers, would have stood no chance in the housing market. In essence it worked as follows:

[iii]   The percentage of owner-occupiers (10 per cent in 1901) fell temporally after the war as a result of bombing but recovered to 44 per cent by 1961.

a house builder deposited an agreed sum with the building society which had rejected his prospective buyer's mortgage application. By doing so he both partly financed the purchase himself and provided the building society with the comfort of a secondary security. The mortgage would then be granted, the sale completed, and when the buyer had repaid sufficient capital, the deposit reimbursed to the house builder.

The 'builder's pool' continued to be widely employed until 1937 when the case of *Borders versus Bradford Third Equitable Building Society* ended its short but invaluable existence. Counsel for Mrs Elsie Borders of West Wickham successfully argued that the practice contravened the Building Society Acts, after it emerged that Morrell (Builders) Ltd had 'misled' her by failing to properly explain the arrangement. Regardless of the fact that Mrs Borders had fallen well into arrears, the court invalidated her contract and forfeited the Bradford building society's rights of repossession.[42] Though the judge ruled that the builder's collateral *per se* was not illegal, the Building Societies Association (BSA) immediately made successful representations to the government for it to be banned. And with the passing of the Building Societies Act 1939, the builder's pool was outlawed and forgotten.[43]

It is perhaps worth briefly pausing here to reflect on how many of the losses on so-called 'sub-prime' mortgages in recent years might have been avoided had the builder's pool remained legal or had similar arrangements been subsequently sanctioned.

The pre-war Act did introduce some long-overdue protection for future mortgagers. Among other provisions it eliminated conflict of interest by prohibiting the use of the same solicitor by both parties to a mortgage contract. It also incorporated the BSA members' code of conduct, endowing it with statutory recognition and the societies with professional status. Since their first conception in the early nineteenth-century building societies had asserted that their prime mission was, without prejudice or favour, to assist all lacking the capital to buy a home outright. According to Burnett,'by 1938 1.3 million borrowers were taking advantage of the buyer's market to move into home-ownership and a growing proportion of them were wage earners': 37 per cent claimed the Abbey Road Building Society,[iv] one of the largest in the country.[44] The level of prejudice and favour employed by societies in selecting their wage-earning borrowers nonetheless remains open to question. In common with all BSA members, the Abbey Road denied all discriminatory policies and said it would lend to anyone providing evidence of adequate stable income from a legal source regardless of class or political opinion. Historian Paul Johnson is more sceptical suggesting that, however creditworthy, a working-class applicant could seldom expect a warm welcome or a favourable result. In his words:

[iv]   The Abbey Road merged with the National Building Society on 1st January 1944 to form the Abbey National Building Society (acquired and renamed by the Spanish group Santander in 2010).

> The mythology of building societies tells a glorious story of facilities advanced
> to these self-governing groups of working-class capitalists for the erection or
> purchase of private residential accommodation ... But neither in the early years,
> nor during the period of rapid expansion between the wars do the societies
> seem to have made a major appeal to workers whether agitators or respectable
> artisans.[45]

Whatever the truth, the upswing in mortgage advances in the 1930s could not have been achieved without attracting *depositors* of all classes. A highly competitive and evidently antagonistic 'publicity war' developed between the leading societies, which persuaded many working-class savers to abandon their familiar post-office, savings-bank or savings-club account.[46] Transferring their money to a building society purchased a step towards a home of their own, to house, not only themselves and their family, but the material possessions that any savings remaining after payment of the purchase deposit or their future income might buy.

The rise of Britain's 'acquisitive society', to which economists like R.H. Tawney and Ferdynand Zweig attach such great significance, can thus to a large extent be attributed to the housing boom of the 1930s. Acquisitiveness played a key role in transforming attitudes to the use of personal finance both before and after the war, but it must be reiterated that the transformation did not originate in product promotion. In the interwar years the advertising industry was still in its infancy, although developing fast in size, scope and expertise in parallel with new related professions, including brand image creation, marketing, public relations and, most commercially influential, market research.

Market research, though misunderstood, mistrusted and much maligned, to its credit has never claimed to explain the origins of consumer demand, only to attempt to measure its level. Early researchers discovered that markets are protean, cloudlike, incessantly moving, changing in volume and shape, and capable of self-destruction. They also demonstrated beyond reasonable doubt that professional promotion can achieve nothing for any given product other than capture a share, or greater share, of a prevailing market. Often producers and retailers failed to accept this as the invariable truth and, as many still do, put their trust in their own business acumen, experience or 'feel for the market' – occasionally with spectacular success and occasionally with spectacular failure. When put to the test, consumer demand rarely exceeded the ascertained estimates even of interwar researchers working with archaic resources. For all its inevitable inaccuracy, market research proved the businessman's most dependable lodestar. However much he spent on advertising and promotion, his every attempt to thrust his product upon a market demonstrated to be unreceptive was doomed to failure.

Full appreciation of the purpose of advertising and its effect on receptive markets had far to go. Advertisers had yet to learn the impact of remote images on consumer expectancy.[47] A courageous few, nonetheless, did begin to deviate from purely factual information, line illustrations and 'pack shots', by instigating innovative campaigns using lateral association to pursue brand loyalty without resorting to direct persuasion or incentive. Outstanding among the early examples of this type of advertising are the unforgettable images that sold Pears soap and Guinness.

To promote its mundane product Pears employed the pre-Raphaelite artist Sir John Everett Millais's painting of a small boy blowing bubbles. This delightful fantasy blinded the beholder to the reality that in a great many homes there was little delight in the weekly bath night when kettles were boiled to fill a tin tub for the whole family to use in turn.[v] The water grew cold before there was time to blow bubbles, or even to admire the semi-transparency and the pungent coal-tar aroma that distinguished Pears from its competitors. Other soaps performed the same function, some were more pleasantly perfumed, softer on the skin and often cheaper but Pears appeal to romantic expectancy outweighed all of this and won the lion's share of the British soap market for many years.

And nothing could have been more remote from the drab public houses and their sawdust-covered floors, where most Guinness was sold and drunk, than the colourful cartoons that enlivened its posters and advertisements. Their zoo animals and quirky human characters became so familiar that, uniquely for their time, they could convey their message without words. Sometimes a remote metaphorical slogan was added to assist the improbable mental association of simplistic childish images with the flavour of Guinness, but in general they portrayed creatures of few words. That was perhaps as well, since they could never have articulated the quality that distinguished Guinness and ensured its disproportionate percentage of the beer market. These advertisements were to prove the pioneers of the psychological techniques of emotive or romantic correlation that have predominated in advertising since the advent of commercial television in the 1950s.

Meanwhile, most mass-producers chose to err on the side of caution and concentrate only on either long-proven or clearly emerging markets. Increasingly challenged by the demands for liberation from its claustrophobia, Victoriana, with its innate inference of convention and respectability, clung to its dominance of domestic retailing. At the same time growing prosperity and media acclaim for the benefits and pleasures of modernity created interest in the distinctive geometric styles that originated in the France of *La Belle Époque*, now universally recognised as 'art deco'. For British consumers, art-deco architecture, interior adornments, furnishings, practical domestic objects and ornaments provided both a departure from convention and a conspicuous suggestion of culture. They were not just fashionable or useful but were regarded as a superior alternative to the vulgarities and ostentation of Americanisation, ignoring that the art-deco movement was as influential, or possibly more influential, in America as in Britain. Stripped of prejudice, American imports of almost every kind were not vulgar, ostentatious or devoid of culture.

---

[v]   The 1923 Housing Act requiring a fixed bath in all new houses had to be replaced by the 1924 Act, requiring the bath to be installed 'in a bathroom' (Burnett, 1993, 232).

American films, magazines and advertisements depicted clean-lined hygienic, all-electric homes, practically and comfortably furnished with efficient labour-saving appliances, obligatory telephones and large gleaming motor cars parked on private drives. In these fine dwellings lived healthy, well-dressed people enjoying prosperous and fulfilled lifestyles. Such stage-managed scenes bore no resemblance to most British or indeed most American homes or lifestyles, but indicate that expectancies of modernity on both sides the Atlantic had more in common than was generally accepted. The supposed negative influence of Hollywood was particularly exaggerated. Its filmmakers fully understood that the cinema, in Jeffrey Richards' phrase, 'deals in drama, dreams and myths' and that Britons, like Americans, went to the cinema to escape reality and forget their troubles for a few hours.[48] The audience, too, fully understood that they could emulate neither the projected celluloid paradise nor the gaudy art-deco interior and comforting central heating of the picture palace itself. The impressions they left were nonetheless deep and enduring.

The cinema, for example, contributed more than any other media to broadening the appeal of foreign travel. Before the First World War, apart from seamen and men on military service, the wider world was the exclusive preserve of the rich international businessmen and the still richer upper classes who traversed the oceans in the opulence of grand liners or spent their summers luxuriating in fashionable resorts on the Mediterranean coast. Between the wars the development of cross-channel ferry services and continental railway systems made it possible for the British working class to contemplate its first trip abroad. Burgeoning travel agents, notably Thomas Cook, The Polytechnic Touring Association (Poly Tours) and The Workers' Travel Association began to open up the playgrounds of Europe at affordable prices. They were beyond the reach of all but a tiny minority, but the adventurous few made their presence felt. Seemingly half a century premature, 'a French newspaper' reported in 1926 that 'Cannes was full of the British unemployed who had spent their dole money on a trip to the Riviera'.[49] The negligible dole money in the year of the General Strike would hardly stretch to a trip to the French Riviera and there can be little doubt that, regardless of class, all but a very few of the 600,000 tourists per annum who visited the Continent in the early 1920s paid from their own resources. In 1936 pre-war tourism reached its peak. The 1.4 million, mainly middle-class tourists who travelled abroad still represented little over two per cent of the population.[50] Thereafter, as the news from Europe grew more ominous, tour operators found themselves straining to attract business, intensifying their publicity and stretching their imaginations, sometimes perhaps a little too far. In 1938 Poly Tours, offering trips to the Rhine, picturesquely presented Hitler's Germany with its swastika flag as 'The Land of Dreams Come True', while Thomas Cook commended the barbarous Nazi state for its 'art, life and music'.[51] Such promises undoubtedly tempted a few stalwarts seeking the supreme German culture of times past, but the 1939 continental tourist season was ended before it had begun. The now inexorable yearning for foreign adventure would have to be suppressed for six long years.

By 1937 the majority, unable to afford a trip abroad, had been given the chance of a holiday within Britain's shores – often their first and some fifteen million people per annum were taking a break from work for a week or longer, most with a financial contribution from their employer.[52] Paid holidays were enjoyed by about nine million workers earning less than £250 per annum by the time that the Holidays with Pay Act 1938 entitled everyone with a job to a minimum of one week per annum paid leave and all bank holidays. In response to the growing appetite for holidaymaking, the local authorities of popular seaside resorts made unprecedented investments in new amenities, attractions and the promotion of their towns.[53] Hotels, boarding houses, restaurants, fairgrounds and entertainment venues mushroomed around the coast. Families unable to stretch to a whole week could at least find the cost of a day's outing; perhaps to spend the morning on a beach, now cleaned by the local council and equipped with public conveniences, changing facilities, deckchairs for hire, and with cafes and amusements parks close at hand; the afternoon enjoying the bright attractions of a recently purpose-built pier or promenade; and the evening admiring sea-front animated illuminations, before returning exhausted on an overcrowded special excursion train or coach. Whether they stayed a few hours, a week, or a fortnight they took home nothing tangible, except perhaps one or two cheap souvenirs, but few believed they had wasted their money. Seaside holidays had become an indispensible form of ethereal consumption and for some even a form of conspicuous consumption, a status symbol for aspirants to the middle classes. A fortnight at a smart resort like Bournemouth or Torquay, in a grand hotel providing every comfort and exclusive in-house entertainment could out-boast acquaintances spending a few days in a bed-and-breakfast at Southend or Margate at the mercy of the weather.

A new phenomenon appeared for those who did not wish to spend their holidays at the mercy of the weather or felt, often with good reason, that the British seaside hotel and boarding house offered neither a relaxing break nor good value for money. The camping holidays organised by charities and youth clubs for deprived urban children since the end of the nineteenth century were to prove the inspiration for the commercial exploitation of the communal holiday camp. Among early entrepreneurs in the field (literally and metaphorically) were Joseph Cunningham and his family who had set up a male only 'tented city' in 1894. After the First World War they gradually developed their site near Douglas on the Isle of Man until at its peak it could boast a host of entertainments and facilities, including a large swimming pool, a football field, a cricket pitch, tennis courts, a cinema, a camp orchestra and a monumental dining hall capable of seating 3,600 campers. The sleeping accommodation varied from military-style bell tents, to chalets built by internees in the First World War, to bungalows, and for those who could afford them, indoor apartments.[vi] Among Cunningham's visitors was a young fairground proprietor called Billy (later Sir William) Butlin who, observing the extraordinary growth in the vogue for this style of family holiday,

---

[vi]   Cunningham's did not reopen after the war.

set about planning a communal camp to improve and modernise the concept. Butlin's blueprint bore no resemblance to any prior concept of camping, except perhaps the short open-air walk to a bathroom block from an individual purpose-built chalet containing all the amenities of a superior hotel room of the period. He would provide a bath for every four campers, proportionally more than in most top hotels. As well as continuous activities and entertainments, he would offer unique attractions, such as baby-sitting and childcare services, to ensure that parents could relax together away from their children – a holiday within a holiday for which working-class couples would happily forego their savings. Butlin's pre-war camps, opened at Skegness in 1936 and Clacton-on-Sea in 1938, provided a week's accommodation, all meals and guaranteed continuous fun, whatever the weather, for £2 10s per head. This was almost a week's wages for a worker whose holiday pay, if any, would seldom cover a Butlin's family holiday, travel costs and extras such as drinks and excursions, but the camps were filled to capacity every week of their three pre-war seasons with the employed determined to enjoy the money in their pocket while it lasted.

Among those who copied Butlin's winning formula were travel agents Thomas Cook and the LMS railway, together investing in a more luxurious and expensive 'Chalet Village by the Sea' near Prestatyn in North Wales.[54] This too initially enjoyed great popularity with the burgeoning moneyed classes but was not destined to last long in the post-war ambience. With the popularisation of air travel and packaged holidays in the 1950s the communal holiday camp became increasingly less attractive to the moneyed and middle-classes. Butlins of course reopened after the war and enjoyed a period of extraordinary success (see Chapter 4) thereafter surviving, together with some of its imitators, by adapting to the cheap and cheerful demands of a new working-class market.

Also due to the growing prosperity of the 1930s a very different form of ethereal consumption came to prominence. A new generation increasingly disinclined to save for material purchases, now discovered the benefits of investing in instant credit through the media of hire purchase. A host of providers emerged ready to assist anyone in employment or enjoying regular income with their first cautious, and sometimes not so cautious, step into the uncharted waters of the 'never-never'. Among the first to recognise and publicly extol the potential of this increasingly used financial product was the improbable figure of the long-serving governor of the Bank of England, Montagu Norman. Norman initially expressed grave doubts, but having fully appraised the small finance house United Dominions Trust (UDT) became convinced that more accessible hire purchase would be advantageous to business and individual interests, as well as to the economy. With his seal of approval, the Bank, still in the private sector, seized the opportunity to acquire a major stake in UDT and went on to support its expansion through four decades and its emergence as one of Britain's largest and most prestigious finance companies.[55]

The long and chequered history of hire purchase and analogous credit arrangements was beset with the same brand of moral condemnation as conspicuous consumption itself. The ancient Greeks railed against the supposed evils of instalment plans for land sales. The orators of Rome denounced similar arrangements. Indeed the merits of extended term payment were afforded no recognition until the early nineteenth century, and then with only subdued enthusiasm.[vii] Among the select few enamoured by the concept was society hostess, renowned beauty and prolific writer Marguerite Gardiner, Countess of Blessington (1789–1849). The Countess's, to put it mildly, adventurous lifestyle frequently resulted in financial embarrassment from which, on one occasion, she rescued herself with an early variation on the theme of hire purchase:

[The Countess of Blessington] was attracted by the practice in Paris of hiring 'rich and fine furniture by the quarter, half or whole year, in any quantity required' and reported that she had made an agreement that if she wished to purchase the furniture then 'the sum agreed to be paid for the year's hire is to be allowed in the purchase money which is named when the inventory is made out'.

So impressed was she with her arrangement that she commended this 'usage that merits being adopted in all capitals' and hailed it as a new 'Aladdin's Lamp'.[56] This over-enthusiastic metaphor, with its suggestion of a bountiful genie empowered to grant every wish, was to endure as one of the less derogatory synonyms for hire-purchase.

Such approbation from an articulate aspirant to the aristocracy notwithstanding, hire purchase was not to be freed of high-minded criticism. In the 1890s, William Booth, the founder of the Salvation Army, condemned it because 'The decent poor man is charged ten or twenty times the amount that would be a fair rate of interest [and] if he should fail in his payment the machine is seized and the money lost'.[57] If Booth had in mind the sewing machine, then this was clearly a prejudiced exaggeration. It is highly improbable that the Singer Sewing Machine Company, with a near monopoly of the market, employed any such draconian measures to administer its low-deposit two-year plan which, until after the Second World War, threw an invaluable lifeline to the multitude of tailors and seamstresses who scraped a living from outwork assigned by Dickensian urban sweatshops. Yet Booth and his successors recognised no such merits. The Salvation Army, in pursuing its mission to save the poverty-stricken souls of all in debt, was not alone nor the last to denounce hire purchase. Paul Johnson observes in his *Saving and Spending: The Working-class Economy in Britain 1870–1939* that:

The writer [Edward C. Warren in 1939] who thought that the inter-war growth of consumer credit 'had succeeded in removing the stigma hitherto attaching to hire purchase in many people's minds' was deceiving himself.[58]

[vii]   The first known British agreement to hire with an option to purchase was in 1821 (Harris et al., 1961, 2).

True as this was, the meteoric rise of hire purchase in the decade prior to the outbreak of war was to be curtailed neither by the high-thinking moralists nor the low-thinking abject abusers who really did ensnare the unwary into unsustainable debt. In 1938, *The Hire Purchase Guide and Record* reported that there were twenty-four million active agreements in Britain and that seven million were being signed annually. In some places, 80 per cent of motor cars, 90 per cent of sewing machines, and 95 per cent of new wireless sets, gramophones and pianos were being sold on credit terms. Almost every manufacturer was providing their retail distributors with promotional credit plans.[59] One 'successful furniture trader' claimed that 'my proportion of instalments as opposed to cash business reached 73 per cent in 1937 and my bad debt losses were less than one per cent'. He attributed this achievement to the proficiency of his credit manager who, along with most of his contemporaries, offered facilities only to those customers he personally judged creditworthy and tailored the terms of their contracts as he saw fit.[60]

Income-tax relief applied to every form of interest payable and was therefore seemingly a valuable incentive. In practice it was rarely a factor in the decision to use hire-purchase. The few individuals liable to an appreciable level of income tax and also requiring credit facilities could usually obtain them from their bank. A bank loan was as tax-efficient as hire purchase: its terms were negotiable in confidence: it carried no stigma: no collectors called at the door: late payment did not result in repossession: there were no penalties for early repayment and banks had yet to invent the arrangement fee.

For the majority unable to secure a bank loan, hire purchase was the best practical option when accessible – although not without hazard. The validity of the contract was only as good as the probity of the finance house, since in most cases legal ownership did not pass until settlement of the final instalment. An unscrupulous provider might, and often did, repossess hired goods when just one instalment was in arrears. Future Education Minister, Ellen Wilkinson, on learning that some six hundred contracts were being terminated each day for no better reason, introduced a private member's bill to the House of Commons to protect the rights of hire-purchase buyers – a shortcoming in the legislation first identified half-a-century earlier.[61] Despite the manifest urgency and supportive representations from retail bodies, the motor trade and the hire-purchase industry itself, Wilkinson had to overcome intense parliamentary opposition before the first Hire Purchase Act was passed in 1938.[62] Its far-reaching measures enabled buyers to sign their agreements with some peace of mind but were of scant benefit to those to whom hire purchase remained a closed door.

The unemployed and the lowest paid workers could seldom budget further than the cash literally in their pockets. The more prudent of those unable to afford insurance or provident schemes earmarked their modest savings for unforeseeable events: job loss, robbery, fire, medical expenses, funeral costs; or for happier contingencies: an addition to the family, a daughter's wedding.[63] Working-class savings were commonly kept in a tin cash box secreted at home but as the 1930s wore on more and more gathered the confidence to trust third parties. A variety of local saving clubs proliferated, providing convenient facilities to set aside money for anticipated expenses: new clothes, replacement of household necessities, holidays, Christmas presents.[64]

A 1939 social survey report claimed that: 'Nearly every shop in Lambeth runs a club of some kind. In the case of some this is a real help to mothers and families; they can choose the goods they want and are not forced to pay more than the ordinary cash price, in others there is no choice and the goods are very expensive'. The surveyor goes on to comment, with an implication of impropriety, that the trustees of such clubs were 'publicans and licensed grocers ... this sort of saving [public-house clubs] for specific acts of self-indulgence were not considered a valid form of thrift – it was all part of that widespread self-taxation of the working classes'.[65] Describing saving clubs as an invalid form of thrift or acts of self-indulgence was an unduly harsh judgement since there can be little doubt that they were 'a real help to mothers and families' and many other small savers. 'Publicans and licensed grocers' did not run savings clubs for profit but as exercises in public relations and usually administered them as scrupulously as any savings bank. No businessman worthy of the name would have been so reckless as to risk his livelihood by cheating his customers of the money they would spend with him in any case.

Whether they patronised local clubs or the established savings banks the interwar working classes were certainly committed savers. The figures published by contemporary statistician John Bray (at his own admission inexact) indicate that in the decade from 1927 to 1937 the small savings and investments (of those with annual incomes below £250) reached £3,811 million, having grown by as much as £1,661 million. Building-society deposits and investments in marketable securities more than trebled from £211 million to over £672 million, while the expansion of private equity in homes valued below £1,000 was still more dramatic, from £92 million it grew fourfold to £378 million.[66] By the outbreak of the Second World War the Post Office Savings Bank (POSB), the Trustee Savings Banks (TSB),[viii] the building societies, the life assurance companies, and other major savings repositories were holding more working-class money than could have been imagined at the end of the First. There was no possible way for Bray to reliably measure the amount of cash saved at home or in private savings clubs, but ignoring it all and allowing a wide margin for error, his data suggests that through the years so often remembered for little else but unemployment, social injustice and inequality of income distribution, the majority of Britain's working class had begun to accumulate at least some measure of financial security.

Among the more ardent savers were the older and more conservative working-class generation, permanently tormented by the spectre of unemployment. They

---

[viii] The autonomous Trustee Savings Banks, constitutionally liable to invest solely in public sector debt, merged and were floated as a public company in 1986, before being acquired by Lloyds Bank in 1995, thereafter renamed Lloyds TSB plc.

had, they told anyone who would listen, earned their money by the sweat of their brow and learnt its value 'the hard way'. They believed in the rectitude of paying cash and, if unable to do so, foregoing their needs. They never resorted to borrowing – the certain road to grief. Such diehard spirits fought a generally losing battle with a new generation, impatient to buy into modernity, and failing to appreciate their anxieties over credit.

Yet the British working classes had long been no strangers to credit and the appreciation of the value of equity. Charles Dickens observed the 'strange forethought of costermongers and fishwomen [sic] – the former often wearing great squab brooches as convenient pledges and the latter massive silver rings'.[67] These pawnshop securities had been their capital, but capital encompassing a degree of pleasure with which no paper bond or savings bank passbook could compete. While it was possible to proffer these conspicuous pledges with dignity, being a known client of the neighbourhood pawnbroker was a matter of pride not stigma. Through the interwar years this perception slowly died away as modernity rendered the pawnbroker redundant. A visit to his shop lost its semblance of propriety and became seen as the act of desperation it so often was. Only destitute wives now pledged their cheap jewellery, their weekly washing for a few coppers to tide them over until pay day and desperate husbands the tools of their trade when unemployed. The familiar three brass balls, the sign of the poor man's banker, were less and less in evidence in the high street. By 1939 the number of pledged articles had fallen to just 23 per cent of a decade earlier, but as the pawnbrokers reluctantly closed their doors, others opened, most of which led to less trustworthy breeds of poor man's banker.[68]

The vanishing neighbourhood pawnbroker would certainly have offered a better deal than the so-called 'tallyman' who called door-to-door dazzling cash-strapped prospective customers with a flurry of hype and enticing them with apparently low-priced luxuries and instant interest-free credit. He required no signature on a formal contract nor demanded a pledge or security. He generously accepted just a small deposit and thereafter collected weekly instalments over a period determined at his own discretion – often longer than he had led his customers to believe. Much of his profit came from inflating the prices on delivery of goods inferior to the samples shown on the doorstep. In the absence of a written contract recourse to the law, even if affordable, was useless. In most cases buyers were not even told the true name or business address of the person with whom they were dealing.

Equally notorious for corrupt practice was 'ticket trading', modified over time into 'check trading', a marginally more respectable variation on the same theme. The 'ticket man' provided an unsecured fixed-term loan in the form of a ticket or voucher with a given face value, perhaps £1, £2 or £5. This could be exchanged for clothing or basic domestic necessities at designated shops but did not have to be spent immediately or in full. The seemingly modest but actually progressively punitive rate of interest was concealed beneath the heavy hand of the ticket man who, with unfailing regularity, called in person to extract his repayments. His designated retailers too were charged a 'discount' on surrender of the tickets, so that their prices, reflecting the extra cost, were inevitably higher than competitors who accepted only cash down. By evoking the dread of social censure the ticket man encouraged permanent debt, luring customers into taking another ticket immediately on settlement of the last (usually at twenty-week intervals). He need do no more than mention the denigrated pawnbroker, the moneylender, or the reputedly violent loan shark, the last buffers against dependence on charity.[69] Despite the many allegations of illegal or sharp practice, not all ticket men were consistently blameworthy. Some, it seems, built up lasting and trusting relationships with their customers. One ex-tallyman explained to historian Melanie Tebbutt: 'In my days as a traveller the key used to be left under the mat or in the potted plant. And I used to let myself in with the key and open the sideboard drawer and there was the money. This is the way it is done – it is complete confidence'.[70]

Mutual confidence of this kind perhaps helps account for the enduring success of The Provident Clothing and Supply Company which, having seen off most of its rivals, survives to lead the remnant of its now niche market. While pioneering a 'charitable self-help scheme' in 1881, Methodist lay preacher Joshua (later Sir Joshua) Waddilove engaged in the insurance business in Bradford, devised the 'provident check' in the belief that it would ease the lot of the 'morally inadequate poor'. Waddilove distributed simple loan vouchers, exchangeable only for those goods he judged appropriate to the needs of a self-helper to ensure that their money would not be squandered on drink. The moral stance and fair trading principles that distinguished his company from the general run of tallymen and ticket men led to enormous expansion (5,000 employees by 1920), and to the readily accessible 'Provi' succeeding to the pawnbroker's mantle of the 'poor man's banker'.[71]

Before the Second World War, and for some years thereafter, a mutual distrust endured between the 'poor man' and what in his view was the rich man's banker, who in response, protested that his doors were open to all and that he never turned away a customer on grounds of financial deficiency. Midland Bank advertisements asserted that the 'smallest depositor is assured of a ready welcome and a desire to meet his special requirements'.[72] And as late as 1950, Lloyds Bank still felt it expedient to explain to prospective customers: 'There is a false impression, still widely held, that banking is a luxury for the well-to-do. It is not'. The same advertisement adds, with more than a hint of patronising discouragement, 'The bank will usually require an introduction from another customer or a personal reference'.[73]

Working-class reluctance to enter the grand banking mausoleums that imposed their dreary dignity on the high streets of Britain, from the greatest cities to the smallest market town, was an open invitation to burgeoning small-scale financiers. Most sought to compete fairly for the bank's spurned business and satisfy market demand, while others, not yet subject to external control or supervision, were often incompetent, prone to duplicity and skilled at exploiting their inexperienced and naïve clients. They thrived while small depositors and modest borrowers remained convinced that their business was unwelcome at the 'rich man's bank' and that, in the event of dispute, access to the civil courts would be denied them. More often than not, they were right on both counts.

Britain's banks not only demonstrated no interest in the mutual benefits of assisting the working classes but demonstrated an extraordinary indifference to the social and cultural changes taking place around them. The developing scope of commerce and industry had taken the first steps on the long road to elimination of demand for totally unskilled labour and was creating more semi-skilled, supervisory, office and professional jobs. Not least due to the expansion of the banks themselves, the number of interwar clerical workers tripled, 'foremen, inspectors and supervisors' doubled, while professional practitioners, 744,000 in 1911, more than doubled to 1,493,000 in 1939.[74] Still the banks refused to change their approach to the market.

The failure to attract working-class customers cannot be wholly attributed to bank intransigence. Ingrained class attitudes to money were not easy to dislodge. Workers daring to pursue financial and social ambition continued to be denounced by their peers as 'class traitors' or worse. The accumulation of money, whether or not employed in conspicuous consumption, was blamed for isolating achievers from their families and friends, while modesty, humility and self-denial continued to be lauded for their unquestioned virtue.

Those who defied such convention and aspired to upward social mobility found that there was no alternative to emulation of the middle-classes in manners, dress and speech, and would often invest in elocution lessons to lose their regional accents. Employers offering positions with prospects of advancement still considered such meaningless social attributes as important as academic or technical qualifications. Thus the less ambitious working class chose to avoid the fish-eyed gaze of the personnel officer, as it did the fish-eyed gaze of the bank manager – but it did not follow that British working-class people were all disinterested in making money.

Those too heavily handicapped in the rat races of employment, business or investment could always try the horse or dog races. That is, provided they were able to ignore the moral condemnation unceasingly dispensed even when unemployed men turned to the bookmaker as their last legal hope of respite from destitution. Mark Clapson writes of the fervid antagonism of the 'National Anti-Gambling League' and of individuals like Canon Peter Green, who for four decades maintained an almost fanatical press campaign to rescue the 'one million cases of demoralisation'. Ramsey MacDonald, evidently convinced that socialism had no place for gamblers, unrealistically lamented that a 'class disease had spawned downwards from the idle rich to the hard working poor', while Beatrice Webb more viciously called gamblers 'parasites eating the life out of the working class, demoralising and discrediting it'.[75] In the eyes of these and other similarly financially comfortable self-appointed judges, money in a working-class pocket was always tainted unless earned by their own probably indefinable concept of 'honest labour'.

Ready-money betting other than within racecourse enclosures had been illegal since 1853 but the law remained unclear and was largely unenforceable while literally streetwise bookmakers and their runners were adroit at dodging the police through urban mazes of congested streets and back alleys. These astute operators undoubtedly circumvented the law and were not always above violence or corruption, but they were not all entirely mercenary. One pre-war punter told Clapson that they were, in fact, 'very generous and would often lend people money to purchase food [and] to the forefront in helping people out in less fortunate circumstances'.[76] This view was far from unique. Like the convenors of savings clubs, bookmakers were in essence local businessmen who understood the value of goodwill, but for them its maintenance had to be more refined and intellectual. They supplied an ethereal market rooted in a mesh of emotions, including superstition, bravado, craved peer respect, hope and hopelessness. They had to possess or develop an intuitive appreciation of their punters' mindset and know how to win their trust. They also had to know how to perform high-speed mental arithmetic (compounded by the idiosyncrasies of pounds, shillings and pence), analyse statistics and calculate risks. At the same time, it was in their interest to ensure that their punters did not become destitute, though gambling has since been demonstrated to have seldom, if ever, been the direct cause of working-class financial ruin or demoralisation. Like the cinema, the music halls and spectator sports, it was a form of escape from the inequities of daily life, and an alternative to the uncertainties of long-term investment in the material trappings of modernity, rapidly losing their charms amidst the unpalatable news emerging from Europe in the late 1930s.

Apart from feigned oblivion to deteriorating international politics, interwar indulgence in conspicuous consumption was persistently inhibited by social conscience. Exorcising memories of the despised profiteers of the First World War proved a long and slow process.[77] Most of Britain's rich, including those with recently acquired wealth, were sensitive enough to avoid the 'playboy' lifestyle that the popular press took such delight in admonishing. But there were also those who could not resist the urge to publicise their financial achievements, and the same popular press offered them the facility to do so with dignity and good conscience.

At spectacular London film and theatre premieres, gala balls and glittering events in aid of charities and good causes, the great, the good and the rich fused with the brightest stars of entertainment to form an irresistible magnet for the purveyors of mass-communication. A personal appearance and a large donation rewarded with a few sycophantic words in a popular journal and perhaps a photograph was a sure step in the direction of the honours list. Most charities, though grateful, were fortunate enough to be independent of publicity seeking donors. The vast majority of their private support was, as always, anonymously endowed via personal gifts and bequests and the unsung heroism of benevolent institutions, such as the Freemasons, the City livery companies and corporate trusts. Britain's many charitable trusts established by frequently unnamed philanthropists, then as now, seldom sought or received media acknowledgment for the vast sums they disbursed.

Not only wealthy individuals and grand institutions but ordinary people increasingly began to disburse their money in the emotive expectancy of self-gratification. When the BBC introduced *The Week's Good Cause* in 1926, it informed listeners, often for the first time, of want and distress beyond their personal experience. These Sunday broadcasts could reach a larger audience in a few minutes than the fundraising orators of the past could address in their lifetimes. The voices of admired and respected figures – actors, entertainers, church leaders and politicians – inspired the same sense of personal affinity that commercial advertisers used to create brand loyalty through the graphic image. In 1932 *The Week's Good Cause* raised £88,874; in 1936, with growth in audience and more professional broadcasting skills, £186,144; while in 1940, as war news became more grievous, listeners' sympathy stretched to £368,238 (over £15 million today).[78]

As yet there was no sign of the widespread disenchantment with charity and philanthropy destined to surface with the advent of post-war state welfare, though its intrinsic virtue did not go unquestioned. Socialists, and others ideologically antagonistic to private wealth, time and again derided the voluntary sector. Playwright and Fabian pioneer Bernard Shaw, who as a humanitarian was seen to personally contribute to disaster relief funds, had little time for rich donors. 'He who gives money he has not earned is generous with other people's labour' claimed Shaw, while social reformer Canon Samuel Barnett thought charity 'sentimental' and 'concealing the injustices of society'.[79] These and similar unhelpful hypotheses would have little impact when the new mass media could now so clearly teach the realities of the human condition and find a response in innate British generosity.

Once the parallel development of mass communication and mass production had precipitated the changes in attitudes to personal finance touched upon in this chapter neither political upheaval nor war itself could suppress the ascendancy of consumer expectancy. Mass communication and mass production had yielded to the underprivileged many, the confidence and right to enter some of the hitherto closed domains of the privileged few. Mass communication and mass production had yielded new expectancies demanding to be satisfied by commerce and industry. Mass communication and mass production had yielded the prospect of private capital through homeownership and other realisable opportunities for lasting prosperity. Still a high proportion of the people of Britain experienced no more than intermittent glimpses of the rising affluence yielded to their fellow countrymen by these manifestations of modernity. Long-term unemployment, social injustice, privation and poverty remained to be overcome but by 1939 a lifestyle inconceivable in 1918 was within the reach of an unprecedented majority.

For a few years personal aspiration, ambition and enterprise would have to be postponed. The priority was preservation – bodily preservation and financial preservation. A brief interlude of broadening financial security had played a significant, if unacknowledged role in heightening those qualities of reserve and self-belief the British would come to claim as their unique shield against the aggression of Nazi Germany. The sphere of 'elegant economy' radiating the virtues of self-imposed financial constraint still loomed large but a partial eclipse by its antithesis, 'conspicuous consumption', had been unmistakeably observed – a fleeting crescent soon to be obliterated by the dark clouds of the Second World War.

Endnotes

[1]   Johnson, Paul, *Saving and Spending: The Working-class Economy in Britain 1870–1939* (1985), citing MO Directive Replies, January 1939, 160.

[2]   Aldridge, Alan, *Consumption* (2003), citing Scruton, 'The Good Life' (1998), 9.

[3]   Ibid., 2.

[4]   Stearns, Peter N., *Consumerism in World History: The Global Transformation of Desire* (2001), 1.

[5]   Berry, Christopher J., *The Idea of Luxury: A Conceptual and Historical Investigation* (1994), 206.

[6]   Hunt, Alan, *Governance of the Consuming Passions: A History of Sumptuary Laws* (1996), citing Phillip Stubbes 'Anatomy of the Abuses in England' (1583), 81.

[7]   Berry (1994), 2–3.

[8]   Ibid., 299.

[9]   Monod, Paul K., *The Murder of Mr Grebel: Madness and Civility in an English Town* (2003), 67.

[10] Monod (2003), 239.

[11] Bocock, Robert, *Consumption* (1993), 11.

[12] Bocock (1993), 12.

[13] Berry (1994), 117, 125.

[14] Veblen, Thorstein, *The Theory of the Leisure Class: An Economic Study in Institutions*, 1899 (2007), 67.

[15] Veblen (2007), 60–61.

[16] Cordery, Simon, *British Friendly Societies 1750–1914* (2003), 98, 160, 175.

[17] Himmelfarb, Gertrude, *The De-moralization of Society: From Victorianism to Modern Values* (1995), 143–145.

[18] Hopkins, Harry, *The New Look: A Social History of the Forties and Fifties in Britain* (1964), 388.

[19] *Daily Herald*, 19th May 1945.

[20] Hennessy, Peter, *Never Again: Britain 1945–51* (1992), 67.

[21] NA, PRO, MO: TC/10/D, 'Ask Your Dad'; *Daily Telegraph*, letter from T. Haslet, 23rd November 1948.

[22] *The Recorder*, 23rd October 1948.

[23] *Daily Mail*, 16th November 1948.

[24] McKibbin, Ross, *Classes and Cultures: 1918–1951*, 1998 (2000), 61.

[25] Crisell, Andrew, *An Introductory History of British Broadcasting* (1997), 22.

[26] Ibid., 13.

[27] Nicholas, Siân, 'All the News that's Fit to Broadcast: The popular press versus the BBC 1922–45' in Catterall, Peter, Seymour-Ure, Colin and Smith, Adrian (eds), *Northcliffe's Legacy: Aspects of the Popular Press* (2000), 124.

[28] Clarke, Peter, *Hope and Glory: Britain 1900–2000*, 1996 (2004), 116–117.

[29] Fowler, David, *The First Teenagers: The Lifestyle of Young Wage-Earners in Interwar Britain* (1995), 95.

[30] Barnett, Correlli, *The Audit of War: The Illusion and Reality of Britain as a Great Nation* (1986), 201.

[31] Clarke (2004), 116.

[32] Hoggart, Richard, *The Uses of Literacy: Aspects of Working Class Life with Special Reference to Publications and Entertainments*, 1957 (1992), 321.

[33] Byrne, Michael, *The History and Contemporary Significance of Book Clubs* (1978), 1, 8.

[34] Howlett, Peter, *Fighting with Figures: A Statistical Digest of the Second World War* (Central Statistical Office, undated), Table 2.19.

[35] Ibid., Table 8.21; Clapson, Mark, *Suburban Century: Social Change and Urban Growth in England and the USA* (2003), 27.

[36] Daunton, Martin, *A Property Owning Democracy? Housing in Britain* (1987), 77.

[37] Burnett, John, *A Social History of Housing 1815–1985* (1993), 236–237, 249.

[38] Idem, *Affluence and Authority: A Social History of 20th Century Britain* (2005), 5, 249.

[39] Ibid., 255.

[40] Bray, John F.L., 'Small Savings' in *The Economic Journal*, vol. 50, No. 198/199 (Jun–Sep 1940), 2.

[41] *Whitaker's Almanac*, *1946*, 579.

[42] *Journal of Land and Public Utility Economics* (vol. 15, No. 2, May 1939), Russell, Horace, 'The Borders Case', 225227.

[43] NA, PRO, BB/WEBS, Minutes of Legal and Parliamentary Committee of the Woolwich Equitable Building Society 15th September 1939, 1023/30; Ritchie, Berry, *We're with the Woolwich 1847–1997: The Story of the Woolwich Building Society* (1997), 74.

[44] Burnett (1993), 254.

[45] Johnson (1985), 117.

[46] Wellings, Fred, and Gibb, Alistair, *Bibliography of Banking Histories* (1997), 6.

[47] Elliott, Blanche, *A History of English Advertising* (1962), 210.

[48] Richards, Jeffrey, *Films and British National Identity: From Dickens to Dad's Army* (1997), 41.

[49] Brendon, Piers, *Thomas Cook: 150 Years of Popular Tourism* (1991), 260.

[50] Pimlott, J.A.R., *The Englishman's Holiday: A Social History*, 1947 (1976), 262.

[51] Brendon (1991), 276.

[52] Cross, Gary, 'Leisure in the Era of the Popular Front' in *Journal of Contemporary History*, vol. 24, No. 4, October 1989, 613.

[53] Pimlott (1976), 221, 244–245.

[54] Ibid., 247.

[55] Harris, Ralph, Naylor, Margo, and Seldon, Arthur, *Hire Purchase in a Free Society* (1961), 29.

[56] Ibid., 20–21.

[57] Johnson (1985), citing William Booth, *In Darkest England: The Way Out*, 1890, 156.

[58] Ibid., 159.

[59] *Hire Trader's Guide and Record*, XIV, No. 543, 1st April 1938.

60 *Hire Purchase Journal*, February 1947, 6.
61 Harris et al. (1961), 26.
62 *Hire Trader's Record*, April 1938.
63 Zweig, Ferdynand, *Labour, Life and Poverty* (1948), 80–84.
64 Hoggart (1992), 133.
65 Johnson (1985), citing 'Social Services in North Lambeth and Kennington' (1939), 149, 151.
66 Bray (1940), Table I, 198, 199–204.
67 Tebbutt, Melanie, *Making Ends Meet: Pawnbroking and Working Class Credit* (1983), citing Charles Dickens in 'Household Words' (6th December 1851), 17, 159.
68 Ibid., 116.
69 Tebbutt (1983), 180.
70 Taylor, Avram, *Working Class Credit and Community since 1918* (2002), 119.
71 Ibid., 117.
72 MO: TC57/2/D.
73 LTSB, 1678 1950–1951, 'Banking for Beginners', February 1950.
74 Burnett (1993), 250.
75 Clapson, Mark, *A Bit of a Flutter: Popular Gambling and English Society, c.1823–1961* (1992), 45–47, 30.
76 Ibid., 51.
77 McKibbin, Ross, *Classes and Cultures: 1918–1951*, 1988 (2000), 54.
78 Nightingale, Benedict, *Charities* (1973), 118.
79 Ibid., 111.

Chapter 3
Petrified 'Capitalists'
(*The Second World War*)

The war could not mean a mere matter of a few minor adjustments in our personal lives and affairs. It meant we had to readjust our whole conceptions and to abandon many of our legitimate prospects and hopes. That is why the National Savings movement is making a special drive this week in order to swell the ranks of the Savings Army at home, no less vital to our success than the armed forces themselves ... and our desire is to see every man and woman a volunteer.

Sir Kingsley Wood, Chancellor of the Exchequer – June 1940

It was small consolation for the trauma of September 1939 to May 1945 that when the Second World War at last came to an end almost everyone in Britain was in a stronger personal financial position than at its start. This chapter will consider some of the causes and effects of this extraordinary progression.

The most, and possibly only, positive effect of the onset of war was that it purged the nation of the most debilitating social factor of the previous two decades – unemployment. In the first four months of 1939, from over one and a half million, the jobless total fell by more than 40 per cent and following the declaration of war on 3rd September intensified conscription and the demands of munitions production contributed to a rapid acceleration in the decline. By the start of 1941 the dole queues had all but vanished and soon a dearth of manpower began to hamper every sphere of commercial and industrial activity. As in the First World War, employers resorted to recruiting women to jobs in normal times the exclusive preserve of men and although they always paid substantially less than to a man for the same work, the money brought home by wives and daughters represented a significant boost to the household income of a working-class family. Family incomes were not only enhanced by the wages of women and men employed for the first time in years but often by the unforeseen earnings of those of pensionable age postponing retirement or returning to their old jobs to assist the war effort.

Both men and women earned more than they had ever known, by working longer hours than they had ever known, leaving them little time to spend the unfamiliar cash they shook out of their bulging pay packets. When they did find an opportunity to go to the shops it was an unfamiliar experience. They found less and less worth buying. Saving before spending became second nature to the people of Britain and the amounts they saved surpassed the most optimistic hopes of their government, desperate to replenish its fast depleting war chest. The savings of these ordinary people would form the true bedrock of the wartime economy.

No other source of revenue proved more dependable or would contribute more. Yet wartime saving was no lucrative investment. National Savings never paid more than 3 per cent in interest, building society returns were no better and the equity growth in endowment policies was almost always disappointing. Inflation rose, albeit with severe fluctuations, by about 50 per cent through the six years of war and few savers were blind to the erosion in the real value of their money. But wartime savers did not invest in anticipation of high income or capital appreciation. The prospect of a stake in the peaceful future of their nation was all they dare contemplate.

The wartime surveys and enquiries carried out by Mass-Observation, the social research organisation founded in 1937 by Tom Harrisson and his associates, time and again recorded the patriotic sentiments of savers. The following examples portray the mood of the nation with consummate clarity:

> I don't feel that I have the right to spend, or keep money on deposit and expect the government to win the war. They can take the lot as far as I am concerned if they need it, as I expect they will before we are done. I shall then only hope to be looked after with humanity when I can no longer work.

> My attitude is, as long as the Nazis are defeated they can have all my money. My attitude towards money has not changed. I only think about it when I can't meet my bills, but, of course, I am pleased when I have any. Since the war I have saved for the first time in my life.

> As the skies darkened, I saved money more keenly and accumulated twenty-one [National Savings certificates] in twelve months. I also proposed the formation of a savings group.

> Now I consider the effects on shipping space of the purchases [of National Savings certificates] I make. I make no fetish of this consideration, but I do let it weigh when contemplating articles above five shillings.

Other savers were less resolute but bowed to peer pressure and accepted the mood of the nation:

> It's just – well one automatically does. It helps the war; – I don't know, they say it's the right thing; – We save more money, but only because the government have asked us to invest in their securities.[1]

> True, I am earning more than in pre-war days, but even so the proportion of the amount I am saving is much higher; – If you are going to save, the Post Office [National Savings] is the best place, because the private concerns will crash first. If there is any money to be had, the government will have it.[2]

These and similar convictions were the deeply engendered hallmarks of a now almost forgotten inherent sense of duty to King and Country. Throughout the war Winston Churchill and morale boosters and propagandists like J.B. Priestley and George Orwell never lost an opportunity to exploit this unwavering national pride and faith in Britain's ability to withstand whatever adversity or misfortune should befall it. In the context of such illusions of national supremacy, Jeffrey Richards cites the actor and film director, and until his untimely death, regular broadcaster for the BBC's overseas service, Leslie Howard:

> [The English demonstrate] qualities which seem to me to represent the best there
> is in human nature: qualities of courage, devotion to duty, kindliness, humour,
> cool headedness, balance, common sense, singleness of purpose and idealism.
> … We have contributed to the civilisation of the world … something which the
> Germans have never known the meaning of – something called tolerance.[3]

Improbable as it is that as individuals most possessed all or any of these flattering attributes, the people of Britain could, and for the most part did, at least help fight the war by entrusting their savings to the nation. A wartime diary maintained by an evidently senior executive of the POSB now preserved in the Royal Mail archives, provides a unique and detailed testimony to the extent of patriotic conviction that savings were safe with the government until certain victory:

> In the period of the crises in March to the end of September 1939 only seventy
> [of about twelve million depositors] bothered to write to the department about
> the safety of their savings. Of those, a number of the letters did not reveal much
> apprehension. [For example] 'I have no doubts as to the government meeting its
> liabilities. My doubts were due to small talk'.[4]

The following month the diary records the receipt of just eight apprehensive letters and deposits soaring to a record breaking £6,370,000.[5] When they went on sale on 29th November 1939, thirteen-year-old Princess Elizabeth was photographed purchasing the first new 3 per cent defence bond and nine-year-old Princess Margaret the first 7th Issue National Savings certificate.[6] In less than three weeks this inspired public relations exercise yielded over £34 million from private investors following the princesses' example, and every subsequent issue brought queues to the nation's post offices and banks. Despite their sluggish rate of appreciation and inconvenience to cash, National Savings certificates became and remained Britain's most popular security, while Defence Bonds, offering similarly uninspiring terms, went on selling long after victory. Until the last vestige of possibility of resumption of war had vanished, investing in Britain continued to be regarded as a personal obligation.

The level of wartime thrift was truly extraordinary. From just over £547 million at the outbreak, by July 1945 the total deposited in the POSB alone had risen to £1,645 million and the number of individual accounts grown from twelve million

to over twenty million.[7] Simultaneously TSB deposits shot up from £252 million
to £603 million.[8] One zealous contemporary statistician calculated the 'small
savings' invested in National Savings certificates, Defence Bonds and savings
bank deposits to the last pound. According to H. Oliver Home, the total saved
between November 1939 and August 1945 was precisely £3,651,869,779.[9]

With declaration of war all house-building work in progress ground to a halt
and the property market slowed to a virtual standstill, stripping would-be home
buyers of their primary reason to save with a building society. The BSA, presuming
an inevitable wholesale transfer to National Savings, made urgent representations
to the Treasury to permit its members to offer more attractive terms. Predictably
the request was summarily dismissed, causing some societies to express fears
for their very survival.[10] Their anxiety was soon to prove an overreaction. They
had overlooked a compensatory incentive about to become increasingly valuable
to their depositors. Building society interest was paid net of income tax and it
remained exempt from surtax too (until 1952/53). As tax rates became ever more
punitive far more accounts were opened than closed and the societies attracted
record numbers of new savers. Through the war years the number of building
society accounts increased by almost 50 per cent – from 2,088,000 to 2,965,000.[11]
These depositors need have no concerns about failing to invest in Britain, since in
common with all savings repositories, building societies were required to divert
the bulk of their funds into national war loans.

Shortly after the outbreak of war, Sir Robert (later Lord) Kindersley, one
of the founding directors of the National Savings Committee (NSC) at the start
of the First World War, was reinstated as president with a brief to raise thrift to
unprecedented heights. Kindersley commenced by making a series of earnest
broadcasts appealing, like all wartime orators, to patriotism and national pride,
employing such rhetoric as:

> If we spend our money in a greedy race for less and less, we are not only making
> fools of ourselves by raising prices against each other, we are just not doing our
> job of saving and so we become Hitler's best allies:. Let each one of us sit down
> and think up how we can reduce expenditure. What about perms, cigarettes,
> sweets, or that extra glass of beer and everything else that is not essential: Make
> it a matter of pride to finish up the first year with as many unused coupons in
> your [ration] book as possible. Ultra-smart clothes today make one shudder. At
> least, if they don't they ought to: Don't let us play at sacrifice; let us get down
> to the real thing.[12]

According to a Mass-Observation survey, listeners considered Kindersley's
broadcasts 'half-hearted' and that they made 'no profound impression', but there
can be no doubt that savers were far from half-hearted and were profoundly
impressed. In October 1941 Kindersley published a letter from King George VI
congratulating him and the NSC on raising the investments of private savers
tenfold in 18 months, to reach his target of £1,000 million.[13] In addition to the

war-generated propensity to curb expenditure, this result was largely attributable to the outstandingly talents of Sir Harold (later Lord) Mackintosh, the then president of the Advertising Association and vice-chairman of the TSB. In marked contrast to Kindersley, his newly appointed vice-president, assisted by the frequent appearances of his wife, possessed the charisma to unfailingly win the hearts and minds of his audience 'with a homely style, interspersing his serious, well prepared speech with jokes and anecdotes which his secretary carefully preserved in a notebook'.[14] Twenty years his president's junior, Mackintosh combined all the qualities of an experienced businessman and banker, a devout Methodist and proponent of the Smilesian virtues, with the boundless energy that he devoted to his assignment. Under his guidance by March 1943 270,450 active NSC groups, including over 80,000 in workplaces, had been established to serve every parish in the land. Every week, in every class, in every school, every pupil bought at least one National Savings stamp.[15] In the half year to March 1941 school saving groups alone raised £3,811,855 (over £160 million today).[16]

During the First World War the National War Savings Committee (later renamed National Savings), with Kindersley as its vice chairman, had set up town centre 'tank banks' where war bonds could be bought directly from the Army's then most advanced weapon, with the intention of evoking a vicarious sense of military involvement. In similar tradition, whenever possible Mackintosh now associated imaginative promotional events with the funding of specific armaments. For a 'Warships Week' he built the full-size bridge of a battleship in London's Trafalgar Square. For a 'Wings for Victory Week' he spectacularly transformed the square into a mock RAF airfield complete with model fighter aircraft. The event attracted enormous publicity, brought many thousands of visitors to London and 'added £160 million to the savings of ordinary citizens'. Hardly a day passed without the NSC making its presence felt somewhere in Britain. Mackintosh silenced the critics of the 'cost of his ballyhoo' by pointing out that every pound spent on publicity for the London Wings for Victory week had produced £9,000, and that it had benefited the RAF Benevolent Fund alone by £192,000.[17] In a war-torn nation his array of creative live entertainment, involving exhibitions, parades, circuses, concerts, films, theatre shows and much more, served to raise civilian morale as much as to raise their investment in the war effort. Among Mackintosh's more persuasive concepts was the never to be forgotten 'Squander Bug', who promoted National Savings through a long and vigorous campaign, admonishing those who dared spend their money when there was a war on. The remnant of the nation's abject money spenders was reminded that this unpleasant little cartoon character:

loves to prowl around on polished counters and hear the cash registers knocking up the pounds, shillings and pence spent on things you can do without. 'Nice work', he chuckles, 'doesn't help the war effort a bit!' Be on your guard against this little fifth-columnist. Make your money fight for Britain.[18]

As well as events and press advertisements, Mackintosh used posters, leaflets, free magazines, the radio, the cinema and, on one splendid occasion, thousands of carrier pigeons to deliver the message of the NSC.[19] It was a message no one failed to receive. Overt non-savers were subjected to the same contempt shown to civilian men judged indifferent to the carnage of the Great War. In November 1941, a Mass-Observation survey reported that even in Coventry, bombed to destruction a year earlier, 73 per cent were saving to the maximum.[20]

Employers began buying National Savings certificates on behalf of their staff, deducting the cost from their wages and in some cases adding a gratuitous contribution. Despite this being precisely the type of patriotic action the government was doing all in its power to promote, in December 1939 the Solicitor General's office, claiming to anticipate trade union hostility, raised a formal objection on the grounds that the deductions were 'contrary to the Truck Act 1830'.[21] Through an ensuing two and a half years of bureaucratic correspondence between the Home Office and the Ministry of Production, this presumably considered legal opinion was ignored by all parties. The matter was finally resolved when in October 1942, following a display of common sense by a TUC official, referred to only as Smythe, the Home Office committed to writing: 'If savings certificates are paid for with the concurrence of the workers concerned it seems unlikely that its legality will be challenged'. Since the outbreak of war the Trades Union Congress (TUC) had continually urged its members to 'save to the utmost' and always remained a loyal supporter of National Savings.[22]

In his *Wartime Patterns of Saving and Spending*, Harrisson's Mass-Observation associate, Charles Madge provides an analysis of the response to a survey on motives for saving. Expressed in a variety of ways, 'for a rainy day' or 'to have a shilling or two behind you' tops the list. The second most common reason, possibly an extension of the first, is summed up as 'specific preparation for post-war unemployment'. For all the publicity and evidence to the contrary, 'to help the war effort' manages only third place, although more than a few of the savers do claim to set personal considerations aside and put 'patriotism' first. Predictably, 'in order to spend' is bottom of the list.[23]

Ross McKibbin cites Madge to argue that there was a 'conventional upper limit on expenditure which [working-class] people felt reluctant to exceed'. Not only was it difficult to spend to the limit in bare-shelved shops but in wartime anyone indulging in overt extravagance, like anyone overtly failing to save, could expect little other than intense disdain. McKibbin goes on to claim that there also 'tended to be a conventional upper limit to saving as well as to spending' and asserts 'some, though, could have saved more', arguing that financial prudence was in approximate proportion to experience of unemployment.[24] Whether or not they had ever stood in a pre-war dole queue, everyone was expecting hard times ahead and surely would not have limited their savings simply to comply with a 'conventional upper limit'. More probably conventional British reserve inhibited some of Madge's respondents from revealing all they had saved, and others, perhaps embarrassed by their unfamiliar circumstances, might well have convinced themselves that the war could not be benefiting them financially.

Madge himself confessed it a struggle to extract reliable information, explaining that his researchers had encountered 'a tendency to conceal some forms of saving'. They had found it particularly difficult to gather reliable information from wealthier families, from whom they reported 'correspondingly higher resistance [and] a high factor of concealment – people are only prepared to disclose regular weekly savings'. On the other hand, Madge suggests that wage earners believed financial prudence a matter of pride and were more prepared to talk about the money they were accumulating, but there is no hint that any believed it unconventional or indeed possible to save too much. A young engineer expresses the most widely held opinion: 'Guess we'll need it after the war. Before the war there was plenty of food and no money; now there's plenty of money and no food. We'll get value for money afterwards!'[25]

Most of the working-class savers interviewed by Madge's team in 1943 indicate that they are well aware of the seriousness of the national economic plight, but, reasonably enough, are looking first to their own future. Regardless of class, those who acknowledge their financial good fortune believe it temporary at best. Attitudes had barely shifted from those of February 1941 when Mass-Observation had posed the blunt question: 'What do you think things are going to be like in London after the war as far as money is concerned?' Only 21 per cent were then optimistic. A lone voice, from perhaps the more forward thinking, had no doubt that 'there'll be plenty of money', but the majority agreed wholeheartedly with the Londoner who unhesitatingly predicted: 'we shall all be broke'.[26] The foregone conclusion of post-war economic doom was officially endorsed by the 'Unemployment Insurance Statutory Commission', when claiming that Britain's 'unemployment fund', though transformed from a seemingly immutable pre-war deficit to a credit of £55 million was 'by no means an excessive provision for the loss we may anticipate in the aftermath of war'.[27]

The breadth of misgivings about future unemployment and financial misfortune are further evidenced by the extent of self-inflicted 'forced saving', then a common synonym for endowment life assurance. Madge reveals that there were currently 103 million active policies: 'two and a quarter for every man, woman and child in Britain'; 95 per cent of families in Glasgow, 88 per cent in Slough, and in Bradford, the lowest of the towns researched, 75 per cent were subscribing to a savings based life policy.[28] Almost every one of these policyholders was also investing in other forms of savings, and in many cases keeping up repayments on pre-war loans and mortgages.

Once the 'phoney war' gave way to full-blooded conflict, it was not long before dedicated consumers found their spending options curtailed by emergency measures. The supply of retail commodities diminished to a fraction of pre-war demand and people began buying all available foodstuffs and necessities to store, more often than to consume. Prices rose in response and inflation rocketed: at the end of the first year of war it had jumped from 3.1 per cent to 17.2 per cent.[29]

Between 1938 and 1940 the average pay of a male manual worker rose by 30 per cent.[30] To curb further rises the government pushed hard for formal wage constraint but aborted its plans on the personal intervention of the Minister of Labour, Ernest Bevin, supported both by the TUC and incongruously by employer organisations whose members were desperately short of labour. Bevin convinced both that wage levels would be better maintained by stabilising the cost of living, and coerced the TUC into agreement to support voluntary restraint.[31]

By mid-1941 rationing had been introduced for petrol, food, clothing and footwear while supplies of basic utilities, including coal and gas had begun to run short. Electric power cuts were occurring with increasingly frequency. The following year the Board of Trade severely curtailed the issue of manufacturing licences, diminishing domestic manufacture to the bare minimum, and totally banned production of a long list of items described as 'fripperies'. Apart from those commodities designated essential or 'Utility', the entire output of the surviving licensed producers was reserved for export only, and severe restrictions were imposed on imports.[32] These compulsory constraints on consumption combined with wage restraint, high taxation, rigid price controls and the general disinclination to spend, to lower the rate of inflation. By the end of 1941 it was brought down to 11.2 per cent and restored to 3.1 per cent in 1944.[33]

The management of Britain's war economy is indeed a heroic story, not only in raising resources to oppose Nazi aggression but in the, albeit temporary, positive influence on the nation's attitude to personal finance. It is never in the nature of the British or probably any other taxpayer to graciously submit to parting with a share of his or her rightful and often hard-won income. Yet when they paid, Britons would come to derive personal satisfaction from having made their contribution to the defence of the realm. The three wartime chancellors, Sir John Simon, Sir Kingsley Wood and Sir John Anderson, would in turn exploit this mindset for all it was worth and fight tirelessly to extract every possible penny from the pockets of their fellow countrymen. With the benefit of hindsight few would dispute that in such adverse circumstances all did their best to be as fair and reasonable as possible.

Not all their contemporaries would have agreed. While most were keen enough to assist the war effort, there was a huge psychological rift between paying taxes with no hope of seeing a return and investing in National Savings or War Bonds, which at least were realisable even if inflation could be expected to erode the anticipated appreciation. At pre-war rates Britain's comparatively few taxpayers, in general, had taken a straightforward approach and paid their dues. Now their liabilities were escalating fast and those most heavily affected were beginning to consider the available options for mitigation. 'Legal avoidance' had not been widely practised since the phrase was dismissively coined by Lloyd George when introducing 'supertax' in 1909. This was about to change and create possibly the least celebrated legacy of the Second World War. Its chancellors were to prove the unwitting founders of Britain's 'tax-planning industry'; an ethereal consumer commodity underpinned by the 1928 *obiter dictum* of Lord Justice General, Lord Clyde, famously commencing:

No man in this country is under the smallest obligation, moral or otherwise, so to arrange his legal relations to his business or his property, as to enable the Inland Revenue to put the largest possible shovel into his stores. The Inland Revenue is not slow, and quite rightly, to take every advantage which is open to it under the taxing statutes for the purpose of depleting the taxpayer's pocket and the taxpayer in like manner is entitled to be as astute, to prevent so far as he honestly can the depletion of his means by the Revenue.[34]

The time had come to exercise the rights the learned judge had prescribed. Potentially high taxpayers began to consult accountants and tax lawyers for advice on how to efficiently arrange their business and financial affairs so as to prevent, so far as they honestly could, depletion of their means by the Inland Revenue and close their stores to its shovel. Most professional practitioners then had neither the experience nor the expertise to devise sophisticated avoidance schemes of the type notoriously publicised in the dynamic commercial ambience of the 1960s and 1970s,[i] but the legislation was a transparent sieve of loopholes and they seldom found difficulties in constraining their clients' tax bills to within affordable boundaries.Among the more commonly used ploys was the 'hobby farm' (not outlawed until the late 1950s); a sham business, not necessarily agricultural in nature, that required a plethora of 'wholly and exclusively' but not *necessarily* incurred expenditure to generate little or no income and thus create a loss for the Inland Revenue to set off against any other type of taxable income.

The more straightforward way to legally avoid direct taxation was to waive or postpone remuneration and live on capital encroachment or investment earnings – preferably in the form of tax-free interest. The retention of cash and accessible investments for such purposes, somewhat ironically, transpired an additional boost for National Savings and therefore the war economy. The 'super wealthy' men, if any,[ii] who followed the column of (later Sir) Oscar R. Hobson, the sagacious City editor of the *News Chronicle*, might have heeded his invariably succinct advice:

A super-wealthy man, paying the maximum rate of 19s 6d in the pound could for example sell £10,000 worth of 3 per cent War Loan and spend the proceeds as income at a cost to himself of only £7 10s a year but at a loss to the state of £150 in income tax and £142 10s in surtax.[35]

---

[i]   See Nigel Tutt, *The History of Tax Avoidance* (1985) – a misleadingly named work on schemes employed in the 1970s and 1980s.

[ii]   In 1944/45 134,209 people were assessed to surtax in the United Kingdom, just over 92,400 (69.8 per cent) on income of less than £4,000, only 1,081 on over £20,000, but *just 52* on more than £100,000 (House of Commons Parliamentary Papers, 'Report of the Commissioners of HM Inland Revenue for the year ended 1946/47', Table 48 (Assessments at 30th September 1947) – as Hobson added: 'A good many rich people have by necessity or choice been living on capital').

Such simple legal sidestepping was still not everyone's preferred defence against the dreaded unstamped manila OHMS envelope containing a ruinous demand from *The* Collector of Taxes, who relieved *His Majesty's* Inspector of Taxes of such unsavoury duties. It is widely conjectured that wholesale undetected tax evasion, with the black market at its root, continued through the war years and beyond. Indeed, the path of the evader was smoothed by an undermanned and under-resourced Inland Revenue grappling with the intricacies of the law and floundering beneath a mountainous backlog of work, while the number of taxpayers escalated by the day.

The civilian workforce too was escalating by the day. From about twenty million it reached a peak in 1943 of twenty-six million, while the strength of the armed forces rose by degrees from 533,000 in 1939 up to about 5.6 million in the final months of the war.[36] Almost the entire adult population was employed for the duration, and even most of the approximately 40 per cent deployed to munitions production were earning as much or more than they had before the war. The shortage of manpower was continuous and creating boundless opportunities for anyone with a modicum of initiative to enhance their income, regardless of ability. The signature tune of the later television series *Dad's Army* typifies the attitude of many civilians happy to help the war effort but happier still to further their own ends:

Mr Brown goes off to town
On the eight twenty-one
But he comes home each evening
And he's ready with his gun.[37]

Mr Brown and those like him, officially described as 'volunteers required to serve without pay on military duty at times which will not interfere with their civil employment', from a financial point of view probably did very well 'in town' – even if not so well from their military commitment. War Office correspondence filed at the National Archives under the deceptive title 'Home Guard Pay and Allowances' records a dogmatic debate at senior level, drawn out over several months in 1940, regarding a proposed expense allowance for volunteers on duty. It was eventually agreed to pay 1s 6d 'tax free' for five hours continuous service or '3s for ten hours for an extra meal [which] cannot be claimed or used honestly for other purposes'. Air-raid wardens, by contrast, could claim up to 10s per day to cover 'loss of civil earnings'.[38] The Home Guard's tax-free compensation, enough for a cup of tea and a sandwich, was eventually granted, but not before Sir Anthony Eden wrote personally on behalf of the War Cabinet to acknowledge the volunteers' 'important and increasingly important work', which in defiance of their Dad's Army image, was often intensely demanding, stressful and dangerous.[39]

The commuting Mr Brown would have been in small need of the occasional 1s 6d or 3s, since he would probably have been employed in a secure job or perhaps running his own business. In either case, his more pressing concern would have been the alleviation of his growing tax liabilities. He might, for example, have been charging his employer's expense account with the train fare for 'the eight twenty-one' and the return journey, while leaving the motor car it provided for him at home.[iii] These and similar benefits-in-kind were all exempt from income tax and increasingly employers began to assist their indispensible staff with beneficial remuneration packages. McKibbin discloses some of the contents of such packages and suggests a justification for them:

> Businessmen and business employees ... were able to escape the worst effects of taxation by the addition to their salaries of untaxed or 'tax efficient' increments. In the 1940s British business began to pay more senior employees in taxed income and 'perks': 'working-day' holidays, life and medical insurance contributions, pension contributions, assistance with children's education, subsidized mortgages, and the 'company car'. By these means style of life and perhaps morale was in part preserved when it could have been dangerously undermined.[40]

For their legitimacy, these lifestyle and morale preserving perks relied on the case of *Tenant v Smith*, fought as far back as 1892. The judge, had shown a singular lack of foresight or clarity of thought when he proclaimed 'the thing sought to be taxed is not income unless it can be turned into money', before ruling that a rent-free house occupied by an employee 'for the convenience of his employer' did not constitute taxable income.[41] Mr Brown then, with a clear conscience, could pocket his package of benefits-in-kind unencumbered by taxation since, indisputably, they were all provided for the convenience of his employer.

Had he been the proprietor of a small or medium-sized business, Mr Brown might well have been making healthy profits which, it must be presumed, he conscientiously declared to be assessed to income-tax. There were businessmen, however, who were not quite that conscientious either in their dealings with the Inland Revenue or indeed with their customers. According to McKibbin, 'shopkeepers, as in the First World War, were notoriously able to sell whatever they had, and were none too deferential when they did'.[42] When any type of restricted goods appeared, as they did sporadically, queues formed and they were sold out in minutes – that is, apart from those concealed 'under the counter'. Private retailers found it hard to resist favouring customers prepared to pay well above the marked or controlled prices but, usually due to lack of evidence, comparatively few were prosecuted until after the war. Service providing tradesmen similarly charged highly inflated prices, often for poor work impeded by shortages of materials and skilled labour, to clients of all classes desperate to buy back a semblance of their vision of pre-war normality. The preponderance of individuals making quick and easy money would not escape the attention of the Treasury.

[iii]   His employer, then as now, could not deduct home-to-work travel expenses from profit for tax purposes.

The Chancellor of the Exchequer since May 1937, Sir John Simon, is now seldom remembered other than as a doyen of income tax law,[iv] but with the outbreak of war he proved himself as capable and energetic as the most revered holders of his office. He immediately set to work on an emergency Budget with an overriding intent to prioritise personal savings. He could not afford to permit anyone to spend their own, let alone borrowed money, other than to directly support the war economy. First he gently prodded Montagu Norman at the Bank of England to 'ask the co-operation of the bankers towards prompt restriction [the word 'refusal' is crossed out in his original draft] of all advances'. He softened his blow a little by adding: 'I am aware that I am imposing on them a responsibility which may embarrass them in their relations with their customers. But I am confident that I shall have their fullest co-operation and that any sacrifices involved will be cheerfully borne'.[43] Two days later, on the eve of budget day, Simon again wrote to Norman, this time in more emphatic terms, telling him that it was 'necessary to impress upon the bankers that this is a long-term policy and as such will require their unremitting attention throughout the period of the war' and warning him of the inflationary dangers of a 'diversion of resources towards non-essential trades'.[44] Two days after that he reduced the bank rate from 3 per cent to 2 per cent to ease the cost of loans for war-related and other key industries – but nothing else. This 'cheap-money' policy fixed the bank rate at that low level for the next twelve years, although in fact the demand for private credit evaporated of its own accord, since nothing surpasses war as a creator of uncertainty, the greatest deterrent to borrowing.

On 27th September 1939, Sir John Simon presented the first of his two war Budgets. As were both, it was a more determined and imaginative performance than he would ever be given credit for.[45] Although discreet in his general approach, by lowering the thresholds at all levels, reducing personal reliefs and raising the standard rate by 1s 6d (7½ per cent) he introduced millions of British people to income tax for the first time in their lives. Together with the 6d he had added in his spring Budget the standard rate now reached 7s (35 per cent). The following year he increased it by a further 6d to a record high of 7s 6d.[46] The newly initiated taxpayer could look forward to contributing as much as 37½ per cent of his taxable earnings to the defence of his country, while the elite who declared incomes above £50,000 could expect to pay an additional 9s 6d (47½ per cent) as the top rate of surtax. Simon was asking them to part with up to 85 per cent of their taxable income.

Their heirs too would also have to endure a new scale of estate duty depriving them of an additional 10 per cent of their inheritance. As with legal income-tax avoidance, before the war taking proactive steps to alleviate liabilities contingent on death had been exclusive to the very wealthiest. The new scale meant that now people of more moderate means would begin to take an interest in the preservation of their swelling capital. As the war years progressed, devices such as family

---

[iv]   Simon founded and was editor-in-chief of *Simon's Income Tax* and related manuals, still leading tax legislation authorities.

trusts, gifts *inter vivos* and designated life insurances increasingly featured in private estate-duty mitigation schemes.

For the majority concerned with the financial affairs of life rather than death, there were no legitimate options short of abstention for alleviating the costs of Simon's additions to duties on tobacco, alcohol and, to the horror of housewives like my mother – who probably then began her secret store – sugar (see Prologue).[47] In one form or another, everyone in Britain was now a taxpayer.

A public still stunned by the declaration of war reacted to Simon's first speech with an amalgam of deference, pragmatism and pessimism.[48] The *Daily Mirror's* report reflected no such attitudes. Its post-budget headline came as news to no one: 'Now You Know There's a War On' and its criticism of the Chancellor for 'accentuating the tendency of business to come to a standstill' was surely of little interest to its working-class readers. The *Daily Mail* similarly complained that 'an unprecedented burden' would cause 'further severe dislocation of trade and industry inflicted without warning'. Both these mass-circulating newspapers, displaying small sensitivity or appreciation of the concerns of ordinary people, many holding their first secure job in years, were offering no more constructive comment than to suggest (wrongly) that higher taxation and the promotion of thrift might discourage private enterprise.[49] The 'editress of a women's magazine' displayed a more realistic grasp of the overall situation when she told Mass-Observation: 'I'm sorry for the younger generation, they'll be chained for life to the debt from this war' and went on to correctly predict that, however much the government extracted from the public purse, it would never be enough.[50] The *Daily Mirror* carried out a post-budget survey which revealed the true concerns, priorities and more positive attitudes of the current generation: 'It hits us, but not so hard as German bombs and if it helps keep them away it will be worth it'; 'We can't hope to win the war without paying for it. I think it's like an insurance'.[51] So often did *Mirror* readers repeat the word 'insurance' it seems almost as if income tax had been elevated from an unpopular imposition to a voluntary premium for an imaginary 'all war risks' policy. The *News Chronicle* need hardly comment: 'Sir John Simon was right to make the country face up to the realities of the situation from the outset'.[52]

Simon himself admonished the 'inexcusable extravagance' of anyone who failed to save and expressed gratitude for the 'flow of humble gifts',[53] while the POSB war diarist recorded a press release which, in similar spirit, showered praise on depositors making direct voluntary donations to the nation: '[The donors were] people of very modest means, who wished to help the country, gifts probably more indicative of a selfless desire than even those from wealthy persons. Most of them wished to remain anonymous'.[54] Each month he meticulously entered the, not always so selfless, gifts effected via direct transfer or by waiving interest and dividends. As they became more affordable and tax-efficient, the voluntary donations steadily grew in size and number, from just 'seven gifts ranging from 1s to £1,000' in January 1940, until May 1945 when 241 depositors waived interest of £971 and 2,673 dividends worth £9,561.[55]

The morning after Simon's final budget speech on 25th April 1940, *The Times* leader headline read precisely as it had seven months earlier: 'The War Budget' but this time spoke more emphatically of 'gigantic figures'.[56] The costs of war were escalating daily and direct taxation settled in arrears was not generating the necessary revenue fast enough. There would have to be a new indirect tax collectable from importers and producers before the consumer, the true bearer of its cost, even put his hand in his pocket. Simon was at pains to explain that he intended purchase tax to be a temporary source of war revenue, just as his illustrious predecessor William Pitt the Younger intended income tax in 1798, but as with income tax, it would transpire too lucrative to revoke on restoration of peace. The new tax would remain concealed in the price of the wide variety of goods selected by successive chancellors until replaced in 1973 by the equally unloved value added tax (VAT). Purchase tax, Simon announced, would come into effect on 21st October 1940.[57]

Of more immediate concern to taxpayers were still harsher reductions in the income-tax personal reliefs and the surtax threshold lowered from £2,000 to £1,500. Simon also raised the excise duties on tobacco and alcohol, and added levies on telephone calls and postage stamps, as if to caution those avoiding direct taxation that there was no hiding place: what they 'saved' would be recouped by indirect taxation. In imposing a 4 per cent limit on company dividends and banning the issue of bonus shares he dashed the hopes of any speculators thinking that investment income and passive capital appreciation would see them through the war. 'Defensive' investment no longer seemed quite such an attractive option. As the Chancellor undoubtedly intended, within days of his Budget, both private and institutional investors began to divert large swathes of their portfolios into governmental securities. *The Times* City column headline announced approvingly: 'A Gilt-Edge Budget', but a few days later a prophetic letter to its editor warned those financial fugitives who still thought they could play safe, that 'the real Budget is, sad to say, still to come'.[58]

Although discouraging extravagance and urging savings were Simon's constant themes, he firmly resisted the entreaties for compulsory state borrowing published in two spirited essays at the beginning of the war by J.M. Keynes.[59] Among the arguments forwarded by the nation's most respected economist was that exorbitant tax rates were bound to reduce the individual's capacity to save. For all Keynes's brilliance this was to prove a misconception. Sir Alec Cairncross later demonstrated that savings as a proportion of disposable income rose impressively from 3½ per cent in 1938 to above 16 per cent in 1944, while disposable incomes rose even faster than taxation due to the constant restriction of spending by shortages, controls and rationing.[60] The 1.8 million middle-income individuals retaining between £250 and £500 after tax in 1937/38, grew to 5.6 million by 1944/45, which for most was adequate to leave a healthy surplus for saving after normal living expenses.[61] Among the many critics of Keynes' proposals, the POSB war diarist demonstrated that the experience of his organisation fully endorsed the Chancellor's faith that the British public required no compulsion to save all they could.[62]

Simon's confidence that individuals and commerce alike would support the nation without formal legislation indeed proved well founded. Once the authoritative voice of Montagu Norman had passed on the Chancellor's message, every bank in Britain henceforth did not simply restrict but refused all private loan applications, regardless of purpose, individual status or strength of security, and suffered no loss of goodwill by so doing. Customers went on depositing their money with unassailable loyalty – and if that money was to be reinvested for the defence of the nation, they had no complaints.

An exceptionally lucid illustration of the consistency of the pattern of banking activity and conformity with the Bank of England's ban on lending can be found in the annual financial returns of the 206 mostly north of England branches of the William Deacon's Bank, held at the RBS archive. These meticulous records highlight both the speed at which money was poured into the bank and how quickly the level of its outstanding advances fell away. Through 1939, at Blackpool Church Street branch deposits had averaged £56,500, of which 67.96 per cent was on loan. By 1943 the branch lending had dropped to barely 10 per cent of the now more than tripled deposits, averaging £170,000. In 1945 the gap had widened still further: of the £255,000 held on deposit no more than 4 per cent (about £10,000) remained outstanding from advances. At the Manchester Moss Side branch lending dropped from 17.1 per cent to 3 per cent, while at the larger Blackburn branch it fell more dramatically from 48.69 per cent also to 3 per cent, while deposits leapt from £119,000 to £421,000.

The returns unfortunately do not indicate the division between personal and commercial activity but by 1943 every branch of William Deacon's had reduced its lending to negligible figures and in some cases to nil. It follows that they could have made few, if any, business advances, yet every branch consistently showed an annual profit (the only recorded loss observed was a mere £143, was at Manchester Moss Side in 1941). Blackpool Church Street had doubled its 1939 profit by 1945 and Blackburn was up by 50 per cent. Through the six years of war most branch reports also indicate a small but steady rise in the number of accounts: Blackpool Church Street, 702 to 942, Blackburn, 1,022 to 1,109.[63] Almost all customers operated current accounts only, and although some might have harboured fugitive funds, in uncertain times instant access was far more valued than a deposit account requiring notice of withdrawal and paying negligible interest while the bank rate was set at 2 per cent.

The war-year annual reports of the leading banks all paint a similar picture: they all conduct more business, remain profitable and pay annual dividends. According to *The Economist* the aggregate profit of the 'seven principal banks' reached a new record level of £9,285,000 in 1945, narrowly exceeding the last full year of war (1944), when the combined total was £9,094,000.[64] Among this magnificent seven, the National Provincial Bank had held £275 million on current and deposit accounts in September 1939, with £140 million outstanding from loans.

By June 1946 its deposits had swollen to £605 million, including £385 million on current accounts, while its outstanding balances (including permitted loans) shrunk to £127 million.[65]

Not only banks but insurance companies, building societies and finance houses remained profitable without granting new private credit facilities. For insurance companies the perils of war, as always, proved conducive to their core business. The generally responsible attitude of borrowers to pre-war mortgage repayment, together with the new deposits and investment income, ensured that the building societies remained buoyant. Despite the credit moratorium, most of the established hire-purchase and finance houses managed to survive on the diminishing returns from pre-war agreements augmented by income from capital reserves.[66] Among the companies which did so was future industry leader, North Central Finance:

> During the war when hire-purchase business in the field of consumer durables and motor vehicles was conspicuous by its absence North Central Finance with a staff of microscopic proportions was fortunate in still having a substantial interest in the financing of railway wagons for colliery companies and merchants. Business came to an end with the nationalisation of railways.[67]

The dearth of revenue from new business and private clients forced smaller and less fortunate finance houses out of business. It was no coincidence that the bankruptcy courts too were almost forced out of business. Among the few positive effects on personal finance to arise from the total cessation of lending was a severe reduction in the number of cases of legal insolvency. Receiving and administration orders dropped from 3,105 in 1938 to 207 in 1945, while the 1,663 deeds of arrangement diminished to just twenty-six (having reached a low of twenty in the previous year).[68] More remarkably the amounts owed by bankrupts fell from close on £7 million to £607,000. Convictions for acts of bankruptcy averaged less than seven per annum and were just two in 1945, the tiny numbers probably more due to shortage of personnel to police the legislation than to debtor probity.[69] Still more remarkably, the *Annual Reports of the Inspector-General in Bankruptcy to the Board of Trade* indicate that when post-war opportunities for borrowing, spending, business venture and speculative investment resumed, the number of cases of insolvency failed to return to its 1938 level. On the other hand, there was a substantial increase in the level of indebtedness. When in 1965 receiving and administration orders surpassed their 1938 total for the first time since the war, the liabilities of the 3,404 debtors were two and a half times greater at £17.7 million. These low insolvency levels provide further evidence that in all sectors of society war-formed habits of attention to personal financial affairs endured beyond the years of austerity.

Among those who found little difficulty in avoiding insolvency through attention to their personal financial affairs were stock market speculators. After the First World War it was estimated that about one million individuals regularly dealt in stocks and shares, and with the easing of economic depression by the late

1930s the popularity of private speculation had grown significantly. Fearing itself a target for the Luftwaffe, the London Stock Exchange (LSE) closed its doors on 1st September 1939 but reopened them just a week later to accommodate the trading that continued unabated outside.[70] It would never again close its doors to business, despite a continuous chronicle of disruption, setbacks and practical difficulties, in particular, loss of capacity due to the absence of members on military service. The market sustained momentum principally by trading War Bonds and gilt-edge government securities and the wholesale transactions of international and institutional bodies, which accounted for more than half the turnover. Wartime turmoil notwithstanding, LSE biographer Ranald Michie claims that it continued to 'perceive the [smaller] provincial stock exchanges as its greatest threat'.[71] Since all the institutional and the most substantial private investors dealt only in the capital, this would suggest that both London and the provincial stock exchanges continued to encourage and value the business of the many small individual investors who traded on regardless.

In peacetime, new share or debenture issues, mergers, takeovers, restructures, boardroom upheavals and similar manifestations of commerce breathe life into the markets. As the war intensified, fewer and fewer such events occurred to add excitement and increase speculation – but it seems an improbable surrogate was provided by enemy action. In September 1940 the City editor of the *Sunday Express* flattered his readers with the headline: 'Investors Don't Get the Jitters Anymore – Air Blitz Shows that British Investors are Tough'. The nation's resilient dealers, according to the article, viewed the first air raids pragmatically and 'rushed' to buy shares in 'brick and cement companies'. Possibly this contained some truth but it is hard to believe that any intelligent speculator presumed that major reconstruction of bombed properties would commence before the end of the war. Greater evidence suggests that investors reacted to the blitz with caution. The many who opted to convert their equities into War Loans might have benefited from a rise of over 15 per cent in the previous year.[72]

Caution might thus have been rewarded but was not essential for successful investment, since almost every class of marketable security appreciated through the war. On average the indices rose 33.5 per cent, British government stocks and UK public bodies provng the best performing sector, with a 74.6 per cent average growth over the six years.[73] Almost all quoted companies continued to post high and escalating profits, and to pay regular dividends up to the legal limit. Anecdotal evidence of quick fortunes made through stock market deals, though undoubtedly frequently exaggerated, is so profuse and enduring that it cannot be wholly discounted as hearsay. Reliable identification of the most astute investors or the extent of their bounty is, however, no longer extant or destined to remain concealed. Stockbrokers bound by client confidentiality had no reason to archive for posterity their records of private wartime transactions. Contemporary Inland Revenue reports confirm significant increases in unearned income, including interest and dividends, but given the growth in savings and other forms of investment, this is to be expected and provides no conclusive guidance to the level of speculative profits.

With the benefit of hindsight, no great depth of appreciation of the whims of the stock market is necessary to see that the surest bets were the industries supplying the rapacious direct and indirect demands of a nation at war, and its people's greater demands for financial security. The speculators who recognised and seized these opportunities could hardly have failed to generate profits – many of them substantial and all of them tax free; it would be another two decades before income tax would be levied on capital gains.[v] A sharp-witted trader might, for example, have done well by selling off insurance stocks immediately war broke out, or better still by buying them back and holding on for a while. On 2nd September 1939 he could have sold Prudential shares at 78s 9d, Pearl for 1s 5½d or Sun Life at 73s 9d and in less than a fortnight bought them back at 50s, 1s 0½d, and 62s 6d respectively. By mid-October all their prices had returned to their 2nd September level and would continue to rise thereafter.[74] For insurance companies, war meant business as usual – better business than usual. In accord with their invariable practice they took immediate precautions to reduce exposure to war risks, raising the cost of all new life assurance and limiting the benefits on policies in force to the higher of paid premiums or surrender value.[75] After every report of destruction and carnage more and more people feared for their lives, their families and their possessions and, at whatever cost, tried to buy some measure of security. Insurance companies, never subjected to any form of price control, did not hesitate to exploit this most emotive of consumer expectancy to the full. The unceasing demand brought them increments in revenues, capital appreciation and profits in every year of the war. The statistics mask a great many tragedies but the number of civilian fatalities thankfully transpired considerably lower than actuarial projections and the claims paid well below budget. Prudential Group's 1943 accounts, for example, indicate in essence that the premium income of its life department was about £15.8 million plus £4.5 million from investments, from which it paid out little more than £12 million to bereaved beneficiaries.[76] The reports of competing insurance companies make similar reading.

These bastions of financial prudence carried on supplying the animated market undeterred by bombed offices, depleted staff, evacuation to improvised premises in provincial towns and similar disruptions. They also carried on promoting business, although it was hardly necessary while Hitler was their most effective publicity agent. The 'man from the Pru', and by temporary necessity the woman too, unfailingly called at the homes of hundreds of thousands of policyholders in every corner of the land, to encourage them to spend still more on self-preservation and family security. These 'ambassadors of thrift' and their competitors diplomatically assured their clients that a paid-up endowment policy would both protect their families and dependants from the financial consequences of enemy action and

---

[v]   Capital Gain Tax was introduced from 6th April 1965 by James Callaghan as chancellor.

would realise their dreams of post-war prosperity. Despite the unfailing profits earned from such improbable doorstep optimism, the insurance companies adopted a cautious, and often over-cautious, approach to the dividends or bonuses they added annually to the equity value of their policies.[77] Yet the British people continued to cherish them, even when aware that the returns they might have been led to expect were unlikely to materialise and that alternative investments could yield greater returns.[78] Under no circumstances would working-class families, like my own, either complain or be dissuaded from entrusting their weekly few shillings and pence to their steadfast ambassador of thrift.

Britain's great life assurance offices had built up their capital on the backs of the lowest paid workers who had constantly struggled for survival in treacherous unprotected workplaces since the Industrial Revolution. In the absence of statutory employer compensation, the Victorian and Edwardian working classes lived in perpetual fear of the consequences of industrial injury. Regardless of the severity of the circumstances, the embryonic state welfare embodied in Lloyd George's National Insurance Act 1911 proffered precious little to the victims of bereavement, accident or sickness and nothing at all to their wives, children and dependants, or to anyone it did not formally cover.[79] Prudent working-class families would spend as much as 10 per cent of their household budget on so-called industrial policies.[80] In insurance parlance the term 'industrial' was to become a euphemism for the poorest social classes able to pay only a few coppers per week for whatever security they might buy. Over time the industrial policy itself evolved into a form of life assurance integral to the working-class tradition of a 'decent' burial, even if in practice its death benefits were barely adequate to cover the cost of the plainest funeral, with seldom a penny over to assist surviving dependants. If an industrial policy lapsed due to inability to continue payment, it carried no rights to refund of its surrender value or even of the premiums paid. In 1943 the Prudential made what it evidently considered a generous concession in offering any industrial policyholder forced to cancel through personal misfortune: 'a free paid-up policy after premiums have been paid for five years and provided the life assured has attained the age of fifteen'.[81]

The press had exposed the demonstrable shortcomings of industrial insurance many times before the war but the little policies never lost their emotive and conventional appeal, and continued to account for the majority of life assurance purchased until the early 1950s. Industrial policies yielded little or no sales commission and against the background of a terrifying war and its austere aftermath, newly moneyed workers became easy prey for the promotion of 'ordinary' endowment policies by representatives not always above the use of emotional blackmail. These more expensive policies offered prospects both of realistic benefit for heirs and rewarding capital appreciation to assist retirement. Like industrial policies they were treated by their buyers as sacrosanct and their premiums paid with unfailing regularity. Even if, as was often the case, capital growth was less encouraging than might have been anticipated, the holder of an ordinary endowment policy could confidently expect to end the war with at least a measure of financial security to his or her name.

An ordinary endowment policy embodied a now almost forgotten additional facility: a percentage of its surrender value could be borrowed back at any time on request. Permitting a policyholder access to his own money defied no government directive or legal requirement and was thus one of the few remaining avenues open to individuals wishing to borrow. From the insurance company's point of view, policy equity was cast-iron security: in the event of default any outstanding interest could be recouped from the retained balance and capital from the death benefit. Prudential agents were trained to advise their clients that they could borrow up to 90 per cent of the surrender value of any paid-up policy.[82] It is to be hoped that they were also trained to advise their clients that taking a loan defeated the basic objective of their policy. Rather than a unique opportunity, this form of loan should have been a last resort and was probably not too often effected by security conscious policyholders with adequate accumulated equity, most of whom would have had savings elsewhere.

Consciousness of the need for financial security was not the exclusive preserve of civilians. Men and women in the armed forces too worried about the uncertainties of post-war life and, contrary to popular legend, were generally in a position to save or invest. Most private and all public sector employers paid their conscripted employees full salaries and standard increments (net of service pay) during absence on military service – though not always willingly. A former Barclays Bank executive, for example, revealed in a later interview that during the war the bank recruited only on a 'temporary' basis to avoid its self-imposed guarantee of full salary in the event of call up.[83] Servicemen also received assistance with payment of ongoing liabilities. In cases of demonstrable depletion of income, mortgage interest and repayments were deferred, while in some circumstances both were wholly written off for the period of conscription.[84] Alternatively, building societies might accept minimal or postponed repayments and replace the outstanding balance with a new advance at the end of the war. Some of the larger societies, led by the Woolwich, provided assistance to buyers of former council houses, since they had taken over a large number of local authority mortgages granted under the Small Dwellings Acquisition Acts in the late 1930s.[85] Similarly, Britain's insurance companies boasted that they never forfeited a life policy, especially one covering a mortgage, for non-payment of premiums while on military service.[86]

The persistent perception that all non-commissioned men in the British armed forces were close to penniless is undoubtedly a myth. Servicemen had nothing to find for food, clothing or accommodation and need spend no more than the occasional few pence on the odd essentials not included in standard issue. The remainder of their pay was free to employ as they saw fit: for leisure activity, to send home to their families or simply to save. Emergency regulations inhibited most of their other spending options, with the notable exceptions of gambling and vice. In 1944, the War Office published a report entitled *An Examination of Army*

Pay and Allowances commencing with an evocation of the spirit of patriotism by Thomas Hardy, writing in 1814:

> If the love of true liberty and honest fame has not ceased to animate the hearts of Englishmen, pay, though necessary, will be the least part of your reward. You will find your best recompense in having done your duty to King and Country – in having protected the wives and children from death, or worse the Death, which will follow the success of such inveterate foes.[87]

This certainly unique document indicates that in August 1942 the lowest paid private received a minimum of 17s 6d per week, 'with proficiency', 21s or 'with three years increments', 29s 9d. A 'private tradesman' did rather better, drawing 43s 6d; while a 'sergeant tradesman' did better still, pocketing 61s 3d a week. By early 1944 the private's basic pay had gone up to 21s or 24s 6d after six-month's service, while an unskilled corporal now received 40s 3d and a warrant officer as much as 91s. The standard weekly pay for officers too had become comparatively generous by 1944. A lieutenant with three years' service received a minimum of £5 1s 0d, a captain £6 2s 6d, and a major £9 19s 6d – all tax free and on top of living expenses. The pay of all ranks was further enhanced by a range of supplements, depending on family circumstances or location. A married officer with two children stationed abroad, for example, might receive up to as much as three times the standard pay for his rank.[88]

The report sets out a meticulously calculated weekly 'budget of a soldier' totalling precisely 14s 9¾d which, assuming it had any basis whatsoever, suggests that, given the stated rates of pay, there was no reason for 'a soldier' ever to be short of a little cash. Curiously, he spent almost a third of his budget (4s 8¾d) on tobacco but nothing on beer or other alcohol. He spent 5½d on 'haircutting, soap, razor blades and cleaning materials', 7d on chocolate, made one visit to the cinema for 1s 6d, and formally saved 2s 11d.[89] Evidently the British soldier was a regular smoker but otherwise, hygienic, sober, plain living, and always had a little money remaining in his pocket.

This so-called budget is at best suspicious but there was no sensible reason or, in most cases, opportunity for spending to rise substantially in proportion to rank or rate of pay. Allowing a wide margin for error, even a newly recruited private soldier should have had some surplus to add to his savings. His family too would not normally have been short of cash. Most service wives could add their own earnings to money sent home and possibly also qualified for the services child allowances that increased regularly through the war years. By 1945 a mother of three, for example, would have been entitled to £1 per week: the equivalent of over 20 per cent of the average wage of a manual worker. Apart from service pay and benefits, more than £318 million was distributed to 'other ranks' in tax-free wartime pensions, grants and allowances, for an assortment of reasons including sickness, war wounds, and dependants in reduced circumstances.[90] On demobilisation every serviceman and woman also benefited from the cash gratuities and other financial assistance to be discussed further in the next chapter.

Despite their legendary 'overpaid, over-sexed and over here'[vi] reputation, the American military personnel, stationed in Britain in increasing numbers from January 1942, did not always have more money than their British counterparts. According to historian Juliet Gardiner, higher ranking officers might have had distinctly less. A US army general, she writes, received the equivalent of £179 4s 3d per month while an officer of equivalent British rank was paid £247 12s 11d. The American officer also more often made a greater financial sacrifice by resigning a highly paid position to serve his country.[91] Lower ranks, on the other hand, were paid up to four times as much as their British counterparts (and indeed far more than most civilian workers in the USA) though the margins might have been narrowed by the supplementary rates and increments mentioned above.[92] Laments such as 'What chance has a poor Tommy with a couple of bob jingling in his pocket?' were ubiquitous, but often the 'couple of bob' might have been worth more than the envied cash the GI jingled louder in his better tailored pocket.[93]

The coins in their pockets were as unfamiliar to young American conscripts as the strange foreign country with an obscure duodecimal currency in which they found themselves. Boys from poor families, naïve and easy prey to sharks and gold-diggers, soon found their generous pay packets depleted by gambling and the mercenary demands of women. Others spent excessively on gifts and gratuities to cultivate or simply maintain the image of affluence bestowed upon them by their austerity-suffering hosts. When their money ran out, the monthly paid Americans borrowed from their weekly-paid British allies, often at extortionate interest.[94] Some resorted to crime. Paul Addison claims that the US forces were the principal suppliers of stolen goods to the black market.[95] The PX (Post-Exchange) stores on American bases demanded no ration points and were better stocked with specially flown-in goods than the austerity compliant NAAFI (Navy, Army and Air-Force Institute). American personnel therefore had ample opportunity to buy, and presumably to steal, supplies for the ready markets in foodstuffs, drink, clothing, cosmetics, tobacco and other luxuries no longer available in British shops.[96]

Activity in the armed forces is by nature intermittent and whether stationed at home or abroad British servicemen regularly had time on their hands, often a great deal of time, and every reason to use it profitably. For those proficient at trades or simply prepared to work, labour shortages created countless opportunities to earn extra cash. Rather than squander the money on black-market luxuries or in emulation of the ostentation of their American visitors, the majority of Britain's soldiers pledged a second allegiance to its National Savings army.

Servicemen and civilians alike heeded Sir John Simon's pleas and put all they could at the nation's disposal but neither this, nor the acquiescence to high taxation, would be sufficient to stay the tidal wave of war costs. Sir Kingsley Wood, appointed Chancellor of the Exchequer in Churchill's war cabinet, lost no

---

[vi]   Attributed to comedian Tommy Trinder.

time in revealing the content of the 'real Budget', that had been so clearly forecast after his predecessor's last assault on the pocket of the taxpayer and consumer. Precisely three months later, on 23rd July 1940, the House of Commons listened to its third budget speech in the first nine months of war. This time no powers of foresight were needed to appreciate that it was not to be the last 'real Budget' and that the pocket of the taxpayer and consumer would again be raided.[97]

Wood left no one in any doubt about the gravity of the situation. Everyone in the land, regardless of class, status or financial means, in one way or another, would have to contribute more. As he spoke a committee headed by the industrialist and distinguished civil servant (later Sir) Paul Chambers[98] was putting the final touches on its blueprint for a new system of fast-track income-tax collection to be called Pay As You Earn (PAYE), but the Chancellor had no time to wait for its completion.[vii] He demanded that employers immediately begin to deduct income tax from salaries and wages 'as directed'. No more could employees delay their biannual settlement until the last moment or longer if they were prepared to pay an interest penalty. Wood went on to demand 'widespread and drastic reduction in personal expenditure' and to announce a catalogue of joyless measures to ensure that there would be no legal option other than compliance. He raised the income-tax standard rate by a further one shilling to 8s 6d (42½ per cent) and also increased all the surtax rates. A wealthy minority declaring taxable income above £30,000 braced themselves to pay 9s 6d in the pound, which with surtax, brought their combined imposition up to 90 per cent. Like Simon, Wood hit the lower paid hardest by lowering the personal reliefs. He made estate duty yet more punitive and even reduced life assurance relief for the first time since income tax itself was introduced. Consumers would again be expected to accept rises in the duties on alcohol, tobacco and entertainment. Finally, the new Chancellor revealed the full impact of purchase tax. The price of 'luxuries and goods not immediately necessary' would conceal 33⅓ per cent and almost every other tangible consumer commodity, including adult clothing, books, publications and many pharmaceuticals, 16⅔ per cent. Essential foodstuffs and little else escaped the net.

The following day *The Times*' budget leader included the extraordinary comment: 'Those on lower incomes [will] escape very lightly [since] 80 per cent of the items in the cost of living index remain exempt from purchase tax'. This inept attempt to comfort the British consumer by throwing some positive light on Wood's Budget, at least won the concurrence of one lower income reader. This high-principled patriot informed the editor that on his birthday he intended to send the Chancellor of the Exchequer a gift of seventy pounds, equal to one pound for each year of his life, and commended the practice to all regardless of income.[99] *The Times* did not report to what extent the commendation was followed by other light escapees content to live on the depleted purchase-tax exempt items in the cost of living index.

[vii]   Wood died suddenly on 21st September 1943, the eve of the scheduled formal announcement of PAYE in the House of Commons.

Kingsley Wood's 1941 spring Budget was predictably dominated by the escalation of inflation and 'the most expensive war in history'.[100] To kill both birds with one stone he imposed the most expensive tax regime in history. First he lowered the income-tax exemption limits and once again all personal allowances, elevating a further two million people to the unenviable status of wartime taxpayer. Then he pushed the standard rate to its zenith – 10 shillings (50 per cent). The richest in the land would now be faced by the daunting prospect that from every pound of their taxable income in the top surtax band the Treasury would extract 97½ per cent.[101] For the next five years that formidable aggregate would extend its shadow across their every spending and investment decision.

The new taxes were calculated to collect one-third of the national income: as *The Times* put it, '[this] may fairly have been said to have reached the limit of what can be raised'.[102] It was still not enough. Wood, unlike Simon, yielded to Keynes' calls for compulsory savings. Every taxpayer would make a loan to the nation by direct deduction from his or her income through the restriction of personal reliefs – uniquely to be refunded at an unspecified date after the war. The concept was applauded by the press, in the House of Commons and given a general seal of approval by the public. Mass-Observation's post-budget poll reported 'unanimous praise' for the scheme.[103] Kindersley described the budget measures as 'rightly designed' to demand 'more drastic self-denial by us all'.[104] The more drastic self-denial involved in 'post-war credits', as the deductions which continued until 5th April 1946 were known, proved rather more than their initial supporters bargained for. The Inland Revenue eked out the repayments (transferred only into POSB accounts) until 1973, to those who survived and retained all their certificates until their sixtieth birthday, or if women, their fifty-fifth.[105] A quarter of a century after the declaration of peace post-war credits were still a sufficiently sensitive issue to be denounced as a 'dishonourable breach of faith' when just how grudgingly the government had reimbursed compulsory savings was fully revealed.[106]

Also in 1941, the Midland, then Britain's biggest bank, began publishing advertisements claiming that 'too many notes are still being hoarded' and recommending hoarders to deposit them in the bank or, at least, invest in Defence Bonds.[107] By then less innocent connotations than traditional working-class distrust of the banks were being attributed to cash hoarding. Tax evaders and black marketeers shunned investing cash for fear of inciting Inland Revenue or police investigation. While such fugitive funds were thought to account in no small part for the wartime growth in current accounts yielding no interest to be declared on tax returns, more knowledgeable culpable depositors did not rely on absolute bank confidentiality. They would have been aware of the case of *Tournier v National Provincial and Union Bank of England*, which established in 1924 that in cases of alleged fraud or theft the courts had the right to require bankers to disclose details of their customer's affairs. It is thus improbable that the Midland's advertisements drastically changed the habits of bank-note hoarders. The majority of current account holders were, in fact, quite innocent savers petrified of the most remote risk, and careless of the value of their money being eroded by inflation.

There is an abundance of anecdotal evidence of questionably legal wartime profiteering, not all well founded and not all involving tax evaders or black marketeers. One Mass-Observation war diary records an encounter with an ostentatiously cash-rich 'man who turned out to be one of the heads of a large munitions factory in the Midlands. He was on holiday in Norfolk. And he actually told my soldier friend that he hoped the war would last ten years. Disgusting!'[108] The diarist spoke for the majority in deploring the attitude of those in positions of responsibility, who not only exploited money entrusted to the nation but were insensitive to the feelings and bravery of those defending it on their behalf. And if the Chancellor could not support that majority opinion by eliminating profiteers and opportunists, he could still reap a harvest of taxation from their attempts to indulge their ill-gotten gains.

When Wood introduced his spring Budgets of 1942 and 1943, the war continued to drain the economy faster than the combined armies of savers, taxpayers and consumers could replenish it. He could raise direct taxes no further without encouraging greater evasion and stifling the incentive of weary war workers. All that was left was indirect taxation and the diminutive Chancellor wielded the last weapon in his arsenal with all the might he could muster. In 1942 he doubled purchase tax to 66⅔ per cent on twenty-six classes of goods designated 'luxury' and pushed it up to 100 per cent the following year.[109] He subjected essential stationery, hitherto exempt, to 33⅓ per cent, though a severe paper shortage had already reduced the national newspapers to a single folded sheet. In both Budgets Wood targeted alcohol, first raising the price of a bottle of whiskey by 4s 8d and then by 2s 4d (the 7s addition alone would be over £15 today). Those so minded would find it exorbitantly expensive to drink themselves into oblivion to their conscience or the horrors of war.

Surprisingly, six months after Wood's second and in many ways most punishing Budget a Mass-Observation survey revealed that there were now 'far fewer completely disgruntled people', with just 3 per cent giving money as their 'main grumble'. Unsurprisingly, their main grumble was the inadequacy of accessible foodstuffs and other shortages in the shops. The only group expressing serious concerns about the cost of living were the elderly and infirm fighting to survive the war on tiny state pensions or small fixed incomes.[110] The other respondents all agreed that their financial position had improved. Two months later, a further survey reported that over 50 per cent voiced no objection to higher taxation or even to paying income tax for the first time.[111]

In both his third and fourth Budgets Wood added duties to the price of theatre tickets. With the outbreak of war, Britain's theatres, cinemas and places of entertainment had all closed down but, in the apparent absence of imminent danger, most reopened within weeks and stayed open for the duration. On deteriorating stages, hampered by lack of equipment and absence of performers music-hall entertainments, dramas and concerts played to packed houses, often confined to matinees to allow audiences to be home before blackout curfews.[112] Every live performance, and many were provided free of charge, was lauded for its invaluable contribution to the nation's morale. To a besieged chancellor, even these all-important cultural diversions were a vital source of revenue, but to the people of Britain they were a vital reminder that less troubled times were sure to return.

In similar spirit, the magazine *Country Life*, as always at peace with the world, somehow managed to publish a new edition in every week of the war. Its advertisers too, untroubled by the tribulations of conflict, continued to extol the luxury motor cars they could neither produce nor deliver. Jensen confidently predicted that 'after victory' it would resume production of its magnificent sports cars – temporarily reduced to artists' impressions. Bentley, similarly resorting to water colour imagery, poetically reassured hopeful buyers that 'these are pleasures we shall know again'. The grand estate agents presented black-and-white photographs of gracious mansions with antique architectural features and landscaped gardens, to a market that the seldom perturbed *Country Life* solemnly pronounced 'dead' – killed by the £100 per house limit on maintenance and restoration expenditure.[113] In the absence of bank or mortgage finance, a private house buyer needed sufficient accessible capital to pay the full price, since the remnant of the highest income after tax would hardly have bought even the cheapest property.

Dealers and auction houses continued to advertise the sale of antiques and fine art to their exclusive clientele, who resolutely continued to invest and deal in paintings, jewellery, furniture and *objets d'art*. It is in the nature of such investors and dealers to thrive on risk. One leading collector who lost over 10,000 rare books in an air raid, some he claimed worth hundreds of pounds, accepted no more than 1s 6d per volume in insurance compensation, yet evidently went on buying.[114] Looking back it is surprising that anyone at all invested in material things when threatened by enemy bombs, yet the prices of all forms of antiques, especially gold and Georgian silver objects, continued to rise with demand.[115] Jewellery sales at leading London auction houses in January and February 1943, for example, each yielded record bids totalling in excess of £33,000 (over £1½ million).[116]

There were also more practical reasons to buy antiques. The stoppage in manufacture of everything nominated inessential spawned active markets in old and second-hand furniture, carpets, crockery, cutlery, glassware and other domestic requisites. Precious objects, often having spent much of their long lives as mere ornaments, were now dusted off, brought out of retirement and re-employed for their intended purposes. In the fullness of time, such seemingly extravagant but pragmatic acquisitions would be transformed into rewarding investments.

At the beginning of 1945 *Antique Collector* produced detailed data to demonstrate that there was no justification for the widely held view that the seller's market was largely due to rich Americans buying up Britain's heritage. According to published official tables, the number of export licences and declared values had in fact steadily declined through the war years.[117] Wealthy Britons, and those becoming so, were by far the most prolific buyers. The saleroom column of *The Times* regularly reported a buoyant local market and 'keen bidding' at Sotheby's and Christie's. As the prospect of peace drew closer, so the bidding grew keener. One jewellery sale in March 1945 generated as much as £60,500;

in July antique silver went under the hammer for £57,000; while in August fine English furniture fetched £20,691, a record for this type of sale.[118] Even at these now appreciably inflated prices, successful private bidders were destined to make substantial gains after the war. And those who acquired one or more of the few investment properties that changed hands by auction or private sale and survived the bombing were destined to make even more substantial capital gains – tax-free capital gains.[119]

Few changes of significance were made to the emergency tax regime after Sir Kingsley Wood's died suddenly in September 1943. His successor, Sir John Anderson, delivered the 1944 and 1945 spring Budgets in an atmosphere of growing but cautious optimism.[120] After both speeches, *The Times* congratulated the him on having established 'stability' and a situation where 'government expenditure was no longer growing faster than the yield from existing taxes'.[121] The credit for these truly remarkable achievements clearly belonged to Simon, Wood, and the co-operation of the British people, but the press, as always, had a short memory. In his second and final Budget, a few weeks before victory in Europe, Anderson uttered some muted hints that taxes might be lowered, but omitted to say when. There were few higher hopes and no one protested. The British people understood that victory came at a high price and that they would have to pay it. The Chancellor offered some consolation by venturing to suggest that full employment could be expected to continue after the war – regeneration would require a massive workforce.[122] Rationing, shortages and controls too could be expected to continue after the war – austerity would require massive restraint.

In such precarious circumstances the people of Britain could be readily forgiven for failing to recognise the improvements in their personal financial positions demonstrated in this chapter. During the long years of uncertainty they had sought physical and financial security and foregone inessential acquisitions and extravagant pleasures. They had petrified their defensive capital, modest and substantial, in trust to the nation for the duration of the war. They had heeded the National Savings slogan: 'The more you lend, the nearer the end'. And when the end came, they found themselves strangers in a devastated land, overshadowed by austerity, and afraid that their petrified capital was illusory or at best temporary.

Endnotes

1   MO: FR 1053, 'Savings Survey (Working Class)', November–December 1941.
2   MO: TC57 2A, 25th October 1939.
3   Richards, Jeffrey, *Films and British National Identity: From Dickens to Dad's Army* (1997), citing Leslie Howard (1893–1943), 'Shopkeepers and Poets' broadcast 14th and 15th October 1940, 15.
4   RM: POST56/146: 30th September 1939.
5   RM: POST56/146: 31st October 1939.
6   RM: POST56/146: 29th November and 15th December 1939.
7   RM: POST56/146: 31st October 1939 and 31st July 1945.
8   Mitchell, B.R. and Jones, H.G., *Second Abstract of Statistics* (1971), 180.
9   Home, H. Oliver, *A History of Savings Banks* (1947), 361.
10 BSA: Minutes of Council Meetings, 19th September 1939.
11 NSI: *Report to the House of Commons of the Committee to Review National Savings*, (Sir Harry) Page Committee, 22nd June 1973 (HMSO), 266.
12 MO: 57/2/B, National Savings Campaigns 1939–1942, Broadcasts 13th August 1941; 25th September 1941.
13 MO: 57/2/B, 'Kindersley's Broadcasts Survey'; 57/2/C, October 1941.
14 Burton, K.G., *A Penknife to a Mountain: The Early Years of the National Savings Committee* (1999), 223.
15 NSI: *History and Development of National Savings and Investments*, 4th February 2004.
16 MO: TC57/2/C.
17 *The Times*, 7th March 1944; Longmate, Norman, *How We Lived Then: A History of Everyday Life During the Second World War* (1971), 382.
18 *Country Life*, 12th March 1943.
19 Longmate (1971), 382–384.
20 MO: TC57/3/A.
21 NA, PRO, LAB/10/415, Somervell, Solicitor General's Office to Speed, Treasury Solicitor's Department, 11th December 1939.
22 MO: 57/2/C.
23 Madge, Charles, *Wartime Patterns of Saving and Spending* (1943), 101.
24 McKibbin (2000), 177.
25 Madge (1943), 1, 42, 84–85.
26 MO: TC57/1/C, 6th February 1941.
27 *The Times*, 8th April 1941.
28 Madge (1943), 45.
29 H of C, 02/44.
30 McKibbin (2000), 63.
31 Bullock, Alan, *Ernest Bevin: A Biography* (2002), 290–291.
32 Zweiniger-Bargielowska, Ina, *Austerity in Britain: Rationing, Controls, and Consumption 1939–1955*, 2000 (2004), 45–47.
33 H of C, 02/44.
34 Carter, Roger N., Public Lecture, *The Taxpayer and the Treasury* (1938), 18.

35 *News Chronicle*, 2nd April 1946.

36 Axford et al., *The British Economy: Key Statistics 1900–1970* (*c.*1971), 9.

37 *Dad's Army* theme by Jimmy Perry, sung by Bud Flanagan (1969).

38 NA, PRO, WO/32/10019, 28B, 'Home Guard Pay and Allowances, 1940–41', 6th September 1940, Director General of Welfare and Territorial Army, Major W.J. Wells to General Officer Commander in Chief, Eastern Command, citing Defence (Local Defence Volunteers) Regulations 1940.

39 NA, PRO, WO/32/10019, 12A, Eden to Wood, 8th July 1940.

40 McKibbin (2000), 63.

41 Carter (1938), 4.

42 McKibbin (2000), 63.

43 NA, PRO, T233/1396, 'Restriction of Bank Advances', Simon to Norman, 24th September 1939.

44 Ibid., Simon to Norman, 26th September 1939.

45 Dutton, David, *Simon: A Political Biography of Sir John Simon* (1992), 290.

46 *The Times*, 28th September 1939.

47 Ibid.

48 MO: TC57/1/A, 'The Budget, Money Matters and Household Budgetary 1939–1950'.

49 MO: TC57/1/B, *Daily Mail*; *Daily Mirror*, 29th September 1939.

50 MO: TC57/1/A, 3rd October 1939.

51 MO: TC57/1/A, 'First War Budget' (*Daily Mirror* interviews).

52 Ibid.

53 MO: TC57/1/A; *The Times*, 28th September 1939.

54 RM: POST 56, 15/146, 17th October 1939.

55 RM: POST 56 /146, War Diary: month end entries.

56 *The Times*, 24th April 1940.

57 Sabine, B.E.V., *A Short History of Taxation* (1980), 142.

58 *The Times*, 25th and 30th April 1940, letter from Manfred Emanuel.

59 Ibid., 14th and 15th November 1939, J.M. Keynes, 'Paying for the War': 'I. The Control of Consumption' and 'II. Compulsory Savings'.

60 Cairncross, Alec, *The British Economy Since 1945: Economic Policy and Performance, 1945–1995*, 1992 (1995), 76.

61 MO: FR 3073, 1949 'National Income and Expenditure of the UK'.

62 RM: POST 56/146, *POSB War Diary*, 14th and 15th November 1939.

63 RBSGA: WD/377/3, 'William Deacon's Bank: Particulars of Branches'.

64 *The Economist*, 12th January 1946, 69–70.

65 RBSGA: NAT/1007/10 'National Provincial Bank: Abstract of Accounts'.

66 Harris et al. (1961), 30.

67 RBSGA: NCF 30, 'The Story of NC Wagon and Finance Company Ltd'.

68 *Report by the Inspector-General in Bankruptcy for the years 1939–1953* (HMSO – Board of Trade), 4–5.

69 Ibid., Table VI, p. 31.

70 Michie, Ranald C., *The London Stock Exchange: A History* (1999), 288, 72.

71 Ibid., p. 308.

72 MO: TC57/1/B; *Sunday Express*, 15th September 1940.
73 Michie (1999), Table 7.2, 321–322.
74 *The Economist*, 2nd, 16th September, 21st October 1939.
75 Ibid., 9th September 1939.
76 PGA: Box No. 273, 95th Annual Report.
77 Dennett, Laurie, *A Sense of Security: 150 Years of the Prudential* (1998), 85.
78 *The Banker*, Little, L.T., 'Life Assurance and the Value of Money', March 1947, 192–196.
79 Rivett, Geoffrey, *From Cradle to Grave: 50 Year of NHS* (1998), 1.
80 McKibbin, Ross, *The Ideologies of Class: Social Relations in Britain 1880–1950* (1990), 114.
81 PGA, *Prudential Bulletin*, May 1943.
82 PGA, Box 1326, 'Ordinary Branch Training Course for New Agents', February 1948.
83 BB/WEBS, Oral History 725/11.
84 Ritchie (1997), 76.
85 Ibid., 72.
86 *The Economist*, 9th September 1939.
87 NA, PRO, WO/32/10975 – 6A, January 1944: Hardy, *The Trumpet Major* 'Address to all Ranks and Descriptions of Englishmen'.
88 Ibid., W.L. Gorell Barnes, Secretary to the War Office, 20th March 1944.
89 Ibid., Table 3.
90 Howlett (*c*.1996), 'War Pensions, Grants and Allowances', 2.10, 24.
91 Gardiner, Juliet, *Over Here: The GIs in Wartime Britain* (1992), 8, 62.
92 Tillitt, M.H., in *Barron's National Business and Financial Weekly*, 'Army-Navy Pay Tops Most Civilians', 24th April 1944.
93 Gardiner (1992), 63.
94 Thomas (2003), 222.
95 Addison, Paul, *Now the War is Over: A Social History of Britain 1945–51* (1985), 45.
96 Longmate, Norman, *The GIs: The Americans in Britain 1942–1945* (1975), 99.
97 *The Times*, 24th July 1940.
98 *Journal of the Royal Statistical Society – Series A (General)*, Paine, Toby, 'Obituary: Sir Paul Chambers 1904–1981', vol. 145, No. 3 (1982), 374.
99 *The Times*, 24th July 1940, letter from Mr Frank Hayes.
100 Ibid., 8th April 1941.
101 Gee and Co, *Tax Factbook*, 'Historic Data', 7/68.13.
102 *The Times*, 8th April 1941.
103 MO: TC 57/1/A 'Responses to the Budget', 8th April 1941.
104 *The Times*, 8th April 1941.
105 *Daily Mail Tax Guide 1947/48*.
106 Longmate, (1971), 377–378.
107 NA, PRO, T/160/1270: 'Ration Your Current Accounts', 22nd October 1943.
108 MO: TC57/1/F, Husband and wife war diary entry, November 1941.
109 *The Times*, 15th April 1942 and 13th April 1943.
110 MO: TC57/1/E, 11th September 1941.
111 Ibid., 11th November 1941.

[112] Gardiner, Juliet, *Wartime Britain: 1939–1945* (2004), 113, 119.
[113] *Country Life*, 16th April 1943.
[114] *Antique Collector*, March–April 1945, 69.
[115] Ibid., 30th April 1943.
[116] *The Times*, 29th January; 25th February 1943.
[117] *Antique Collector*, January–February 1945, 11, 24.
[118] *The Times*, 8th March and 12th July 1945, *Antique Collector*, September–October 1945, 216.
[119] *The Banker*, April 1941, 27.
[120] Sabine (1980), 142.
[121] *The Times*, 26th April 1944; 25th April 1945.
[122] Ibid., 25th April 1945.

Chapter 4

Short Dawn
(*1945 to 1947*)

Mr Bevan can be assured that, once they are given the chance, the people of this country will take steps to purchase their homes in as great numbers as ever. To boast that he has kept them hitherto from doing so stamps him as a dictator rather than a democrat.

Building Societies Gazette[1]

One morning towards the end of 1947 my father took a couple of hours off work. It was time he felt he could ill afford: it would mean the irretrievable loss of a few shillings from his pay. He walked to the nearby post office where he was well known for his weekly purchase of a postal order for the football pools. By prior arrangement but without formal identification he withdrew most, but not all, of the balance on his POSB account. The cashier recorded the transaction in the proffered passbook and in his own daily log and handed over the sum in cash. My father secreted the bundles of one-pound notes inside his jacket, probably less concerned with the remote possibility of daylight robbery in a busy provincial town than with drawing attention to his errand. He was about to complete the purchase of a house and would not have wished to publicise the financial risk he might be thought to have been taking.[i]

He had not applied for a mortgage. He believed it improbable that he could satisfy the conditions to compete for the funds of a local building society limited by the branch quota system which dominated all advances. But far more constraining was his total abhorrence of debt. This and similar attitudes to credit and borrowing would haunt his generation for decades to come. Forty-five years after the war, Richard Hoggart (born 1918) confesses to remaining obsessed with the petty economies instilled into him in his youth:

> There is still, after all, behind every dealing with money and things, the fear and the hatred of waste. That old phrase which I have quoted before – 'you'll pay for this' – is joined by 'it's a sin and a shame to be so wasteful', 'fancy good food being thrown away', 'he doesn't seem to know the value of money', 'I've had to work hard for every penny I've got and I'm not going to squander it', a penny

---

[i]   At the age of eight, I did not of course witness this event but my father described it many times, some documentary evidence is extant; I thus believe it close to the truth. (Though easier to carry, he would not have accepted the large white five-pound notes (withdrawn in 1961) as it was necessary to sign them individually when changing hands.)

saved is a penny earned', ' take care of the pence and the pounds will look after themselves', 'put something aside for a rainy day', 'waste not want not', 'I mean to get my money's worth' and dozens of others expressing the fear of excess; the built-in rules of the siege economy ... So I try to anticipate every conceivable bill for months ahead, even though I know we are lucky enough to be able to pay them without difficulty.[2]

Hoggart could no more explicitly have expounded the financial mindset of ordinary British people like my father, in the aftermath of the Second World War. Musing on this emotive summation of the spirit of the age of austerity, Peter Hennessy recalls: 'how those phrases resonate for me, the domestic standbys of my childhood'.[3] These and similar aphorisms exhorting financial caution also mirror those which governed the daily existence of my own family. One oral history recording I found at the British Library in particular evoked Shakespeare's rarely heeded wisdom but heard repeatedly in my formative years: 'Neither a borrower nor a lender be: for a loan oft loses both itself and friend'.[4]

My father need be unperturbed by such forebodings as he walked on to his solicitor's office to sign the completion documents and pay over the balance of about six hundred pounds to purchase outright the three-bedroom house he had rented through most of the war. He had paid a small deposit earlier but the total was still well below the market price for a house of its kind. Government controls had frozen all rents at pre-war levels and tied the hands of his landlord who, like most others, was unable to make letting pay and left with no option other than to sell to his sitting tenant at a considerable discount.

In joining the 26 per cent who were then owner-occupiers, my father fully understood that he was acquiring a financial asset of potential substance but capital appreciation was the last thing on his mind. His prime motive was to provide security of tenure for his family through a housing shortage of redoubtable proportions with no end in sight. His greatest concern was the maintenance expense he was about to inherit from his landlord. As with most houses, exterior and interior repairs, redecoration and replacement of worn out furniture had all been neglected since before the war, but immediate attention to such matters was out of the question. Building materials, furnishings, appliances and skilled labour were all in short supply and, where and when available, prohibitively expensive. Post-war austerity was at its height.

Having completed the legal formalities and handed over the cash to his solicitor, my father became the owner of the unencumbered freehold interest in a larger than average semi-detached house with a spacious garden. He also owned the balance remaining in his POSB account, some National Savings certificates accumulated through the war years, and his religiously paid-up endowment assurance policies. He had a regular income from a job and owed not a penny, but would have given no credence to the suggestion that he was well off or affluent. Until researching this book I believed, as my father undoubtedly did, that we then virtually lived from hand to mouth. Occasional wartime spurts of higher earnings had enabled him to save intermittently and after a six-year wait the War Damage Commission had settled the compensation claim for the loss to Hitler's bombers of his pre-war home and livelihood, submitted by a London surveyor on his behalf. He had thus accumulated the capital to buy a freehold property outright, but would have considered the suggestion that the war had transformed him into even a minor capitalist totally absurd and probably offensive. But that is what had happened. My family had experienced a passive transition to a new and different middle-class existence.

We lived in a middle-class street, in our own middle-class house in which there was no central heating, washing machine, telephone, refrigerator, vacuum cleaner or television, and no motor car was parked outside. My parents were well aware of the benefits and pleasures such things could provide. They had seen and owned some of them before the war and they were again being extolled by an anodyne mass media, gently sidestepping the unpleasant practicalities of life in the age of austerity. Whether or not they could afford them, their neighbours and the people they knew did not openly crave these supposed modern liberations from drudgery. In their and my parents' parochial daily lives there was little use for a telephone or a motor car, and four hours per day of Reithian television was the last thing in the world they needed.[ii]

Among my parents more worldly needs was sufficient coal for the open fire to warm a single room in the winter evenings and an arrangement with the merchant for deliveries and payments to be spread evenly throughout the year. Coal was dirty, laborious and expensive, but they believed that central heating which warmed rooms not in use was close to criminal waste. Why did they need a refrigerator using gas or electricity all day and night when their terracotta milk cooler standing in a bowl of cold water and their wooden meat safe, with its ventilated metal side panels, kept their food fresh enough at no cost? They could manage without the contemptuously extravagant vacuum cleaner rich or lazy housewives bought only for show, when the simple broom was so much more efficient. No electric machine, according to my mother, could wash clothes as clean as a scrub in the kitchen sink or a boil in her primitive 'copper'. In 1947 'many leading industrialists' would not be persuaded that there was an annual market in Britain for more than a few thousand American washing machines.[5] Dishwashers, first patented in the USA in 1886, were introduced to Britain in 1923 when *House and Garden* condemned them as 'machines of doubtful value' and drove them to near extinction.[6] Domestic mechanisation was for the future.

The overriding priority of the responsible post-war citizen continued to be the accumulation of financial security. Later a great deal of wisdom would be dispensed about the emergence of affluence gauged by overt material possessions and personal assets. Yet, my parents and those like them, a large and variegated middle class in waiting, were for a brief interval arguably more affluent than

---

[ii]   Reith left the BBC in 1938 but its broadcasts remained heavily influenced by his dogmatic principles long after television transmission recommenced on 7th June 1946.

the future generations which openly acknowledged that elevated status, though burdened with financial liabilities constantly growing in size and complexity.

Britain had indeed emerged from the Second World War a nation of small capitalists, but only a tiny minority of its people felt or behaved like any recognisable concept of a capitalist. Money breeds confidence, confidence breeds demand, demand breeds commerce and industry, and commerce and industry breed capitalists. Amidst a culture of defiant restraint, post-war Britons would attempt to deny this inevitable sequence. Callum Brown succinctly captures the prevailing spirit when conjecturing: 'Suburban ordinariness reached its apogee, enjoyed by older generations as the prize for enduring two world wars and a prolonged economic depression'.[7]

Older generations enjoying the apogee of suburban ordinariness were not alone in accepting post-war prizes, but prizes more often of a financially rewarding nature. People of all classes had begun amassing wealth, in some cases on a substantial scale and at a remarkable speed. Many were unable to 'enjoy' the unfamiliar experience of a surfeit of money and took refuge in inhibition from the unsavoury label, *nouveau riche*, with its connotation of war profiteering. While austerity persisted reluctant and unwitting recruits to the middle-classes remained disturbed by the moral question of the rectitude of consumption, whether or not conspicuous. Their dilemma caused often unfounded feelings of guilt to be instrumental in a religious revival on a scale unprecedented in living memory. The Christian churches experienced their 'greatest annual growth in membership, Sunday school enrolment, and baptisms, etc. since the eighteenth century ... traditional values of family, home and piety were suddenly back on the agenda', wrote Brown.[8] Church ministers had never preached to congregations so receptive to doctrines of abstinence, restraint and prudence.

Faith, however sincere, proved no barrier to those who upheld the nation's God-given right to the plundered riches of the British Empire crumbling under the demands of nationalism, or to the fruits of still dark satanic mills ailing in the face of foreign competition and lack of capital investment. Britons, ingrained with pride in their great tradition, could not bring themselves to acknowledge that the money filtering down to their pockets no longer flowed naturally from these founts. The true fount of their disconcerting capital was American goodwill, but they would not be humbled into expression of gratitude to their allies, who had suffered no bomb shelters, blackouts nor blitz. It was more consoling to thank God for their deliverance from the Nazis, or simply pray that their good financial fortune would prove more than temporary. Prayer was a virtuous alternative to resentment, and the note or few coins slid discreetly onto the plate would not, it was trusted, be judged conspicuous consumption by fellow worshippers. The consolation of private piety was as a feigned gesture of independence akin to the 'sour grapeism' that Elizabeth Gaskell aligned to 'elegant economy' in the days when Britain really was independent. Its people were rightly proud of their role in winning the Second World War but could find little pride in an economic outcome that inhibited their deep nostalgia for the independence of pre-war consumerism.

Hopkins would not be the last historian to evoke Wordsworth's noble aphorism 'plain living and high thinking' and extend that model of post-war demeanour into a paradox: 'There existed side by side, often overlapping in baffling fashion, an England of "plain living and high thinking" and an England of "high living and distinctly low thinking"'.[9] In every sector of the community lifestyles were divided between these camps but, contrary to many accounts, the former were clearly the majority – that is, for a few early post-war years. Would-be high livers, unwilling or unable to curb the urge to spend, continued to find their endeavours obstructed by thinly stocked shops and exorbitant unreliable services. Some took advantage of the ubiquitous opportunities to circumvent emergency legislation and buy their luxuries on the black-market, but there was no need to break the law to indulge in ethereal pleasures. The dilapidated music halls, cinemas, pubs and racecourses might have lost some of the glamour of their pre-war heyday, but they were still a lot more fun than buying functional Utility clothes and National Savings certificates. A dearth of material products need not equate to a dearth of prodigality.

Low thinking and high living, however widely practised or privately coveted, could never be countenanced in public. At best it smacked of Americanisation, the most despised defiler of all held dear by the high-thinking-plain-living majority. To them, anything originating in America was intrinsically devoid of merit. Even the highest thinkers of all portrayed conspicuous consumption itself as an inferior and unwanted American import gratuitously thrown in with the economic aid. George Orwell argued that 'an English murderer ... a little man of the professional class ... living an intensely respectable life somewhere in the suburbs, and preferably in a semi-detached house' was superior to 'the brutal violence of American imports, with all their tawdry overtones of dance halls, movie palaces, cheap perfume, false names and stolen cars'.[10] This appeal to the lowest common denominator of nationalist instinct from an old-Etonian socialist intellectual, whose experience of the things he mentions was no more than peripheral, reveals not only an unfounded thesis but blindness to the realities of consumerism. Orwell was among the creators of both false emotive expectancies of banal British products and false romantic expectancies of the 'brutal violence of American imports', few of which could be so described by any stretch of the imagination. Consumerism could not and did not 'murder' deeply rooted appreciation of all that was best in Britain.

On 26th July 1945, Winston Churchill, the half-American living embodiment of all that was best in Britain, having been rejected by its electorate, returned his prime-ministerial seals of office to the King and left Buckingham Palace in the back seat of a Rolls Royce, driven by a chauffeur.[11] Shortly afterwards the Labour Party leader, Clement Attlee, educated at Haileybury and Oxford and with impeccable English credentials, famously arrived at the palace gates in the front seat of a small pre-war family car, driven by his wife. Although certainly unplanned by the unexpected victor of a landslide general election, this characteristic display of self-effacement proved a masterpiece in public relations. It was a portrait of the virtue of suppression of conspicuous consumption, which precisely reflected the prevailing attitude of most British people to personal finance.

Twelve years later, Harold Macmillan again reflected the prevailing attitude to personal finance with his most celebrated utterance: 'most of our people have never had it so good'. Had Attlee made any such statement he might have been hounded from office, but had he paraphrased his successor's words and suggested 'most of our people have never *been* so good', he would have spoken a greater truism. Patriotism, prudence, sensitivity and self-denial were so prevalent that Kenneth Morgan could later confidently portray post-war Britain as 'the very model of social control'.[12] With equal truth the new Prime Minister might also have reminded most people that their personal financial position had never been so good. He did nothing of the kind.

Attlee intended to allow no one to forget for one moment the enormity of the nation's economic crisis, amidst the celebration of victory and peace. As Ina Zweiniger-Bargielowska puts it, 'There were numerous changes of the control orders while the public had to cope with an avalanche of new laws and regulations'.[13] In the next five years the avalanche would bury the scope of legal consumerism beneath no less than '13,551 new statutory rules, orders and instruments' – not one of them conducive to the celebration of victory and peace.[14] As consumers, his contemporaries would have forgiven Churchill his deliberate overstatement: 'Seven hundred thousand more officials ... have settled down upon us to administer twenty-five thousand regulations never before enforced in time of peace, supported by a rate of wartime taxation [which] has hampered ... recovery in every walk of life'.[15] The Attlee government would continue to promote frugality and thrift with the same vigour as in the darkest days of the war and leave few stones unturned in restraining consumer freedom – in effect, challenging to the limit the British resolve to remain the very model of social control. Most of its people accepted the challenge, stoically complied, and avoided inessential expenditure – for a while.

In essence post-Second World War attitudes to expenditure differed from those of the First in two respects. Firstly, no evidence emerged of a probable quick return to mass unemployment and widespread poverty. Secondly, and more significantly, the addiction to the nascent affluence of the 1930s, whether or not personally experienced, remained inexorable. Yet it was not in the national character to surrender to a mere addiction while the economy remained in crisis and dependent on American goodwill.

Peter Hennessy explains: 'We were morally magnificent but economically bankrupt, as became brutally apparent eight days after the ceasefire in the Far East when President Truman severed the economic lifeline of Lend-Lease without warning'.[16] After Keynes returned from Washington, having temporarily repaired the severed lifeline by negotiating immense, though barely adequate and heavily conditioned loans, what became brutally apparent to ordinary people was that austerity was here to stay. Among the less than morally magnificent brutal apparitions was the spectre that the nation's long trusted economic lifelines, its empire and traditional industries, were already beyond repair. The people of Britain were nonetheless determined to defend their war-enhanced personal finance against these and any other indirect or direct threats – if by no other means then through temporary self-denial.

One observer cited by Hennessy paraphrases the dignity of this stance: 'The selfish set of attitudes revealed in pre-war studies gave way to a sense of purpose which went beyond self and immediate convenience'.[17] This temporary altruistic sense of purpose undoubtedly played a leading role in electing a party with socialist aspiration, but a definitive explanation of Labour's unforeseen vanquish of Churchill's Conservative Party has so far eluded historical commentators. The most popular theory is that Labour was more trusted to implement Sir William Beveridge's blueprint for universal care from cradle to grave. It has also often been suggested that voters saw the wartime Coalition as Conservative led and simply wanted change. For traditional Labour voters, the image of a 'new Jerusalem', a phoenix of prosperity rising from the fires of slum demolition and bomb-site clearance and bringing a resurgence of British supremacy, overshadowed their fears of reversion to financial injustice. As Hopkins so accurately perceives 'The war-born sense of community and social purpose … had swept Labour to power in 1945 but it had gone by 1949'.[18]

This short-lived sense of community and social purpose is prevalent through a series of essays to be found in the Mass-Observation archive, with the given title *Post-War Hopes*, entered for a competition convened by the British Legion in 1944. In a variety of styles, servicemen of all ranks express, above all else, their desire to return to a civilian life free of Beveridge's five metaphorical giants: Want, Disease, Ignorance, Squalor and Idleness. 'By our efforts and sacrifices we have earned the right to demand and obtain better conditions', concludes one entrant, and more than a few others echo his sentiment. But a competition judge, seemingly lamenting the general weakness of content, comments: 'It is somewhat striking that in all these essays there is no wish expressed to throw off war restrictions and discipline, or to exercise any individual freedom or initiative. Few seem to desire a more adventurous life, or one offering more scope'.[19] The generally disheartening themes of these supposedly hopeful essays dwell on security, employment, housing and better pensions for all, but studiously avoid the spirit of enterprise or the pleasures and benefits of consumption. Personal aspirations hardly deviate from high-thinking platitudes, such as:

> A man asks only very little when he leaves the hell of battle; he asks only some kind of paid employment, a home and comfort for his family at a cost within the compass of his wage; the right to enjoy his leisure time.

One perhaps more pragmatic officer does venture to remind his left-leaning contemporaries that: '[In striving for] a better and happier world the great danger is that in caring too much for the majority we may hamper the progressive few'. Little truly original thought is apparent in the twenty or so essays I perused but one entrant did put aside political issues for a more imaginative idea. He suggests that the British Legion itself be disbanded and transformed into an organisation, perhaps similar to a building society, aimed at creating employment by constructing houses on 'model estates with shops, clubs and transport' and providing affordable mortgages for ex-servicemen to buy post-war homes on them – all to be financed by 'the capital from the huge NAAFI profits'.[20]

While none of the entrants comes anywhere near to envisaging Britain as a future affluent society, they are generally optimistic that living standards will improve. They do not expect to succumb to austerity for long. But succumb they will. They will join the overwhelming majority in the quest for an honest path through the often barely comprehensible rules and regulations of civilian austerity. Their acquiescence will be far more prevalent than dissent and violation. In observing the extraordinary level of acquiescence, Kenneth Morgan unwittingly suggests an admirable model for the vogue of 'elegant economy':

> Controls on personal consumption were invested with an aura of patriotism. The ration book was a badge of good citizenship, queuing for food a necessary privation. The government relied it seemed on promoting a kind of secular religion.[21]

Hennessy goes further by arguing that 'selling rationing to the people ... was the most successful government public relations exercise that I ever encountered'.[22] It was predictable enough that the creed of 'fair shares' created by a wartime Coalition government would continue when succeeded by one pretending socialism.[23] It was, however, remarkable that so many people, including Labour's most vehement opponents and those who soon turned their backs on the Attlee government, would accept voluntary restraint in peacetime. Six years of uncertainty, perils and tensions had mesmerised the bulk of British people into passive acceptance of unpleasant necessity.

Interspersed with patriotic restraint, nostalgia became the predominant emotion in post-war personal consumerist expectancy. People in every walk of life found solace in the purchase of the most remote or irrational sign of a resurrection of the best of pre-war Britain. Most of the *Post-War Hopes* essayists, for example, including men serving abroad, took it for granted that the British Empire would survive intact and return to supplying their nation's shops and factories as it had before the war. This was a view unreservedly championed by the Canadian-born newspaper baron, Lord Beaverbrook. In the face of manifest evidence to the contrary, his *Daily Express* constantly portrayed the dominions and colonies as content to remain forever the deferential acolytes of their mother country. In September 1947 Beaverbrook himself published a lengthy article characteristically lauding the Empire's service to the 'whole of the human race' and predicting that 'if we divest ourselves of these assets, Britain and the Empire will fall in ruin and crumble in decay'. In the same edition the *Express* reports a 'glut of guns', supplied by returning Canadian, Australian and British servicemen selling off war-surplus revolvers in Soho for £5. The previous day it had carried a similar story of sales of German cameras at as much as £100, gold sovereigns changing hands at black-market prices, and a series of other illegal dealings on the streets of London.[24] Not everyone conformed to Beaverbrook's intransigent image of British supremacy.

Self-deceiving nationalistic fantasies were, nonetheless, widely enshrined. Whether or not they had served in the armed forces or played any direct role in the war, Britons convinced themselves that they personally had met adversity with innate stoicism and fortitude. The cinema in particular, initially seriously, and later satirically through characters like James Bond, provoked blind faith in the supremacy of English reserve. The film critic, C.A. Lejeune, could not have flattered her readers more than by characterising their celluloid paradigms with the words: 'These people are real people; they do not make much of their private emotions'. In the dark private world of the cinema, anyone with a modicum of patriotism in their veins might transform themselves into a latter-day Saint George, bravely slaying the fascist dragon without deviating from the time-honoured rules of chivalry. On the screen, England's gentlemanly patron saint wore the uniform of an RAF pilot, had an exaggerated Oxford accent, never for a moment lost his composure, and in Jeffrey Richards' words, 'ran rings round the humourless, ranting, dunderheaded Hun'.[25] It was easy to be convinced that the best of Britain's allies could never possess such qualities. When victory in Europe was announced *The Times* had no need to remind its readers that 'The British rose to the full stature of their ancient greatness'.[26] Via a succession of celibate, high-thinking-plain-living stereotypes, craving nothing but to uphold Britain's glory, its films expounded the fine tradition that, as Alan Hunt writes: 'A nation is put in peril when its young men are corrupted by luxury'.[27] One step from the dilapidated cinema, its young men and everyone else were confronted by a Britain put in peril by ration books, shortages and black markets, where there was little chance of being corrupted by luxury. Still their faith in national superiority was unshaken. That this faith mercifully failed to excite extreme xenophobia or social upheaval, as had similar delusions of indigenous supremacy in Nazi Germany, was not unconnected to prevailing attitudes to personal finance. Post-war Britons admired piety, self-help and thrift, untainted things of the not too distant past, and abhorred abject conspicuous consumption, a tainted thing of the not too distant future. The dutiful and the industrious had no inclination, let alone time, to crusade against alien scapegoats, while struggling to revive their own lifestyles to a model seeped in nostalgia.

Britain, of course, was not wholly peopled by the dutiful and the industrious, and the financial corruption synonymous with the era is an undeniable reality, but circumvention of the emergency legislation was, in general, less malevolent than legend has it. Inspired by a BBC *Brains Trust* debate on whether it was possible to lead 'a life of normal English freedom without breaking the law', eminent King's Counsel and prolific publicist, C.K. Allen, put pen to the practicalities:

> The butcher gives an old customer more meat than she is entitled to because
> otherwise he cannot get rid of his expensive joints; is it in feminine human
> nature to say, 'Cut off those offending five ounces or I will denounce you to the
> police'?[28]

Many transactions were more reprehensible than Allen implies but his argument
that petty violation of bureaucratic regulation did not fall within a reasonable
definition of 'black market' is widely supported. The wartime Minister of Food,
Lord Woolton, an experienced businessman himself, must have been aware of
ubiquitous illegal trading, yet would later assert: '[The] fact that, in spite of all the
scarcity … and the rigidity of rationing, that there was little or no black market
in Britain was a tribute to the British people which I hope the historians of this
period will proudly record'.[29] In 1971 the historian Leonard Mosley fulfilled
Woolton's hope by recording, if not proudly, then categorically: 'In Britain, and
even in the nation's capital, a very few ever dabbled in it [the black market]'.[30]
These improbable claims are plausible only where black market is defined as
trading illegally on a commercial scale and on a consistent basis. Ex-servicemen
and entrepreneurs who made fortunes by buying up the substantial quantities of
war-surplus armaments and munitions, for example, were frequently censured on
anecdotal evidence but if their source of supply was the government itself, their
trade *per se* could scarcely have been illegal.

This is not to say that no one took advantage of post-war opportunities for
activity of questionable legitimacy. Innumerable cases of goods obtained by theft
or deception and sold at extortionate prices were alleged and many successfully
prosecuted but since the most obvious precaution against detection of an illicit
transaction is to leave no documentary evidence, there can be no reliable
assessment of the full measure of the black market. Statistics, official and unofficial
enquiries, journalistic investigations, court records, press reports and empirical
comment have time and again been exposed as inaccurate, biased or unfounded.
Retrospective testimonies, including those confessing involvement, have similarly
proven inconclusive or embellished. Researchers and commentators generally
concur that the majority of transactions dubbed black-market were victimless
and of little consequence. Given the complexity of the law, there can be little
doubt that perpetrators and beneficiaries were usually genuinely ignorant of their
wrongdoing.

Other perpetrators and beneficiaries, not genuinely ignorant of their
wrongdoing, might have plausibly justified their actions by arguing that they
were simply exploiting the weaknesses in laws and regulations which created
abnormal demand in themselves. In 1947 a Mass-Observation voluntary war
diarist, described as a 'partner in a Sheffield firm of accountants, born 1901',
records his disapproval of a wily 'pawnbroker client': 'This man buys carpets,
pays a £1 tip to get into a warehouse … when he has obtained the full quota for
his firm [under manufacturing control regulations] then classes himself as a new
business to get another quota and puts his main assistant down as a dealer and gets

a third quota for him'.[31] This enterprising opportunist was evidently manipulating the rules to serve his customers and deprive his competitors of business and as such was ethically and probably legally culpable, but it is improbable that the Board of Trade would have taken action. Although it could hardly have been unaware that deceptions of this kind were commonplace, it lacked the resources to adequately police them or gather sufficient evidence for successful prosecution. The pawnbroker's manoeuvres had not, in effect, altered the total quota of carpets available in his designated area or defied the principle of fair shares. At a time of severe shortage, a customer in desperate need to replace his worn-out or war-destroyed carpet was happy enough to find a well-stocked retailer and did not question his source of supply, expect a competitive price or take account of the rectitude of the transaction.

'Fair shares' had become something of a sick joke, while the potency of 'make do and mend', the wartime slogan of consumerist restraint, was wearing as thin as the pre-war garments with which victorious Britons had grown tired of making do. In the autumn of 1945 the King himself appealed to Attlee: 'We must all have new clothes – my family is down to the lowest ebb', but the Prime Minister had no concessions to offer.[32] The war was over but rationing and controls were not. Regardless of status, everyone was expected to make do, but not everyone had the time or the skills to mend. Every type of service provider able to undertake the simplest repair or maintenance job was overwhelmed by demand from frustrated customers prepared to pay whatever they were asked. Employees, (and doubtless some registered unemployed), housewives, pensioners and anyone else working in their free time could earn extra cash and, in some cases, a great deal of extra cash. Most of this income slipped quietly through the tax net while an understaffed Inland Revenue struggling with a workload now two years in arrears, like the Board of Trade, had little capacity to pursue defaulters. Although some moonlighters might have reflected their 'tax saving' in modified prices, most had no qualms about charging all the traffic would bear – and more – yet gratitude accompanied payment more often than complaint.[33]

The volume of moonlighting cannot be gauged with any greater accuracy than the black market in general but it can be deduced that overcharging could not have been practised on the vast scale implied by anecdotal evidence, since had that been the case it would have caused a rapid escalation in inflation. The rapid escalation in inflation in 1940 was, as has been seen, caused mainly by severe labour shortages and largely predated the introduction of rationing, production controls and import restrictions at the root of the wartime black market. Having been returned to stability, inflation was restrained at about 3.4 per cent for the three years to 1946 but rose to 7.4 per cent the following year, before falling back to just 2.6 per cent in 1949. The temporary surge was largely attributable to a bout of high wage awards and there is no evidence that price exploitation was a material factor. Not everyone in post-war Britain could be fairly described as 'the very model of social control', but the majority did manage to abstain from yielding to the more excessive demands of exploiters of shortage.

It was to a Britain acclimatised to dealing not only with excessive demands but excessive taxation, rationing, rules and regulations that on 23rd October 1945 the new Chancellor of the Exchequer, Hugh Dalton, addressed his first peacetime Budget. He made a sincere attempt to maintain the goodwill of an electorate that had so recently put its trust in a Labour government by offering a mixed package of positive but responsible measures. Trumping the pessimism of his predecessor, Sir John Anderson, he reduced the standard rate of income tax for the first time in eleven years – by a full one shilling, to 9s in the pound (45 per cent). For the first time in five years, he increased the personal allowances and broadened the bands, thus completely exempting large numbers of the lower-paid from income-tax. Dalton did all in his power to help both consumers and taxpayers. He brought to an end the already despised post-war credit scheme and lifted purchase tax from domestic heating products and a selection of widely sought necessities. Even the richest did not complain inordinately when he increased the top rates of surtax up to 10s 6d, retaining the maximum imposition at 19s 6d (97½ per cent), nor were there many objections to his introduction of a duty on new motor cars – there were none to be bought.

Anderson, among others on the Opposition benches, expressed unreserved praise for a Budget that offered, as he said, 'the greatest incentive to the greatest number'.[34] The pro-Labour *New Statesman's* appreciation of Dalton's efforts is more ambiguous: 'Every working-class elector would recognise [the Budget] as straight socialism ... but also as a bid for the support of the well-to-do'.[35] The Chancellor's commendation of continued support for National Savings was also endorsed on all sides of the House, and by the press and public.[36] But this warm approbation would soon turn literally cooler than the self-assured Dalton or anyone else could possibly have predicted.

Meanwhile his colleagues on the Labour benches became increasingly critical of his failure to adequately address the issue of class biased wealth distribution. They especially resented the retention of the punitive wartime scale imposing duty on every estate valued above as little as £100. In Dalton's second Budget on 9th April 1946, he alleviated the concerns of small potential beneficiaries by reducing the lower bands and raising the threshold to £2,000, permitting most private houses (average price £1,459) to be passed on without encumbrance.[37] At the other end of the scale, he increased the duty by substantial margins on estates exceeding ten thousand pounds. The fortunate few, bequeathed over £2 million could expect to pay 75 per cent on the excess, while the time the donor of a gift *inter vivos* was required to survive for his or her heirs to escape estate duty was extended from three to five years.[38] These measures would incite the most fundamental transition for centuries in the attitudes of Britain's aristocratic families to their personal financial affairs.

Just four months short of the fifth anniversary of disposing of 97 per cent of his interest in the Chatsworth estate, the tenth Duke of Devonshire, among the richest men in the country, died on 26th November 1950. His heirs, as recipients of a taxable gift *inter vivos*, were faced with three daunting alternatives. They could raise 75 per cent of most of the value of the palatial house, extensive lands and illustrious collection of art treasures and put themselves into crippling debt; they could sell up, almost certainly into American hands; or they could earn the duty from the market potential of their inherited asset. Contrary to their stereotyped and often self-cultivated image, Britain's privileged classes were seldom strangers to trade and industry. As did many of his similarly placed contemporaries, the eleventh Duke opened the doors of his stately home to anyone prepared to pay for the ethereal pleasure of admiring the privately owned opulence within, eventually settled the duty by his own endeavours and died leaving a thriving business at Chatsworth.

Dalton's second Budget was a shadow of his optimistic performance in the post-war euphoria of the previous autumn but he did his best to maintain the momentum. To the growing number of returning private stock-exchange investors his most exciting proposal was withdrawal of the 'excess profits tax'. Although not due to take effect until the start of the following year, the freedom granted to public companies to appropriate a greater proportion of their profits to expansion and dividend distribution generated an immediate spate of market activity and price rises. The *Investor's Chronicle* attempted to curb inexperienced speculation by predicting that Dalton's simultaneous purchase-tax increases would result in loss of business for those companies permitted to supply the home market and currently enjoying demand beyond production capacity. It cautioned investors to support the conventional wisdom and stay with traditional forms of saving.[39] This would indeed prove sound advice in the light of the declining production and export figures, of which the Chancellor was acutely aware.

Dalton dare give away no more than, in the words of the *News Chronicle* headline, 'tit bits for everybody'.[40] His own words, as before, were filled with promise but his gifts, as judged by the press, were thinly spread and empty of promise. Again he supported the lowest paid, but now their income-tax reliefs were smaller and as consumers they could look forward only to inadequate purchase-tax reductions on a few necessities. Dalton did throw in some concessions, possibly calculated to win popularity, among them a cut in duty on sport and theatre (but not cinema) tickets and the establishment of a £50 million fund for the National Trust and similar organisations to acquire beauty spots and preserve the landscape. At the end of his speech no one felt appreciably better off.

Anderson, this time in less charitable mode, complained that taxation still 'obtruded itself on every transaction and was a constant irritant' and admonished Dalton's 'cynical indifference' to those paying above the lowest rates.[41] The press joined the Opposition in applauding the former Chancellor for airing the widely held opinion that until higher earnings left proportionately higher net pay after tax, there could be no incentive to increase production. Oscar Hobson, as ever, was more pragmatic and succinct in his reflection:

> Recovery, in spite of the weakness in money incentives goes on. In the face of
> war weariness and a tax system which mitigates against initiative and energy,
> the supply of consumable goods increases, and incentive, in spite of everything,
> in a measure also revives. That is the case – and it is a strong one for 'hastening
> slowly' and not rushing into further considerable reduction of taxation, for
> which we may pay dearly in the end.[42]

Dalton too reflected that people had come to accept the rationale of high taxation
and that further reduction would not necessarily stimulate economic revival.
In practice, his strategy proved more complex while incentive was constantly
hampered, not only by punitive taxation, but by growing intolerance of extended
austerity. The Chancellor's 'tit bits', nonetheless, had put a little extra money into
the consumer's pocket, full employment and revival of private enterprise were
continuing apace, and export production had begun to revive.

By November 1946, it looked as if Dalton's strategy was working and people
were looking forward to appreciable reliefs from taxation and austerity regulation.
Dalton himself went so far as to boast that his export based programme for
recovery had 'succeeded beyond expectations and beyond estimate … [and that] I
have been able, as chancellor, to meet all the demands of the public purse literally
with a song in my heart'.[43] For Britain's consumers, this song should have sung to
the disappearance of 'for export only' labels and the reappearance of the imported
produce so long denied them. It might also have sung a valediction to the rationing
system, that summer made more abhorrent by its extension to bread and flour;
an unnecessary and ineffectual inconvenience, considered to have 'entailed no
hardship'.[44] C.K. Allen emotively called it 'a protracted farce [when] thousands
of bakers ignored the whole hocus-pocus and nearly every housewife despised
and defied the law'.[45] His words mirrored the nation's changing attitude to the
increasingly irritating irrationality of rationing in peacetime.

Anyone persuaded that Dalton would soon put an end to the whole projected
farce and hocus-pocus was about to experience a rude awakening – rationing would
again become rational. It would not be the threat of an enemy, foreign competition
or the shortcomings of British industry that thwarted the Chancellor's unrelenting
efforts, but nature itself, literally blocking all roads to economic recovery. Two
months after his joyful pronouncements of success, that least predictable of factors,
the British weather exacerbated Dalton's problems beyond probability. For seven
more years the ration book would remain an unwelcome adjunct to the purse of
every housewife and an unwanted symbol of her and her family's stoicism.

Never would that stoicism be more tested and not found wanting than through
the arctic winter of 1947, with the heaviest snowfalls since 1814 and temperatures
close to the lowest on record. For more than fifty days the thermometer seldom
rose above freezing point. On 24th February the *Daily Express* reminded its
readers of their duty to the government's unpoliceable restrictions on the usage
of all domestic fuels: 'On Your Honour'.[46] And honoured it was; often in the
face of hardship to young children, the elderly, the sick and the housebound.

People warmed their beds with glass bottles filled with boiled water – the rubber hot-water bottle was yet another victim of austerity. Production and distribution in almost every industry was obstructed for weeks on end; first by snow and ice then, when the thaw came at last, by floods. Dalton could do nothing but watch his employment, production and export graphs, so recently in the ascendant, droop, descend and descend again, and possibly pray that his once singularly ill-fated forecast would come to pass: '... the shortages and frustrations which still afflict us will disappear like the snows in winter and give place to the full promise of springtime'.[47] This was not to be Britain's destiny for 1947. What followed the winter snows was a springtime of little promise and a summer of stifling heatwaves to further compound consumers' frustration with rationing and pervasive shortages – and then an autumn when potatoes were added to the list of rationed foods, although only until the following spring.

As rationing became more intense people resorted to barter for the necessities of life that they could not buy for cash. Even on the smallest scale, barter was an indictable offence: swapping a couple of eggs for a few ounces of meat, or even giving them away carried a potential fine. In practice, most such transactions were acts of neighbourliness, intended to help out in emergencies, with neither party giving thought to the legal niceties. Self-righteous critics who found virtue in acquiescence to austerity and unable to differentiate between barter and black market denounced it, not simply for violating 'fair shares', but for causing *inflation*. Exchanging unneeded food for needed could hardly be described as unfair, and barter by its very definition could in no way affect retail prices or inflation. Some barterers experienced more soul searching than gratification, while others openly justified their action by condemning the manifest inequity of the whole rationing system. But neither self-imposed penance nor protest impressed the vigilantes whose job it was to expose and prosecute exponents of an indefinable black market and to defend the 'considered' policy that 'the ration is a maximum and if not required ... should not be drawn' and that 'it should not be transferable whether by sale, barter or gift except within ... [the] household'.[48]

These plain-clothed guardians of the culture of austerity sometimes received little more sympathy from the courts than their victims. Shortly after the war the *Daily Express* reported that two clerks from the Ministry of Food had received a firm dressing down from an unimpressed Old Street magistrate for their 'ghastly amateur policework'. Posing as traders they had persuaded a wholesaler to sell them forty pounds of cucumber and then immediately prosecuted his firm for exceeding the controlled price by just 8d for 'porterage and cartage'. The defendant plausibly pleaded that he believed he was legally entitled to pass on his additional expense, but regardless of the tiny sum involved and the furtive nature of his detection, was required to pay the extortionate fine of five pounds with fifteen guineas costs.[49]

The penalties for successful indictments involving the merest hint of black marketeering were invariably out of all proportion to the severity of the offence, especially if judged to contravene the rationing regulations. The *Daily Mirror* reported in January 1946 that 'A licensee who bought a clothing [ration] book from a man in his bar for £3 5s and a drink, was fined £300 [over £12,000 today] for possessing a clothing book not issued to him'. The judge, taking no account of the first-class character report provided by the police themselves or of the defendant's record of service as an officer in both world wars, placed him in custody until the fine was paid and informed him, it must be assumed ungrammatically: 'You were trying to get what other honest people cannot get'.[50] C.K. Allen later commented: 'If you lose or are robbed of your clothing coupons, you can with great difficulty recover half the original number. Is it any wonder that people buy coupons in what is now an open market?'[51]

There can be little doubt that many cases of far more serious crime falling within the wider definition of black market remained undetected but some did reach the courts. A few *causes célèbres* involving allegations of large-scale war profiteering proved an open invitation to the press to indulge in an orgy of sensationalism and condemnation of the ills of commerce and consumerism. The most notorious, the 1948 Lynskey Tribunal, (after the judge, Sir George Lynskey) after weeks of hearings at enormous cost, ignominiously failed to convict the loquacious 'super-spiv', Sidney Stanley. This courtroom farce resulted in the resignation of a junior Board of Trade minister, John Belcher, for having accepted the modest gift of a suit although he evidently granted no favours in return. Stanley, who was transparently guilty at least of sharp practice, took full advantage of the extraordinary ambience of the times to make an ass not only of the law but the whole system of controls and rationing. Britain's most distinguished barrister and chief prosecutor at the Nuremburg trials, Sir Hartley Shawcross, floundered in the face of Stanley's outrageous smokescreen of verbiage. Apart from providing the most amusing conversation piece of the day, the tribunal exposed the regulations, with which every British consumer was expected to comply, as so chaotic and enmeshed in bureaucracy that they could not be untangled by even the clearest legal minds in the land.[52]

Stanley was not the only person to show no remorse for actions totally indefensible in normal times and circumstances. Addison cites the oral testimony of 'East End resident Mr Franklyn' on the matter of theft from a building site:

> You could go along there and take exactly what you wanted. You could take
> the bathroom taps. You could take fridges. There was asbestos, everything you
> wanted that you'd seen during the war but you had never had ... All in all,
> everybody was on the nick shall we say ... I think the people as a whole thought
> that after six years of war they was entitled to these things. Never having had
> anything at all they didn't steal it as such. They made the best of what they saw.[53]

'The people as a whole' did not go so far as to steal building materials or anything else, but it did not follow that they were all content to meekly accept privation and abide by the letter of the law of austerity. Motorists, in particular, resented petrol rationing denying them the freedom of the open (if unrepaired) road. Private use of petrol had been completely prohibited from 1942 until the end of the war.

Thereafter a small private fuel allocation was introduced, increased slightly in 1946, but again rescinded from October 1947 to June 1948 when a modest ration was restored until May 1950. While such meagre allowances prevailed, a private motorist prepared to risk a fine would need to forfeit few of his precious points to reach a source of black-market fuel. Business transporters received generous worst-case-scenario fuel allocations and, provided they completed their deliveries without incident, always found themselves left with a ready saleable surplus. This, as an article in the *Manchester Guardian* put it, more scornfully than diplomatically, 'sometimes found its way into the tanks of private motorists ... or commercial vehicles [being used] for private purposes'. The writer, accepting that the national 'leakage' had never amounted to more than an estimated 3 per cent, went on to accuse motorists of treating 'contempt for the law as almost a virtue'.[54] Yet this was written in 1948 when the petrol black market had passed its peak. In 1945 the police had successfully prosecuted 6,852 individuals for illicit possession of petrol but after the private ration was restored, even to a low level, the number of offences rapidly fell away. Convictions, down to 1,583 in 1947, showed no significant increase during the second period of revocation and continued to decline through the final two years after restoration.[55] The figures support Mr Franklyn's view that people believed they had an implicit right to 'these things' they had enjoyed before the war, and when wholly deprived had few qualms about breaking the law to reacquire them; still it took only a resumption of a small ration for their law-abiding instincts to predominate.

As with all forms of alleged black-market activity the true extent of illegal trade in fuel was never reliably established. The report of the 1948 Committee of Inquiry to the Minister for Fuel and Power (the theme of the *Manchester Guardian* article) exposes all contemporary official statistics as little more than guesswork. Of the published estimates of illegal consumption cited, the highest, produced by an AA and RAC joint committee, indicates that 180 million gallons or over 27 per cent of commercial vehicle allocations had been misused for private purposes. The lowest estimate, the work of the Ministry of Transport itself, claims that no more than thirty million gallons or about 4½ per cent could have been misappropriated.[56] The truth must lay somewhere between but the figures are too divergent to draw any meaningful conclusion and the Ministry inquiry, though detailed and thorough, effectually established nothing – that is, nothing that was not common knowledge.

At the beginning of 1947 *The Policy Holder*, avoiding direct reference to the black market, published a subdued appraisal of the post-war petrol situation:

> Private motoring received something in the nature of a fillip by the increase in the petrol ration, but when this took place [in October 1946] there was no great rush to put cars back on the road again, for the number laid up was less than one would have imagined. They had been trickling back into normal use ever since the total ban on private motoring was rescinded and it is doubtful whether there will be any appreciable rush when petrol rationing ceases.[57]

Even the mildest indication of a revival of the emotive and romantic expectancies of private motoring, in practice, could have done nothing other than cause a 'great rush' to put cars back on the road, but as the article suggests, petrol rationing was not the sole delaying factor. Manufacture of private vehicles had ceased for the duration of the war and no new models were yet on the market. A motorist who had sold his car or was unable to restore one still laid up because of scarcity of parts and skilled labour, might have searched long and hard to find a reasonably priced second-hand replacement. If he succeeded, he would have to pay cash down. All hire-purchase and private credit remained frozen.

Even so bleak a prospect might be turned to personal financial advantage. In September 1947 Mass-Observation's accountant diarist records (possibly omitting some detail) that his client had ordered three new cars 'to get one first. ... [He will] lay up the second and third until the anniversary of the licence is reached – when he is allowed to sell. He should rake off a nice profit out of the two, probably enough to pay for the new one'.[58] If this opportunist carried through his plan the chances were indeed in favour of him making 'a nice profit', but it would have been no quick or straightforward process. Among the gems in the Museum of London's oral history collection is an interview with a former West End car showroom assistant, who relates how men offered her bribes or brought gifts of chocolates and nylon stockings simply to get their names on the two-year-plus waiting list for a new car, with no guarantee of delivery. The Standard Vanguard,[iii] the first post-war mass-produced motor car, was not released on to the general market until 1949.[59]

Clearly a sizeable minority were determined to revert to money spending and material conspicuous consumption at the first opportunity, but the majority still retained the conservative habits acquired in the war. Goaded by a government constantly wrestling with economic deficit and forebodings of recession, saving was still the British people's top priority. The total investment in National Savings, having grown from £1,500 million in 1938 to £5,500 million by 1945, would consistently exceed £6,000 million until the early 1950s. Simultaneously the level of investment in endowment life assurance continually grew to new heights. Even before the sales forces of the leading insurance companies had resumed their pre-war strength, the number and value of new policies had surpassed all records. In 1945 alone, Prudential's life department underwrote additional cover of estimated at £68 million, compared to £28.3 million in 1938. Among the contributing factors was the so-called 'top hat' scheme popularised during the war, whereby directors and senior executives were paid low salaries while their employers contributed to large endowment policies enabling them to receive lump-sums entirely free of tax. The Finance Act 1947 brought this crude form of tax avoidance to an end by clarifying that all employer contributions to life assurance or pension schemes were taxable as income of the employee.[60] For the overwhelming majority whose

---

[iii]   The Standard Vanguard was named after HMS *Vanguard*, the naval battleship used by the Royal Family for their tour of South Africa in 1947.

employers provided no contribution[iv] there were more practical reasons to take out life or pension polices, as *The Banker* explained:

> Demobilised men have found life assurance an obvious necessity at the beginning of an ordinary settled life, more particularly a family life, and most of them have not lacked the means ... thanks to a fairly substantial Forces gratuity and a fairly high earned income in civilian employment ... to secure some assurance protection.[61]

The Attlee government could boast unqualified success in maintaining full employment but the beneficiaries of its most fundamental policy, rather than risk the failure of the promised welfare state to ensure prosperity from cradle to grave, opted to save for their own long-term security. Victims of the housing crisis, unable to escape bomb-devastated, smoke polluted, over-populated town centres, seldom recognised any signs of the supposed income redistribution, let alone that within a decade they would be told that they were enjoying a state of affluence. According to McKibbin 'the proportion of personal wealth held by the top 1 per cent declined from 56 per cent in 1936–1938 to 43 per cent in 1954'.[62] This decline cannot be attributed to a significant reduction in the personal wealth of the top 1 per cent or even top 5 or 10 per cent, but to the appreciation in the savings and investments of the rapidly escalating proportion of the population who now found themselves in the middle brackets, and however reluctantly, in the middle classes.

Post-war social mobility was not always upward. In his 1947 annual report, the secretary of the Distressed Gentlefolk's Aid Association (DGAA), a more professional and robust charity than its anachronistic title suggests, expressed concerns over 'the marked increase in [largely female] applications for assistance in the prior two or three years'. People under the aegis of the DGAA, the Family Welfare Association and similar support organisations were often down to no more their 26s per week old-age or widow's pension. Typically they were women who had devoted much of their lives to the care of their parents, relatives or friends, and as a result of bereavement were left penniless, alone and often themselves incapacitated by war-related infirmity. Among the secretary's gravest concerns was that people at the point of despair would go to any lengths to conceal the truth from their wealthy family or friends. Inhibited by pride and class consciousness, they would never seek assistance or even claim their rightful state benefits and, in the words of the report, 'therefore died in extreme poverty and obscurity'. The inability to come to terms with post-war inflation, in particular, left many confused and demoralised, as their comments in response to a Mass-Observation survey illustrate:

[iv] In 1936 only 2.6 million employees were in pension schemes, rising rapidly in the post-war period to eight million in 1956 (Blake, 2003, 133–134).

The confusion is the old one between the cost of living and the cost of being alive: I should say, if you got £2 in 1939 you need £4 15s now: Smoking has almost doubled ... and who in these psycho-serratic days would dare to say that cigarettes are less of a physical necessity to those who smoke than butter: The real cost of living is the cost of carrying on the habits one is used to ... of the people who find the cost of living has increased most are those whose established tastes have always been relatively costly – the upper and middle classes.

The greatest problem was accommodation. As the DGAA's Miss Owen put it, '[there is] the choice of either the Poor Law institutions^v which are a disgrace or the river'.[63] The distressed gentlefolk who declined either option eked out a miserable existence, often in cheap lodgings, devoting their depleted means to maintaining a show of 'elegant economy' for the benefit of a diminishing audience doing likewise. Numerous testimonials to such anguish are recorded, including the case of an 'extremely depressed seventy-year-old 'Mrs B' whose 'well-to-do' husband died in 1941. Suffering from loneliness, she had left their country house for a seaside hotel where she stayed until it became unaffordable. During the wartime bombing her son and his family, unable to find a place to live, moved into her home and remained there. Mrs B was 'at loggerheads with her daughter-in-law and so could not go to live with them'. Now she was surviving on severely reduced investment income in an uncomfortable north London boarding house, unable even to afford the fare home to see her son and grandchildren. 'Her son pays her no money since the family has always been well off and it has not occurred to him. She, for her part, finds it embarrassing to ask', wrote Miss Owen. 'Embarrassing' here was probably a considerable understatement: in Mrs B's class-dominated pre-war time warp, entrenched convention would have rendered a request for money unthinkable.

The DGAA, like all contemporary charities, relied entirely on private donation for its funding and its ability to help was limited. In the atmosphere of post-war austerity and anticipation of universal state welfare, people were not inclined to give away their private security in the expectancy of nothing but virtuous self-gratification. A Mass-Observation survey report entitled *Aspects of Charity* in August 1947 contains some revealing insights into prevailing attitudes. The observers comment that:

Overwhelmingly, among both panel and general samples, the main feeling against charity derives from the belief that there should no longer be any need for it, at any rate in organised form: that the State should be responsible for providing relief wherever it is required.[64]

---

^{v} The Poor Law Institutions (workhouses), first introduced in 1833 by Earl Grey, were intentionally harsh to discourage scroungers. They retained their 'disgraceful' reputation long after they were taken over by the NHS in 1948.

The general view of the interviewees is that voluntary donation is 'a bad thing in itself but until the state takes over all its present functions it will remain a necessary evil'. Charity is 'bad both for the donor and the recipient'; 'a hindrance to social reform'; 'often a racket'. More than a third express disapproval. A young housewife succinctly voices the general response:

> I think that the more one is called upon to give money for charity the worse the reflection on the social system. The one who receives loses his dignity and the one who gives has a false sense of superiority.

Convictions of this kind were underscored by the rarity of appreciative comment from potential beneficiaries, who complained that the charities they approached were either not prepared to help at all, or that the help had failed to meet their expectations. Or as one 'Bethnal Green housewife' said: 'I don't know no charity that does anything, I have never had anything out of them'.

On the positive side, two-thirds of those interviewed expressed no criticism of specific charities and almost all professed to have donated at one time or another. Over 20 per cent said they had privately answered an advertisement or radio appeal, and only 5 per cent confessed unreservedly to have never supported a good cause at all. The claimed motives for giving, however, generally indicate no deep commitment to the relief of suffering and injustice. A 'middle-class engineer' commented: 'I feel it is regrettable that charity should be necessary. On the other hand I think the instinct to give is a good one'. Surprisingly, in view of the concurrent revival in churchgoing, no more than 1 per cent associated charity with religious faith or supported the concept that voluntary donation is a duty to the community or to God. Nor was it equated with the fulfilment of the basic tenet of Christianity stating that the giving of alms is 'the result of an act of goodwill and therefore a virtue'.[65] According to a 'commercial traveller', claiming to be a practising Christian, 'The rise of capitalism, the profit motive, our get-rich-quick mentality, all tend to make us behave like animals in the economic jungle and allow charity to become a forgotten virtue'. When asked about various methods of charitable fund raising, such as raffles and the then frequently held flag days, respondents repeatedly made direct or indirect allusions to blackmail. Nuns calling door-to-door were viewed with particular disfavour and, together with the Salvation Army, considered the worst of emotional blackmailers. An 'artisan', with reference to the latter, commented indignantly:

> Of course they work on a proper business footing, there's nothing haphazard about it. They've got millions invested in their insurance [company]; if you buy a policy from them you go straight to Heaven and if you take one out with an opposition insurance company you go straight to Hell. ... They'd cadge and cadge but in the long run it didn't do them any good.[66]

An earlier Mass-Observation survey of *Attitudes to the Salvation Army* had found that 74 per cent of interviewees were favourably impressed by its compassion, services to the community, and religious sincerity. Only 2 per cent were 'very critical', the most common complaint being that they found 'the music and religion irritating'.[67] Others concurred that the true aim of the intimidating uniformed officers, who knocked at doors and appeared at pubs and clubs at inconvenient moments, was more to prick religious conscience and spread their evangelistic message than to collect money.[68]

Since 1864 the Salvation Army had been among the nation's most active charitable institutions, promoting faith and an array of social services in Britain and around the world. The spare change proffered by individuals wanting rid of its obtrusive collectors could never have supported the cost of its prodigious work. As perceived by the disgruntled artisan, the greater part of its revenue was generated by the profits of the Salvation Army Insurance Company, founded in 1892 for the specific purpose of 'the raising of funds substantial, continuous and increasing for the support of our great Salvation Army'.[69] These, together with the gifts and bequests of wealthy patrons, philanthropic organisations and its private bank provided the bulk of the money that enabled it to surmount post-war antipathy to charity. Remarkably for a religious institution, in publicising its work to attract revenue, it matched the best of its commercial contemporaries. In 1945–1946, for example, when the advertising budget of Lloyds Bank's was £24,000, the Salvation Army, financially a comparative dwarf, spent over £20,000 on publicity.[70] Within a year of the end of the war it was producing promotional films and planning a major documentary for the Festival of Britain, heedless of the attitudes of private individual donors.[71] In 1944, the annual broadcast appeal by Mrs Beatrice Eden, wife of the future Prime Minister, had yielded a generous £8,343 with the news of war-related suffering, but thereafter donations reduced year by year. In 1951 the BBC's most successful fundraiser, Richard Dimbleby, could not persuade listeners to part with more than £3,000. The Salvation Army attributed the diminishing returns, not to growing apathy for its cause, but to the widely held conviction that a comprehensive system of state welfare should or would render charity redundant.[72]

There was also a widely held conviction that the welfare state should or would create greater social equality; a challenge the upper and middle classes thought neither achievable nor desirable. Along with the higher thinking of the plain-living working classes, their most common defence of the status quo was to conspicuously reject abject materialism – but not everything material. Second only to the pre-war motor car of prestigious marque, the most coveted of their exceptions was their domestic telephone. In April 1946 the *News Chronicle* reported that Major S.W. Digby MP had complained in the House of Commons that he 'was in the *embarrassing* position of being the only person in his village with a telephone. People were constantly asking to use it. ... [He] wanted a *public* telephone in every village' (my italics).[73] The embarrassed Conservative Member for Dorset West evidently saw no reason to demand a private telephone for every person in his village or indeed anyone else. Between the wars, when not used as a business necessity, the telephone had been elevated to a symbol of class status. For the upper and middle classes, it had replaced the post office or servant-messenger as the polite medium of appointments and social contact, while the working classes called in on friends and neighbours unannounced. In the mid-1950s Margaret Stacey observes in her incisively researched *Tradition and Change: Study of Banbury* that the upper classes were distinguished because 'they own cars and have telephones', and with an implication that the working classes had neither the means nor the desire to own either, adds:

> So too do many members of the middle class in Banbury ... who make the most trunk calls ... [because] they have some relationships with their next-door neighbours, but their social circle is principally drawn from members of their own class with like interests living in the town or nearby villages.[74]

Few people in Britain could have been unaware, if not from contemporary literature then from the cinema or radio, that in America a home telephone had long been an indispensible normality used casually by all classes, often for trivial purposes. The Labour government did nothing to dispel the middle-class image of the telephone and evidently lacked the foresight to invest in extending the network to reduce costs with economy of scale. The nationalised General Post Office (GPO), jealous of its monopoly of the supply of all equipment, lines and calls, was adamant that the telephone was not a domestic necessity and delayed its mass distribution for as long as possible.[75] It did not commence modernisation of its pre-war plant until 1954, by when its application list had grown to 450,000, of whom a third had been waiting for three years or longer.[76] From the perspective of today's universal telephone reliance and, given the dependency on public call boxes in wartime emergencies, the level of demand is rather less than might be expected. The working classes continued to perceive the home telephone as an unseemly middle-class luxury, exaggerating the cost of its usage as their reason for rejection. It was not until well into the 1970s that a black receiver (white or other colours being disdained as conspicuous consumption) was seen as a normality in a working-class home. Meanwhile, in moments of crisis, they paid by the word for a telegram to be delivered at best within an hour or two by a uniformed GPO motorcyclist, whose approach invariably struck dread into the heart of its recipient.

Post-war consumer attitudes to material needs like telephones and motor cars could be restrained by convention, scarcity and expense but these could not restrain attitudes to arguably the most emotive ethereal need of the time: to recapture cherished memories of pre-war holidays – often a once-only experience. People in all walks of life had worked hard through the war, with little or no time off and annual holidays, if granted at all, had been spent literally at home. Victims of stress and trauma needed rest and recuperation. Young married couples still living crammed with their families were so desperate for a brief respite that they would forfeit their precious savings for a home of their own. Young children had grown up in a world without holidays and parents felt a deep obligation to make reparation. The media promoted an annual holiday as an essential ingredient of a normal healthy lifestyle and the Holidays with Pay Act 1938 now guaranteed almost twelve million employees payment for between twelve and eighteen days leave per annum (including bank holidays).[77]

Few begrudged the money, but the road to holiday nostalgia was strewn with obstacles. Larger resort hotels had been war-requisitioned or taken over by evacuated businesses, schools and institutions and left in no condition to be reopened. Seaside promenades, piers and amenities had been damaged, more by defence barricades than by enemy bombs. Restaurants, cafes and entertainments had been closed, neglected, and remained closed. Reconstruction had to be postponed: money, labour and materials were prioritised elsewhere. Surviving or reopened hotels and guest houses offering generally poor and expensive accommodation were 'deluged with applications'. Hotel bookings were made many months in advance (always by post) to avoid a 'full up for the coming season' postcard or a letter offering a stay possibly rationed to a few days.[78] The cost of accommodation was racked up not only to cover skilled staff in short supply but to exploit a cash-rich market, ready and able to pay a heavy price for the taste of retrospective luxury – even if the food tasted of contemporary austerity. Discreet private hotels catering for the high thinking offered less than plain living beneath a veneer of respectability, frequently inserting the word 'Christian' in their names – The Sunnybeach Christian Hotel – a euphemism for no blacks, no Jews, no Irish, no working class and not much food. Away from the sea, the spas and health farms that had come into vogue in the 1930s and where the deficiency of food might pass for a healthy light diet, were reopened to serve those craving bodily reinvigoration – at a price.

Resort residents with little or no training or experience cashed in by converting their ill-equipped homes into boarding houses. Tales are told of up to twenty boarders sharing a single toilet and bathroom with the landlord and his family, hotel guests sleeping on the floors of rooms screened off to segregate the sexes, and in beds made up in baths or on billiard tables.[79] Bed-and-breakfast residents joined day-trippers in long queues for a plain meal at a cafe or restaurant, also often a run-down catchpenny demanding valuable ration points and circumventing the meal price limit. Pubs were packed to capacity and the licensing hours short. On a bank holiday, weekend or any fine day it was hard even to find space to sit on the popular beaches. Sugar rationing and frequent milk shortages meant no ice-creams, sweets or rock. Public toilets were closed or derelict. Yet every day in the summer months every urban railway and bus station was packed with people determined to get to the coast, regardless of the probability of standing there and back, while long progressions of pre-war private vehicles crawled along single-lane roads, burning up rationed petrol. And who was to say that a trip to Brighton was not on essential business?

In this desert of disillusioned nostalgia appeared five blossoming oases. Within two years of the end of the war Billy Butlin had reopened his two pre-war holiday camps and added the three more he had contracted to build as training camps for the Navy and RAF, at Filey, Pwllheli and Ayr. A master showman and one-time campaigner for holidays with pay, Butlin displayed a unique perception of the post-war growth in propensity to defy austerity and spend money on family holidays. He restored and refurbished his camps to exemplary standards and, although never cheap, kept his prices within the reach of an average family. As were his competitor hotels, boarding houses and burgeoning imitators his camps were continuously filled to capacity through the holiday season. What made Butlin's special was the 'eggs, bacon and fresh peaches' and other scarce foods offered in greater quality and quantity than elsewhere, that attracted the new middle-class visitors, (although perhaps not quite as many members of the upper classes and celebrities as Butlin would have the world believe).[80]

For those prepared to spend a little more it again became possible to venture abroad. In April 1946 Stanley Adams, the chairman of Thomas Cook, wrote: 'With the coming of the first peaceful spring, the urge to travel is sweeping through this and other war-weary lands like an epidemic'.[81] This was no exaggeration, but the epidemic was generally contained by inadequate transport and travel facilities. Heathrow Airport opened to much acclaim on 1st January 1946 but at first tourist flights were few and far between. Until air travel was popularised in the mid-1950s, with the emergence of chartered-flight low-budget packaged holidays, there were only cross-channel ships or ferries. Early post-war travellers could expect to be burdened with bureaucracy, frustration and no great comfort or joy on arrival. War-damaged continental roads, railways, hotels and restaurants were in desperate need of restoration and it would be years before all the major tourist attractions were reopened. Yet at the start of the 1946 tourist season, Thomas Cook announced that 'thousands of requests are being received daily ... about travel ... and continental holidays' and apologised for being unable to meet the demand because so many of its trained staff were yet to be demobilised. It hoped 'in the near future' to announce 'tours to Switzerland and other countries'.[82]

For determined travellers the inconveniences paled into insignificance against the prospect of respite from austerity. Mass-Observation's Sheffield diarist records booking his own train ferry and hotels for his family summer holiday in 1947, co-incidentally to Switzerland, and surmounting difficulties such as 'unannounced changes in railway timetables and the tiresome form filling to obtain adequate currency ... What a difference from pre-war days!'[83] His account loses its exasperated tone after arrival at his destination. Then he cheerfully writes:

> We did not trust the hotel with our passports so we went ourselves to the Food
> Office to collect more meal coupons. And what a supply! They gave us sheets
> of coupons, amply sufficient for another fortnight and we are only staying for
> another three days.

In the dining car on the sleeper train home, he seems delighted by the quality and quantity of the breakfast provided: 'bacon, two eggs, rusks, excellent and abundant marmalade, grapes and Nescafe (there was no butter, sugar or milk however) – 154 francs each'.[84]

Anyone who answered an advertisement in the October 1947 issue of *Modern Motoring and Travel* might have fared still better. Motoring enthusiasts were offered a continental holiday unencumbered by food shortages, petrol rationing or even tourist currency regulations. They could transport their pre-war or second-hand car to a place with 'supplies of petrol unlimited'. £50 per head would buy them first-class accommodation aboard a luxury liner, transport for their vehicle, the chance to take part in a two-week motor rally in Norway with full board at 'the best hotels – in association with the Norwegian government'.[85] These intrepid motorists need not be concerned that the tourist currency allowance had been reduced from £100 to £75 in October 1946 and then suspended altogether in the winter of 1947–1948. The restrictions, it seems, did not apply to Sweden, Denmark or Norway.[86]

Among other continental tourist attractions was a visit to one of the casinos that had lost no time in reopening, regardless of state of repair. Gaming remained illegal in Britain apart from at exclusive licensed clubs or at parties for invited guests in private houses or hired venues, run (at least ostensibly) on a non-commercial basis – both frequented only by the richest in the land. For ordinary Britons doubtless this hazardous European entertainment added a touch of extra excitement to the escape from austerity, but it is improbable that many visited France, Belgium or Switzerland primarily to chance their currency allowance on the roulette wheel. There were plenty of ways for them to lose their money at home.

The editor of the *Policy Holder* chastened people who went in for 'the usual gambling counters' and expressed relief that those wanting 'a flutter on change' were few. As did every other conservative luminary, he commended only investment in British government stocks and similar cautionary bets to the 'watchful, careful and thoughtful [aiming for] fundamental security'.[87] No doubt speculators who prided themselves on falling into this category followed the editor's advice but Britain certainly contained no dearth of gamblers wanting 'a flutter on change' or on almost any uncertainty. The post-war gambling boom ran the post-war holidaymaking epidemic a close race for the title of the nation's most popular surrogate for material conspicuous consumption.

The football pools had all closed down with the outbreak of war but, like the cinemas and theatres, soon reappeared albeit in a modified format. Against a background of declining interest in football, absence of players and erratic fixtures, the major promoters formed an alliance called Unity Pools, the effect of which was to reduce their industry to a shadow of its former self. This did not stop self-appointed guardians of national morality pronouncing football gambling 'a negative factor in wartime' and worse. There were even complaints that it created 'an unreal demand for newspapers' when Unity Pools co-operated in alleviating the paper shortage by publishing their coupons (betting forms) in advertisements rather than distributing them in individual envelopes through the post.[88] On restoration of peace and the revival of professional football leagues, Littlewood's,

Vernon's, Cope's and other leading promoters resumed their vigorous competition. Each week they sent their printed coupons to homes throughout the land, receiving in response 136 million postal orders in the 1946–1947 season alone.[89] 'Doing the pools' quickly became Britain's favourite pastime with greater numbers trying their luck than attended the football grounds or even the cinema. Few regarded it as serious gambling, spending an average of no more than between 2s 6d and 3s 4d per week and filling their leisure hours with an inflexible weekly routine: study the newspaper sports columns, tick the boxes with 1, 2 or X, make a copy, buy a postal order and a postage stamp, post the coupon, check the results on the wireless, throw away the copy. Pool losses per se were never the cause of hardship, and most devotees gained nothing but a topic of conversation, romanticising the expenditure of a large prize – always in modulated and unassuming terms. Fantasy winners never gave up work, bought a grand house, a Rolls Royce, indulged in a world cruise and certainly did not forget their friends and family. Under no circumstances did they aspire to higher social status. Most football-pool gamblers might have agreed with an opinion expressed in a 1948 report commissioned by the 'National League for Education Against Gambling' (NLEAG), which suggests that the popularity of the pools stemmed from 'the dispirited feeling that, though something can be done by the individual, it doesn't amount to much'. Debateable as this is, there can be no question that post-war gambling, at best, was only marginally associated with striving for a more fulfilled lifestyle.[90]

The NLEAG report accentuates not only the enormity of the activity as a whole, but provides some remarkable evidence of the amount British people were spending on this ethereal pleasure – over and above the far greater amounts they saved and invested. Forty-nine per cent claimed to regularly gamble on horses, 18 per cent on dogs, while 25 per cent admitted to playing cards for money at home.[91] Card playing had returned to vogue through the interwar recessions, increased as a diversion from the dreary evenings of wartime blackout, and endured in the ambience of austerity, almost certainly on a larger scale than the figures suggests. It was impossible to reliably gauge the cash changing hands behind closed doors and covered windows but there were a number of contemporary attempts to calculate the total staked on horse and dog racing. *The Economist*, contending that illegal gambling was more prevalent than before the war, estimated that in 1946 off-course bookmakers took in as much as £351 million.[92] In the following year, according to Addison, it was estimated that less than a million people attended the racecourses but about £400 million was bet on horses and a further £300 million staked on greyhound racing. For all their huge following the football pools were among the lesser factors of the gambling boom. The ten million or more people who habitually completed their coupons laid out only slightly over £70 million between them in the season.[93] If this data, published by Mark Abram, among the most respected researchers of the time, is to be accepted, then in 1947 the total staked on horses and dogs was ten times greater than the turnover of the football pools. Allowing a substantial margin for error, if nothing else, Abram's estimates demonstrate that there is some truth in the plethora of empirical evidence of enormous reckless bets being regularly placed by individuals.

Generally less reckless, mainly working-class gamblers were attracted in vast numbers every Monday to Saturday evening to the uninviting open terraces of Britain's rundown greyhound stadiums. In 1946 alone some 6.3 million attended the leading tracks, of whom, according to Ferdynand Zweig, 25 per cent were 'People who do nothing but gamble at [dog] racecourses ... professional punters, mainly lonely bachelors, often ex-servicemen, who tend to shun the responsibility associated with more regular employment and having no family life'.[94] It is well documented that many ex-servicemen delayed seeking regular employment for as long as possible after demobilisation but Zweig's summation is not entirely convincing. A great deal of money was indeed squandered away at the dog tracks but within two or three years of the 1946 peak, attendances had begun to fall away rapidly. It is improbable that many of the men shunning employment remained 'professional punters' for long. In no circumstances short of fraud, can gambling *per se* ever be a consistent source of income. Zweig goes on to contend more credibly that the heaviest losers were 'fairly well-off, from lower-middle and upper-working-class occupations, (including cash-rich small businessmen) treating the tracks as a hobby'. These inveterate losers were, he claims, the largest numerical category, suggesting that their prime motive was not to win but to display their financial successes elsewhere. Legend has it that such men cultivated an easy-come-easy-go manner to maintain their resilient reputation, boasting of their occasional win to anyone who would listen and immediately staking their entire prize on another dog, as conspicuously as possible, to show how little the money mattered to them.

Gambling as a form of conspicuous consumption was as much a badge of honour to the working-class punter as to his wealthier contemporary. In similar spirit, to be judged by his friends and cohorts a good sport, not afraid to lose, outweighed his expectancy of winning a few shillings to buy a round of drinks or place another bet.[95] This perceived prestige value was the only reason that illegal off-course betting retained its popularity.[vi] A win at the short odds offered by the back-street bookmaker, if paid at all, would have never made an appreciable difference to the lifestyle of a working-class man, and his loss might have been considerably greater than the stake money. With the purchase of each brief period of exhilaration or show of bravado came the risk of arrest and penalty.[96]

A bookmaker's wife explained to Mass-Observation in 1947: 'You'd be surprised if you knew how heavily and regularly the working man bets. It's his kind of religion. It brings him some hope. He's got no interest in religion. He knows that's only a money-making racket. The parson's getting a good living out of it – same as my chap gets out of his'.[97] If the working man was betting as much as she and the above cited research suggest, her husband was getting

---

[vi]   Cash off-course betting remained illegal until May 1961 when the first betting shops opened.

a much better living 'out of it' than most parsons. Yet by likening gambling to religious faith, the bookmaker's wife shows that she understands that his punters were motivated more by psychological need than by winning money for its own sake. The well-dressed upper- and middle-class men and women who attended fashionable horse race meetings were similarly motivated. To them it was a social obligation to be seen by their peers placing bets as a casual amusement irrelevant to money-making. Again, taken together with the estimated figures cited above, the mass of anecdotal evidence demonstrates that at the bookmakers' stands in the members' enclosure, as well as at the offices of the turf accountants legally registered to accept credit bets, middle- and upper-class gambling took place on an enormous scale.

The press and the moralists remained so persistent in their contention that the post-war gambling boom was the root cause of crime, vice, suffering and poverty that in 1949 the government, possibly reluctantly, convened a Royal Commission on Gambling under Sir Henry Willink. This sat for just short of two years before concluding that as 'a factor in the economic life of the country or cause of crime [gambling] was of little significance [and] its effects on social behaviour much exaggerated'.[98] Mark Clapson provides an alternative argument for the innocence of post-war gambling:

> To the end of the 1950s there is evidence to suggest that gambling coexisted with saving among the casual poor. Together they were part of a strategy for self-help for those who could not bring themselves to conform to what Orwell called 'Smilesian aspidistral standards.[99]

There is probably as much evidence to suggest that the casual poor who employed this strategy of self-help were as likely to become the *permanent* poor as the conformists to aspidistral standards. The gambling boom in practice transformed a small number of non-conforming self-helpers into the permanent rich. The pools promoters, their associates and senior staff, as well as many bookmakers could hardly fail to make money. Stars of the profession, such as William Hill and Joe Coral, used their phenomenal talents for high-speed £ s d arithmetic and astute business acumen to achieve enduring success, float their 'entertainment' companies on the stock market, and retire respectable millionaires.

It is open to question whether they would have done so well had there been greater opportunity for their punters to use their money to more material purpose. There were surely more than a few of them among the thousands who, in November 1946, queued at the Victoria and Albert Museum for a glimpse at all that was most creative of British post-war design.[100] Scottish architect, Basil Spence's *Britain Can Make It*[vii] exhibition displayed 6,000 material items, produced by 1,300 British firms, for Britons to admire and desire.[101] These marvels of ingenuity were

---

[vii]   Apart from the obvious double meaning, the name was an intentional reminder of Churchill's morale-boosting pronouncement during the Blitz – 'Britain can take it'.

almost all destined for the 'export drive', the pivot of Dalton's strategy to redress the economic deficit. None would reach the high-street shops. British consumers were expected to remain content with functional clothing and furnishings bearing the 'double C' Utility label[viii] – the trademark of austerity. As contemporary cynics commented, 'Britain can make it, but Britain can't have it'. The visitors nonetheless overwhelmingly expressed their admiration for modernity and native inspiration. Of the 1,250 people interviewed on behalf the recently established Council for Industrial Design, 'only 4.7 per cent expressed disappointment'. The lack of price tickets caused little or no concern that the exhibits might be unaffordable. Only 10 per cent had come expecting to be able to buy anything, and some assumed that they would never be able to do so. As one interviewee pragmatically commented, 'If we could buy home improvements where would we put them? First we have to get a home to improve'.[102]

However convinced by what they had seen, all the visitors expected a long and patient wait for a home to improve and concurred that for Britain to 'make it', it would need to make housing its priority. 475,000 houses had been destroyed or rendered uninhabitable through the war and many more fallen into dereliction through neglect.[103] The War Damage Commission estimated: 'out of approximately 14½ million rateable hereditaments in Great Britain and Northern Ireland at the outbreak of war, about one in four were notified to the Commission as having sustained war damage'.[104] Now an accelerating birth rate meant that each day more and more young families were adding their names to the housing lists – seldom with optimism. Demographic changes emerging from a transforming industrial landscape further compounded the problem, as increasing numbers of workers chose to relocate. Where there were most jobs, there was least accommodation.[105]

The government tackled the crisis head on: housing was to be among the top priorities of its new welfare state. The Minister of Health, Aneurin Bevan, divided his peerless energy between driving on monumental building programmes, including the grand designs for 'new towns', and the monumental task of creating the National Health Service. To compound the problems of constant shortages of money and building materials, Bevan's efforts were hampered by the number of skilled men still retained by the forces. He overcame the fierce opposition from politicians of both parties and senior military officers, who foresaw grave risks in dismantling the nation's defences too quickly. But, while speeding up demobilisation assisted productivity, it also increased the number of names on the local authority housing lists.

A fortunate few did not have to wait long. As a temporary solution, the government revived the project to re-house victims of bomb damage first mooted by the wartime Coalition in 1942, and began to construct prefabricated dwellings.[106] In comfort and quality the prefabs belied their much mocked reputation and would prove anything but temporary. Most remained occupied until well into the 1970s

---

[viii] The double C originally stood for 'civilian clothing': improved Utility designs on display at the exhibition were never produced.

and a handful of stalwarts still remain devoted to their 'rabbit-hutch palaces'.[107] Of the half million proposed only 156,667 were completed but the recipient of a greatly sought-after key found it unlocked a door to surroundings truly palatial compared to the cramped obsolete pre-war tenancy he gladly left behind. As late as 1951 no more than 37 per cent of Britain's houses contained a fixed bath, while every 1946–1948 prefab not only contained a fixed bath but it was in a modern bathroom with hot water on tap. It also had an internal toilet, an electric cooker, a three-cubic-foot refrigerator, wall-mounted electric sockets, a multi-fuel heater, separate rooms for children and often a small private garden too – all exemplars of pre-war affluence and unavailable post-war luxury.[108] The prefabs did not simply provide better living conditions; they were more economical. The average cost of construction at £1,365 turned out 50 per cent over budget but no local authority passed on the excess.[109] The rent for a three-bedroom prefab was initially 14s 2d per week and with exemption from rates comfortably affordable from a typical tenant's wage (estimated at about £3).[110] Still in 1950 the weekly rent for a four-bedroom prefab was no more than 19s 9d.[111]

The number of prefabs completed was too small to cause an appreciable shortening of the waiting lists. Bevan did all in his power to accelerate house construction without losing sight of his dedication to closing the gap between the living standards of the rich and poor. His eloquent, although possibly a little confused, words spoke of 're-creating the *classless* villages of the seventeenth and eighteenth century' with well-built spacious homes incorporating the conveniences of modern life 'for the *working classes*'.[112] But even the silver-tongued Bevan would never be able to sincerely claim to have created a classless council estate. However well appointed, tenants or their children aspiring to the middle classes abandoned their local authority homes at the first opportunity and bequeathed them to the less aspirational working classes. The Labour governments' house building achievements, however, should not be underrated or allowed to be overshadowed by the later negative social consequences of demographic evolution. By 1951, 961,000 new houses had been completed and 338,000 more adapted or restored, providing rent-subsidised homes for almost five million individuals.[113] What is more, the winners of the lottery for one of Bevan's *classless* houses appreciated their good fortune and, unlike the tenants of his successors' cheaply built, fast-deteriorating properties, took a pride in their homes and were often prepared to spend their own money on maintenance and improvement.

Bevan's visionary brand of socialism took no account of an ambition close to the heart of Britons of all classes – to own a home of their own. He railed with all the rancour in his prodigious repertoire against the resolve encapsulated in Eden's celebrated phrase, foreseeing Britain as a 'property-owning democracy'.[ix] To discourage investors, speculators, as well as ambitious owner-occupiers, in November 1946 Bevan predicted that property prices would fall substantially as

---

[ix]   Eden's friend, Scottish politician and journalist, Noel Skelton (1880–1935) is reputed to have originated the phrase in *Constructive Conservatism* (1924).

soon as sufficient homes had been completed. He was neither the first nor last to deceive himself with that elusive possibility. The Prudential Group instructed its trainees that:

> Houses with vacant possession are in many cases fetching fantastic prices and
> even taking into account the general increase in building costs including labour,
> there is little doubt that many people buying their houses at the present time
> will eventually be faced with a substantial drop in the value of their property, as
> and when the supply of new houses begins to catch up with the demand and the
> authorities' programme covering the building of houses gets underway.

> The main reason why the Company does not favour loans on such properties
> [priced below £600 in 1939] is that, by and large, such houses are generally
> purchased by those who fall within what may be termed the lower income group.
> It often follows that these individuals' experience of ordinary business procedure
> is very limited … [and] should default occur and it become necessary for the
> Company to exercise its rights as mortgagee, such persons are likely to feel very
> aggrieved at pressure being put upon them by a powerful Corporation.[114]

The implication that the powerful Prudential's propensity to lend to 'what may be termed' the *higher* income group, that is, those with the means to buy expensive properties and absorb the eventual 'substantial drop in value', is analogous to Bevan's censure of working-class home ownership. His confidence that, given time, the housing demand could and would be fully satisfied proved a convenient excuse for the Prudential and its competitors to refuse mortgage applications from wage earners.[115] A retired 'Man from the Pru' told me in a personal interview of the struggles he had had with his employer on behalf of loyal policyholders to secure an occasional advance from the late 1940s, even though the feared 'substantial drop in value' was never to materialise.[116]

Similar fears provoked by politicians and pundits caused insurance companies to remain wary of mortgage business until the property boom of the early 1970s. In accordance with their cautious stance, their terms and conditions were as and often more demanding than those of building societies. Yet after the war, seemingly with little reason, the societies became increasingly resentful of the competition, fervently maintaining that home loan provision was their sole prerogative.[117] The BSA went so far as to admonish the insurance companies simply for promoting mortgage protection policies, among their core activities for decades, due to the: 'awkwardness of sharing mortgage business with organisations capable of competing with them in the mortgage field, whose methods of approach to the borrowers might not be in accord with best building society practice'.[118] This apparent paranoia was not only unjustified but superfluous given that the BSA's members were as conservative as the insurance companies and did not always themselves scrupulously adhere to the 'best building society practice'. Building societies, though far more numerous than today, were then mostly comparatively small; serving perhaps a single town or designated area and dependent on local investment. The managers, often also the proprietors, granted mortgages to members (depositors) they knew personally or who were recommended by known sources. They also usually worked hand-in-glove with neighbouring bank and insurance company managers, which meant that a rejected applicant's had little chance of raising a mortgage at a second or subsequent attempt in the area.

The many difficulties faced by individuals endeavouring to raise mortgage finance did not stop the unrelenting housing shortage forcing prices to rise and to go on rising. In the House of Commons, a frustrated Bevan thundered his demands for legislation to control the market. He venomously denounced the private housing sector and its financial supporters, exclaiming to the press: 'This time we are not going to allow the moneylenders [building societies] to take a fat rake-off from the people's homes'. He threatened to 'resign rather than allow speculative builders to drive up prices in a speculative market'. Most of all, he detested private landlords, who 'owned other people's homes' and reflected the building societies' 'crippling interest charges in their burdensome rents'.[119] For all Bevan's powerful rhetoric, no legislative action detrimental to the private sector transpired under the Labour government.

The *raison d'être* of a building society was to assist those with insufficient money to buy their own home outright: speculative builders were immobilised by licensing restrictions, and private landlords were bound hand and foot by rent controls. It was in none of their interests to drive up prices. Prices rose for no other reason than demand for an estimated four million dwellings – as many as had been built in the twenty-one years between the wars.[120] The *Estates Gazette* claimed that the 'hardening' of prices was due to ending of the 'much-criticised war-damage contribution' and the continuance of the cheap-money policy. It is improbable that either was at the root of the problem, but nowhere in the *Estates Gazette* (or any other publication) was there a house to be found for sale, and there were practically none to let either. It collated a series of reports from estate agents around the country all of which underscored the enormity of the famine. At the beginning of 1946 no residential property of any kind, regardless of age or condition, stayed on the market for longer than a few days. One leading provincial agent reported that 'the large majority of sales are effected by public auction: others by private treaty and take place so quickly that properties are usually on the market for only a matter of days'. Another claimed 'we have no difficulty in disposing of houses of any age or condition. Prices are on average double 1939 values'.[121] Behind these and similar reports lay a million stories of private anguish and dashed hopes.

Building land alone lingered on the estate agents' books. A man bold enough to buy a plot to build his own house or even set out to rebuild his bombed out former home, faced a mountain of controls, restrictions, permit requirements and similar bureaucracy. The *Estates Gazette* hardly needed inform those so minded, that the 'building licences, introduced at the start of the war, were continued by the post-war government in order to limit private building'.[122] Towards the end of

1946, Bevan demanded that those local authorities issuing the highest proportion of the few, far-between, and highly coveted CL1138 building licences cease to do so until further notice. He did leave some councils with limited discretion. A few would-be builders managed to surmount the paperwork, secured their CL1138 and were permitted to commence construction. Then, they had to raise the finance. And their problems did not end there: recruiting and organising tradesmen, workers and obtaining building materials, as *Good Housekeeping*, exercising considerable restraint, put it, 'was an adventure'.[123] It was perhaps as well that most good housekeepers chose not to go down that adventurous road.

The fortunate who survived the war and kept their house intact or adequately insured found themselves on an adventurous road leading to capital appreciation. The less fortunate, whose homes fell to the Luftwaffe, found themselves on an adventurous road leading to compensation. The War Damage Act 1941 introduced a special tax on private and commercial property owners to create a fund for the payment of compensation for destruction to buildings, plant and machinery, business equipment and household chattels.[124] To supervise the claims and administer their settlement, Sir Kingsley Wood established the War Damage Commission (WDC), probably with little or no concept of the mammoth task he was setting. By the end of 1942 over two and a half million properties, an estimated 92 per cent of them dwelling houses, had suffered varying degrees of bomb damage.[125] Before it was disbanded, after two decades of continuous service, the WDC, with a staff never exceeding 83 at its head office and 347 at regional offices, received no fewer than 4.7 million claims from individuals, processed them manually, and paid them over £700 million. The smallest were disposed of quickly, generally without contest; the majority being settled between 1946 and 1949. Claims for substantial damage involving thorough investigation and a process of negotiation, in some cases, were protracted over several years, but claimants were seldom disappointed with the compensation they accepted in the end.[126] The WDC was briefed to reinstate values as at 31st March 1939 but its inadequate staff had no means of differentiating between war damage and prior deterioration, especially where a property had been heavily devastated or totally destroyed. The Commission's official and only chroniclers, Sibyl Clements and her colleagues, were quite aware of the shortcomings. As they wrote: 'There was plainly ample scope for fraud at one end of the scale and for innocent mistake at the other and a variety of mixed possibilities in between'.[127]

During the blitz, Mass-Observation's Sheffield war diarist, with characteristic reproachfulness, recorded hearing that 'one of the men in town put in a claim for £5,500. I estimated the damage at £150 for stock and £80 for building'.[128] The WDC took such alleged greed in its stride, coped patiently with the multitude of claims, dealt with each on its merits, settled disputes with quiet diplomacy and only in the rarest of cases resorted to legal action. In its first year it sued just six claimants, five of them successfully. Through its entire history only one prison sentence resulted from a fraudulent claim.[129] This near-forgotten but heroic organisation has never received the recognition it deserves for helping to restore the financial position of millions of people, among them my own family.

Another often forgotten source of post-war financial restoration is the gratuity paid to every serviceman on demobilisation.[x] All gratuities were tax-free since the War Office did not wish to be accused, in its own words, 'of giving with one hand and taking back with the other'.[130] Conscripted servicemen were unconditionally entitled to a financial package calculated on a complex scale based on rank, time served and family status. Addison cites the examples of an unmarried private with three years' service receiving £83 and a married major with one child, £196.[131] Based on the official published tables (the source of Addison's figures), had they completed five years' service, the private would have received a minimum of £121 and the major £324.[132] In practice, there were other facets to the calculation. As demonstrated in the previous chapter, service pay varied widely for men of the same rank and gratuities had to be adjusted proportionately. For the purpose of calculating the gratuity, the War Office required that 'a major who joined the army in 1939 as a private be treated as if he had been a major for the whole war'.[133] The hapless Major Pollock in Terrance Rattigan's *Separate Tables* confesses: 'I only got it [his commission] by a wangle – it wasn't difficult at the beginning of the war'. As a single major with five years' service Pollock would have received a minimum lump sum of £292 tax free (over £12,000 today) and probably would have had little problem 'wangling' a few other benefits and an army pension. For all his troubles, he could afford to brush aside the small loan sympathetically offered to him.

In addition to the gratuity there was also a package of benefits including the much maligned 'demob suit', other clothing, travel vouchers or cash in lieu. The enterprising or ambitious received a further £150 to assist them to set up in business, study at university or train for a vocation.[134] There were further generous resettlement grants on offer in appropriate circumstances. In the event of death in service, widows received pensions based on a scale rising with rank, heavily biased in favour of the dependents of men who had died overseas.[135]

Young working-class men leaving the services had more disposable cash in their pockets than ever before in their lives but neither their education nor military training had prepared them for any such eventuality. Personal finance was not a subject thought appropriate to a school curriculum or a training programme, nor were there as yet newspaper 'money' columns or radio programmes offering free investment advice. Not until the advent of affluence, when it can be contended they were least needed, did a host of Fleet Street financial wizards appear, simultaneously dispensing wisdom and disclaiming liability. In 1945, the only public guides were advertisements vested with commercial interest. The National

---

[x]   Originally denied, on 18th March 1945, following trade union representations to the Government, regular policemen, firemen, reservists and auxiliaries also became eligible for gratuities on a par with military service, if they had served over six months under Civil Defence conditions (NA, PRO, WO/45/19898; 'Gratuities Policeman/Firemen').

Provincial Bank, for example, published an unusually expansive announcement, under the banner 'Hard Earned Money' explaining that:

> The advent of Peace will find an unprecedented number of people in possession
> of moderate capital derived from war savings, service gratuities and tax refunds.
> Before investing in business concerns it is wise to be assured of the bona fides
> and reputation of contracting parties ... National Provincial Bank Limited offers
> to customers an experienced credit information service.[136]

Deprived of much of their traditional lending business, Britain's banks found themselves in the unprecedented position of having to proactively maintain the goodwill of their existing customers, and at the same time proactively attract new depositors. Never intentionally inviting the fugitive funds of black marketeers or tax evaders, they began to take an interest in a hitherto untapped but now substantial market – the small businessman dealing exclusively in cash. This cash, they believed, could enhance their reserves while its depositors would have little or no requirement for credit. To attract such individuals in 1947 the Midland Bank, in an imaginative new departure, risked the substantial production budget of £2,000 and £14,000 for distribution to 1,800 cinemas for 250 prints of each of four films – called *Starting Trouble* (changed to *Small Beginnings*), *Money to Burn*, *The Cap Fits* and *Paper Money*.[137] The last is a cautionary tale of a street-corner newsvendor called Joe, whose cash savings of some four hundred pounds are stolen from the cardboard box kept, in legendary tradition, under his bed. But never mind! His 'friends and relations' with unheard-of generosity rally round and make up most of his loss. Now he owns his long coveted smart newsagency and banks with the 'sympathetic' Midland, according to Joe's final proclamation, 'safe h'even from the h'atom bomb'.[138] No copies of the films are evidently extant and only the one script has survived, but the titles alone define their target market. How many cash traders were inspired to embrace the ways of traditional banking is not recorded, but it would be many years before cinemagoers were treated to another bank commercial.

Those who chose not to put their cash in the bank included young ex-servicemen irresponsibly celebrating their return to civilian life. Our Sheffield war diarist once again registered his indignation on learning that a friend's son had dared spend his entire gratuity on a second-hand motor car that 'takes every penny of his income, in fact he cannot pay his proper board at home'.[139] The income of the young man in question, like that of many of his peers, probably came from just enough casual work to run the car and pay his basic expenses, while he delayed for as long as possible commencing a regular job and (perhaps literally) a pedestrian lifestyle.[140]

Other young men enhanced their income by dealing on the black market. They had no difficulty finding customers ready to pay high prices for virtually unobtainable luxuries, such as cosmetics, cigarettes, coffee, chocolate, nylon stockings, jewellery and watches, but acquiring such things for sale presented increasing problems. American servicemen, once the main source of supply, returned home when the war was over, and British producers, importers and wholesalers had few rejects or surplus goods to sell off. The so-called 'spiv' later depicted on stage and screen as an overdressed sharp-witted character, flashing money and enjoying a carefree existence, was certainly a myth. His nearest real-life equivalent was generally an unsavoury individual leading a shadowy and unconstructive existence, who quickly vanished when choice returned to the shops.[141]

Despite their reputation for ubiquity these work-shy petty criminals represented only a tiny minority. Most ex-servicemen gratefully accepted the offers of a state-funded start in civilian life, and in general used the money to advantage, often achieving success in the professions, commerce and industry – in some cases spectacular success. Many chose not to return to the anachronistic atmosphere of their native towns and migrated, usually southwards, to find jobs with prospects. The majority who secured a regular income wished for little more than to settle down to a conventional family life, but even this was not necessarily straightforward.

Britain was still suffering the economic wounds inflicted by the winter snows, when on the 15th April 1947 Hugh Dalton delivered his penultimate Budget. He commenced on a positive note, asserting that the progress over the previous year was 'not a bad start for today's excursion' but for consumers and taxpayers, hoping for help in rebuilding a sustainable conventional family life, his message soon turned negative. They would have to pay additional purchase tax on a range of necessities including domestic heating and cooking appliances, 50 per cent more for cigarettes, and if they succeeded in buying a house, doubled stamp duty.[142] The Chancellor nobly claimed to have rejected the introduction of a betting tax 'with regret [as] it would be … not very difficult to tax the totes, horses, dogs and football pools … but we stand for justice'.[143] Indeed, this would have been the worst moment to tax one of the most readily accessible escape routes from austerity. The *Daily Express* delivered an unequivocal verdict of disappointment: the Budget, said its editorial, 'failed to provide a stimulant to the unapplied energies of the people'.[144]

The unapplied energies of the people were being sapped not only by the ongoing impact of abnormal weather conditions, high taxes and poorly stocked shops, but the mountainous national debt they were expected to help diminish with greater exertion and prolonged privation. The exported product of Britain's under-funded and hastily-revived industries was failing to generate the necessary revenue. On 6th August 1947 unrelenting economic deterioration forced the Prime Minister, Clement Attlee, to announce yet another round of frustrating austerity measures. House building was to be cut back, imports, especially of food and building materials were to be drastically reduced, the petrol ration was to be cut, and dining at hotels and restaurants further restricted. Attlee reminded the people of a nation at peace that they were fighting 'another Battle of Britain … which could not be won by the few'.[145]

The many needed no reminder that they were fighting a battle of Britain on the battlefield of austerity and taking pride in the ground that they, as individuals, were regaining. The nation had a multi-digited debit balance on its account but no red ink was in evidence on the private bank accounts of its people. The ascent of savings and investment continued apace. The promised welfare state to endow all with lifelong security drew near to fruition. Everyone knew that beneath the surface the best of British life and tradition had weathered the storms. Stoically its people fought on – paying their income tax, buying their National Savings certificates, accepting 'suburban ordinariness', thinking highly and living plainly – but not for much longer. The short dawn of post-war 'elegant economy' was over and the shadow of its eclipse by conspicuous consumption was about to appear.

Endnotes

1   *Building Societies Gazette*, May 1946.

2   Hoggart, Richard, *A Sort of Clowning: Life and Times, vol. II, 1940–1959* (1990), 188–195.

3   Hennessy (1992), 307–308.

4   British Library Sound Archives, C900/02589: 'Bank manager born 1929'; (Shakespeare, *Hamlet*, Act III).

5   Hopkins (1964), 307.

6   Hardyment, Christina, *From Mangle to Microwave: The Mechanisation of Household Work*, 1988 (1990), 152–153.

7   Brown, Callum G., *The Death of Christian Britain: Understanding Secularisation 1800– 2000* (2001), 174.

8   Brown (2001), 170, 172–173.

9   Hopkins (1964), 97.

10 Orwell, George, 'The Decline of the English Murder', in *Collected Essays, Journalism and Letters: Volume IV*, 1946 (1980).

11 Howard, Anthony, 'We are the Masters Now' in Sissons and French *Age of Austerity* (1963), 15.

12 Morgan, Kenneth, O., *The People's Peace: British History 1945–1990* (1992), 61.

13 Zweiniger-Bargielowska (2004), 151.

14 Idem, *The Historical Journal*, 37. 1. 1994, 'Rationing, Austerity and the Conservative Party Recovery after 1945', 187.

15 Idem (2004), 229.

16 Hennessy (1992), 94.

17 Ibid., 78.

18 Hopkins (1964), 91.

19 MO: FR 2220, March 1945.

20 MO: TC40, 'Post-War Hopes' March 1944.

21 Morgan (1992), 67.

22 Hennessy (1992), 47.

23   Zweiniger-Bargielowska (2004), 10–11.

24   *Daily Express*, 16th and 17th September 1945.

25   Richards (1997), 87, 89.

26   *The Times*, 8th May 1945.

27   Hunt (1996), 80.

28   Allen, C.K., 'The Pinpricked Life' in *The Spectator*, 5th November 1948, 584–585.

29   Zweiniger-Bargielowska (2004), citing Lord Woolton, *Memoirs* 1959, 152.

30   Mosley, Leonard 'Back to the Wall' (1971) in *Journal of Economic History*, vol. 47, No. 1, March 1987, 198.

31   MO: Diaries 1939–65, No. 5067, 10th September 1947.

32   Howard in Sissons and French (1963), 25.

33   *The Banker*, June 1946, 148.

34   *The Times*, 25th October 1945.

35   *New Statesman*, 27th October 1945, 275.

36   *The Times*, 25th October 1945.

37   *Housing Market: House Prices since 1930*: Office of the Deputy Prime Minister.

38   *The Times*, 10th April 1946.

39   *Investor's Chronicle and Money Market Review*, 13th April 1946, 573, 576.

40   *News Chronicle*, 10th April 1946.

41   *The Times*, 10th April 1946.

42   *News Chronicle*, 9th April 1946.

43   Hennessy (1992), 214.

44   Zweiniger-Bargielowska (2004), 214–218.

45   *The Spectator*, 5th November 1948.

46   *Daily Express*, 24th February 1947.

47   Hennessy (1992), 276.

48   Zweiniger-Bargielowska (2004), 174–175.

49   *Daily Express*, 5th September 1945.

50   *Daily Mirror*, 5th January 1946.

51   *The Spectator*, 5th November 1948.

52   Thomas, Donald, *An Underworld at War: Spivs, Deserters, Racketeers and Civilians in the Second World War* (2004), 385–389.

53   Addison (1985), 63.

54   *Manchester Guardian*, 8th April 1948.

55   NA, PRO, MFP, BS.69 (6/26), *Evasions of Petrol Rationing Control*; *Report of the Committee of Enquiry to H. T. N. Gaitskell* (Ministry of Fuel and Power, April 1948), 6.

56   Ibid., 23.

57   *The Policy Holder*, 1st January 1946, 9.

58   MO: Diary, 5067, 10th September 1947.

59   Museum of London Sound Archives: 96.25, 'Showroom assistant, born 1929'.

60   Blake, David, *Pension Schemes and Pension Funds in the United Kingdom* (2003), 39.

61   *The Banker*, March 1947, 192.

62   McKibbin (2000), 41.

63   MO: TC57/1/G, 9th January 1947.

[64]   MO: FR 2508, 8.
[65]   Nightingale (1973), 103–105.
[66]   MO: FR 2508, 21.
[67]   MO: FR 2387, 'Attitudes to the Salvation Army', March 1946.
[68]   Salvation Army Heritage Centre (SAHC): Minutes of Publicity Council Meeting, 31st October 1945.
[69]   *War Cry*, 5th January, 1935.
[70]   LTSB: HO/GM/Adv/2, 1678, 'Advertising 1931–1972', Advertising Committee minutes, 21st April 1947.
[71]   SAHC: Minutes of Publicity Council Meetings, 31st October 1945.
[72]   Nightingale (1973), 118; SAHC: Minutes of Publicity Council Meeting, 22nd February 1951.
[73]   *News Chronicle*, 13th April 1946.
[74]   Stacey, Margaret, *Tradition and Change: A Study of Banbury*, 1960 (1970), 155.
[75]   Marwick (2003), 91.
[76]   Barnett, Correlli, *The Verdict of Peace: Britain Between her Yesterday and the Future* (2001), 137.
[77]   Pimlott (1976), 236.
[78]   *News Chronicle*, 23rd February 1946, 8th April 1946.
[79]   Pimlott (1976), 223.
[80]   Addison (1985), 116–117.
[81]   *The Times*, 'Peace Time Travel Again', 27th April 1946.
[82]   *Financial Times*, 8th and 10th April 1946.
[83]   MO: Diary 5076, 22nd and 30th July 1947.
[84]   Ibid., Entries 7th and 16th August 1947.
[85]   *Modern Motoring and Travel*, October 1947, 16–17.
[86]   *Financial Times*, 5th November 1951.
[87]   *Policy Holder*, 31st December 1947, 987.
[88]   Longmate (1971), 463–464.
[89]   MO: FR 2560, 'Mass Gambling', Commissioned by the National League for Education against Gambling, January 1948, Table VII.
[90]   Ibid., 270.
[91]   Ibid., 22.
[92]   *The Economist*, 29th March 1947.
[93]   Addison (1985), 24.
[94]   Zweig (1948), 31–36.
[95]   Hoggart (1992), 139.
[96]   McKibbin (2000), 372.
[97]   MO: FR 2560, 59.
[98]   Addison (1985), 125.
[99]   Clapson (1992), 64.
[100] MO: TC26/2/A.
[101] Hopkins (1964), 51.
[102] MO: TC26/2/B and C: Questionnaires.

[103] Burnett (1993), 284–285.

[104] NA, PRO, IR.83.207: Sibyl Clements et al., *A Short History of the War Damage Commission 1941–1962* (undated), Appendices B and E, 24.

[105] Marwick (2003), 35.

[106] Stevenson, Greg, *Palaces for the People: Prefabs in Post-War Britain* (2003), 38.

[107] Finnimore, Brian, *Houses from the Factory: System Building and the Welfare State 1942–74* (1989), 31.

[108] Stevenson (2003), 103.

[109] *Daily Express*, 17th October 1945.

[110] Stevenson (2003), 147.

[111] Rowntree and Lavers (1951), 86.

[112] Marwick (2003), 35.

[113] *The Economist*, 10th November, 1951.

[114] PGA: Box 1326, Booklet, 'Ordinary Branch Training Course for New Agents', February 1948.

[115] *Policy Holder*, 8th January 1947.

[116] Personal interview, H. Kaye.

[117] *The Banker*, Little, L.T., 'Life Assurance After the War' July 1946.

[118] *Building Society Gazette*, January 1949.

[119] Ibid., January 1946, 4 and 10.

[120] *Building Societies' Gazette*, January 1946, 19.

[121] *Estates Gazette*, 5th January 1946.

[122] Ibid.; Daunton (1987), 78.

[123] *Good Housekeeping*, May 1947.

[124] NA, PRO, IR 34 /1362, 'Survey of the Organisation and Work of the WDC'.

[125] Ibid.

[126] NA, PRO, IR 83 /207, Clements, Appendices B and E.

[127] Ibid., 63.

[128] MO: Diary 5076, 14th January 1941.

[129] NA, PRO, IR 83 /207, Clements, 63.

[130] NA, PRO, WO/32/10293, 'Grants and Gratuities'.

[131] Addison (1985), 23.

[132] Table of 'Gratuities for Release on 30th June 1945', 7th February 1945.

[133] NA, PRO, WO/32/12856, 'War Gratuity and Post War Credits: Second World War policy'.

[134] Addison (1985), 24.

[135] NA, PRO, WO/32/9817, 'Payment made after death 1940–1944' (figures *c.*1941).

[136] *The Times*, 1st February 1945.

[137] HSBCGA: 0200/040, 12th May 1947, Intelligence Department Manager to Sir Clarence Sadd, Vice Chairman of the Midland Bank.

[138] HSBCGA: 0200/040; *Midland Venture*, October 1947, 245.

[139] MO: Diary 5076, entry 2nd June 1947.

[140] Addison (1985), 23.

[141] Thomas (2003), 310.

142 *The Times*, 16th April 1947.
143 *Daily Express*, 16th April 1947.
144 Ibid.
145 *The Times*, 7th August 1947.

Chapter 5
First Quartile
(*1948 to 1951*)

Retaining class ties with his kin will not assist the upwardly mobile individual to establish himself at a higher status level than that of his family of origin, and to achieve this will mean giving time to the cultivation of a new lifestyle and acquaintances.

John H. Goldthorpe[1]

Until Cripps reminded the nation that it could not have its cake and eat it, the people had not seemed to realise that free teeth and spectacles were just another form of consumption and rationed, at that. It had not been appreciated that social services, subsidised houses and controlled food prices were just as much a part of the standard of living as another pound in the pay packet ... Few realised they were not paid for by the weekly insurance stamps.

David Marquand[2]

As the first half of the twentieth century drew to a close the Labour government sustained its determined and in many ways fruitful efforts to change the face of British society, but the face of British society had no great desire to be changed. Its long ingrained class and gender conventions had survived both war and socialist government unscathed; or in the words of Kenneth Morgan's simple summation: '[by 1948] it was clear that the belief that the British class system dissolved or was basically modified during the war is a total myth'.[3] Morgan was right: Britain had dissolved into a welfare state but the bases of Britishness and British prejudice were not to be dissolved. This chapter will consider some of the differing attitudes to the defence of the national character, to consumption, and to personal finance through a simultaneous low of austerity and high of social reform between 1948 and 1951.

The upper class, in general, feigned oblivion to post-war change. For this diminishing minority it remained vital to keep Britain's time-honoured unwritten social and cultural laws intact and to camouflage their potential redundancy with a show of outdated uniformity. Under no circumstances would it loosen its old school or old regimental tie. Its birthright was to preserve old traditions, old stately homes and old money and to ostensibly distance itself from modernity, commerce and industry. Upper-class parents resumed spending lavishly on 'coming-out' balls for their debutante daughters and would continue to do so long after the Queen abandoned her commitment to receive them in 1959. These expensive charades, bought by families to conserve inherited grandeur for posterity through marriage, were now affordable only by proactive management of income and capital, inevitably demanding ventures into the shark infested waters of modernity, commerce and industry.

These same families also believed it their bounden duty to go to whatever lengths necessary and to pay whatever it cost for the next generation to be tutored in the perpetuation of old class privilege at old British public schools. The government, for all its equality-of-opportunity rhetoric, never seriously considered legislation to the detriment of these great establishments, whose alumni included no dearth of its own upper-class and upper-middle-class leaders and luminaries. Not one Labour Member of Parliament had voted in favour of an amendment to the 1944 Education Act proposing compulsory state schools for all.[4] They did not say it, but they could hardly deny that the public schools had always produced the finest of Britain's military, literary, scientific, professional, artistic and political leaders. Nor did they say that expensive education had produced most of the captains of modern industry and modern commerce upon whom the survival of their 'mixed economy' was dependent. When the Conservatives came to power in 1951, they found the taxation benefits of charitable status, 50 per cent rating reliefs, tax-free endowment income and all the other financial privileges bestowed by tradition upon the old public schools, and therefore upon the parents who paid for them, untouched by the two Attlee governments.[5]

Exactly why these governments, the architects of so many radical changes, disregarded educational establishments whose constitutions flew in the face of socialist ideology remains the subject of unresolved historical debate, but a possible explanation might be found in the charismatic images of popular school fiction. No writer of the time wasted his or her talent on the crude realities of a state school when free to embellish the lives of fictitious young gentlemen, whose real life models were hidden from the public gaze by the old high walls of old private estates. Without resentment or question, readers of all classes accepted that the anachronistic privileges as depicted were immutable and desirable realities of the great British tradition. With specific reference to public-school fiction Jeffrey Richards writes: 'It is generally acknowledged that popular culture holds up a mirror to the mindset of the nation. It confirms sets of values, attitudes and ideals which for good or ill cohere to form the national identity'.[6]

That most devotees of popular culture in the form of public-school fiction had not been privately educated, in no way obscured their conviction that the imaginary establishments and their students were the seedbed of national identity. In similar recognition of the mindset of the nation, McKibbin cites the classless approbation for the book and 1939 film of James Hilton's *Goodbye Mr Chips*.[7] When the film was remade thirty years on, still the idyllic English public school with its gowned teachers, wholesome boys in bright blazers and champagne-sipping parents casually clapping the cricket on bright summer days was accepted as authentic and perpetual. In fiction, the end of term bill was an unmentioned irrelevancy. In fact, more people than ever, not all of them born to the upper classes or even aspirants to the moneyed classes, now paid the end of term bill by whatever means at their disposal. In 1948 Roy Boulting confronted the themes of money, class and the public school head-on in his groundbreaking and thought provoking film *The Guinea Pig*.

As part of a government wartime experiment Jack Read (Richard Attenborough), a young boy from a working-class home, is sent away to a tradition-bound public school. After an unpromising start, Jack soon adopts upper-class tastes, mannerisms and speech and becomes accepted by his stereotypical snobbish classmates. Following a bout of derision painfully administered on his first return home for Christmas he promises not to forget his old friends – none of whom are again seen or heard of in the film. Indeed the transformed hero evidently has no further truck with anyone remotely working-class apart from a school porter who he learns to treat as an inferior, and his parents, who by the time they venture to make their first visit to the school after five years, seem themselves to have acquired middle-class attitudes. The experiment can be deemed a success, since it results in Jack's grant of a partial scholarship to Cambridge, naturally with the intention of becoming a public-school teacher. Historian G.S.R. Kitson Clark observes that: 'If the [public school-boy] returned to work in his native place [he was] no longer quite a native of it, he spoke a different language from most of its inhabitants'.[8] This apparently applied regardless of his class.

The Guinea Pig offers more commentary on contemporary attitudes than to melodramatically underscore the ineptitudes of the British class system. Jack's parents are not ignorant of the ways of the world and are prepared to deny themselves every luxury, give up their precious free time, forego their savings and mortgage their little shop, and save to invest in the *inequality* of opportunity they themselves have been denied. They express unqualified admiration for the dignity of the public school and would never wish to see it changed. Jack's dedicated teacher, on the other hand, concludes the film with an impassioned speech advocating changes in the school's outdated ethos to accommodate the influx of state-funded working-class boys 'on their way'. In the real world, the public school ethos was impervious to change, no influx of state-funded working-class boys was on its way and personal expenditure on private education continued to be an investment priority the middle and upper classes expected to pay dividends to the next generation, both in cash and kind.

The Labour governments safeguarded the universal freedom to opt out of state education and never considered applying price controls to school fees. Nor did they sponsor experiments or schemes like that which benefited the fictitious Jack Read. Real parents made real sacrifices to exercise their right to buy private schooling and the privileges that went with it. Supportive parents felt it their only option when, as was so often the case, state teaching standards fell short of expectation. Teachers' salaries were shackled to an esoteric system known as the Burnham Scale, which trailed the retail price index and, in the name of fairness, offered little or no financial incentive for achievement. The never popular scale was a false economy which, in effect, cleared the way for the private schools to lure Britain's most able teachers with superior facilities, higher salaries and the opportunity to work with pupils encouraged by their fee-paying parents to learn and to participate. Private education was destined to remain at least one ethereal consumer commodity where demand would always outstrip supply.

For the majority, unable or unwilling to pay, the 1944 Education Act had created a three-tier system of grammar, secondary modern and technical schools, predominantly aimed at the provision of so-called 'equality of opportunity'. It provided nothing of the kind. The county councils demanded that eleven-year-old children compete for places at grammar schools and access to lifelong opportunities that no school in the other tiers could hope to equal.[i] In practice, a pass or fail depended on the quality of preparatory teaching, far more than individual ability. Two letters appearing in *The Spectator* in 1948 from independent Member of Parliament, Sir Ernest Graham-Little, in vain exposed the 'farcical preparation' of primary school teachers by citing Ministry of Education advertisements offering women aged between twenty-one and thirty-five intensive one-year training courses with 'free tuition, generous maintenance grants and out of pocket expenses' – subject to no formal qualification or entrance test.[9] A retired teacher told me in an interview how she completed one such course, received her certificate without examination at the end of the year and, barely turned twenty-one, found herself 'fully qualified' to teach in the state system. She was immediately put in charge of fifty-two children, squeezed into a small classroom in an aging and neglected Birmingham school with no indoor toilets, no games facilities and inadequate basic teaching equipment.[10]

Not all state education was quite so perfunctory. There were primary schools with competent and committed teachers who overcame all obstacles for their fortunate pupils. Supportive parents armed only with word-of-mouth information, my own among them, were presented with the challenge of finding the local primary school with the best record of success. When I took the eleven-plus test in 1950, every one of the forty or so pupils in my class passed. At another state school down the road, half my contemporaries were not even entered and those who were all failed. Nationally over 75 per cent failed and were herded off to secondary modern schools, where in general the education could barely be called secondary, let alone modern. A local headmaster spoke for the majority when he told my horrified parents: 'We prepare our boys for the factory here'. This sentence resonated with them for the rest of their days as the epitome of the prejudiced British belief in the normality, rectitude and desirability of a working class without cultural, social or financial aspiration. A remarkable proportion of secondary modern leavers, nonetheless, educated themselves at their own expense or funded by non-governmental institutions, and salvaged their ambitions, financial and otherwise. The majority, however, could hardly wait for their fifteenth birthday to leave school, take a dead-end job and earn some spending money.

---

[i]   A small number of brighter eleven-plus failures were allowed a second attempt at age thirteen.

By contrast, children who passed the eleven-plus, overwhelmingly from middle-class or aspiring middle-class families, received an education that opened the doors to universities, further education and careers with prospects of advancement, and a good chance of an adult life unfettered by financial problems. It is not surprising that so many parents were prepared to invest in private tuition to ensure a grammar school place for their child.[11] A comparatively small outlay might relieve them of the heavy private school fees their neighbours would stretch their resources to pay rather than allow their slower learning children to suffer the indignity of a secondary modern education. Yet no government of any persuasion would ever openly acknowledge the personal financial concerns of those who shunned the system.

The strongest influence on the committee led by R.A. Butler when drafting the 1944 Act on behalf of the wartime Coalition government, had not been the financial or any other practical concerns of parents, teachers or children, but the religious instruction the Church of England believed indispensible to the nation's spiritual welfare.[12] The underlying premise of the Act, as depicted by Correlli Barnett, was 'the ideal of knightly Christian conduct' which, as he aptly observes, does not 'necessarily make for the amassment of material riches, either in the individual or the nation'.[13] Both might have been more materially enriched had the grammar schools placed less emphasis on the classics and more on science and technology, and the secondary moderns more on vocational training. Heedless of the manifest need for every type of skilled technician, the Ministry of Education allocated by far the smallest budget to the supposed third tier, the technical schools. These should have been the most progressive element of the revitalised state system but were simply too few and far between. The standard of education edged above the secondary moderns, but was below the worst of the grammar schools and the technical standards of inadequately trained teachers often left much to be desired.[ii] When their sons or, in a few cases, daughters left the technical schools parents might encounter the anachronistic custom of demanding a heavy premium for an indentured apprenticeship. The integrity of this enduring extortion was widely accepted until the mid-sixties, in accord with the time-honoured conviction that the best way to learn a trade is to be treated as the lowest form life in a grossly underpaid or even unpaid job.

With the exception of the demobilisation grants mentioned in the previous chapter, the state did not consider it appropriate to fund professional training either. Ambitious parents of aspirant solicitors, chartered accountants and similar supposedly prestigious professions invested in iniquitous premiums, as well as to tuition fees and maintenance costs, for their sons (and, again in few cases, daughters) to serve up to five years as articled clerks without pay or at negligible salaries and similarly be treated as the lowest form of life. Since the war university

---

[ii]   Technical schools, entered by voluntary examination at age twelve or thirteen, were never attended by more than 11 per cent of secondary schoolchildren. Many of the teachers had received only wartime training in the forces.

education had been available through grants and state-funded tuition to students who, or whose parents, were able and prepared to pay for their living expenses. Even if long-term financial penury resulted, parents of all classes accepted the price of apprenticeship, vocational training or further education as a sound investment, sure to pay a dividend in the form of a secure job for their child. Whether this would be inevitable is open to question, as Hopkins explains:

> Before the war the complaints of businessmen about the waste of money on education had been a continuous note in the soundtrack of the times. Now business pressed for educational expansion; yet it might be here that the dilemma of 'take-over or be taken-over', confronting our society as a whole, might assume its most acute and critical form.[14]

The attitudes of post-war businessmen had not yet really changed sufficiently for them to press for educational expansion any more than they had before the war, or assume it acute or critical to their own survival or long-term interests. The young applicant seeking a position with prospects soon discovered that still what mattered most was not academic, vocational or even professional training but 'who you know'. Businessmen in general and public sector employers in particular continued to treat family connections as paramount. Fathers went on investing in the exorbitant fees of London's Pall Mall clubs and their provincial equivalents for the specific purpose of making influential contacts to further their sons' careers. McKibbin cites the study by economist R.V. Clements exposing that until the late 1950s school leavers wishing to enter managerial training were '"fixed up" by their fathers, family friends or golfing companions ... Given the importance of these kinds of contacts it would not be surprising if men came to regard membership of the Masons or similar organisations as a prudent act designed to benefit their offspring'.[15]

The offspring in question were invariably sons. Fathers seldom invested in the same way to benefit their daughters' careers in management and might have expected little return if they had. Executive appointments in the world of commerce remained a male preserve. Women did work beneath the dignity of men: telephonists, typists, filing clerks, bookkeepers. It was unthinkable to an employer of the time that a woman could possibly make a financial decision or compete with men in commercial negotiation. Her education and proven ability to control a household budget were considered irrelevancies. Michael Verey, the former chairman of the merchant bank, Schroder's, precisely encapsulates the attitude of financially orientated businessmen in the brief sentence: 'Women were totally disregarded'.[16] Dealing with money retained a Victorian 'not-quite-nice' connotation, unsuitable for ladies. For many years into the post-war era it was widely held to involve some sort of indefinable subtlety of thought beyond the female mental capacity. In 1963, at the induction to my first job as a chartered accountant, I was told that the female staff (naturally only secretarial) 'are not expected to use one iota of intelligence'. Women were actively discouraged from qualifying as accountants until well into the 1970s and the London Stock Exchange (LSE) felt 'passionately ... that it was quite inappropriate for women to subject themselves to the rough and tumble of the floor, or the "scramble [in] the hurley-burley crowd"'. It did not admit its first female stockbroker member until 1973.[17] The world of finance was, as David Kynaston puts it, 'like Ancient Greece, a world untroubled by gods or women'.[18]

Much in the same way as it left the public schools untroubled to lead the sons of the privileged to financial security, the Labour government did not trouble the clear-cut gendered roles that most women seemed contented enough to accept. And as with the public schools, fictional portrayal played a key role in maintaining the status quo. Women were constantly portrayed by the media as exemplary middle-class mothers and housewives, taking pride in their homes and families and whose only exposure to money was the sensible management of the allowance provided by their breadwinning husband for the household budget. Yet for all the post-war conservatism, media imagery and government policy, hairline cracks were becoming detectable on the iron mask of social convention. In January 1949, perhaps sensing this mild evolution, Mass-Observation pose the question: 'Middle Class – Why?'[19] The mostly female interviewees agree that 'middle class' is difficult to define but accept that it applies only to those 'close to the top of the financial tree'. Most backtrack on further probing with revisions such as: '[it is] a question of being born into a family with particular customs, outlook and way of life'.

Plainly the middle class remains a force to be reckoned with, but as more than one interviewee observes, it is experiencing a 'crisis of identity'. The most prevalent opinions speak of a crisis of status, a desire for an identifiable anchor and a concern that diminishing financial distinctions would mean 'the middle-classes shrinking out of existence'. A common complaint is that 'income ... is not a deciding factor nowadays, as many working-class people get higher pay than lower-middle-class, and many upper-class new poor get less'. Comments consistently emphasise the struggle to maintain status, nostalgia for pre-war lifestyles, and dread of encroachment by the *nouveaux riches*. The following are among the more succinct examples:

> Twentieth-century mentality has rejected the more rigid class demarcations but it has not yet formed an alternative class pattern of its own. In the eyes of middle-class people, the traditional class moulds, undeniably worn, are by no means ready for the scrap heap.

> Middle-class people look backwards, sometimes nostalgically, to the nineteenth century when laissez-faire economics ensured middle-class supremacy ... when Victorianism embodied most of the middle-class virtues and vices – stability, initiative, humanitarianism, high moral tone on one side of the coin, solidity, philistinism, and business ethics on the other.

If income or visible possessions are to be used as the criterion of class assessment, many middle-class people may be arbitrarily displaced from the group they themselves still feel they belong to, and whose mores they are still helping to develop and establish. Even if in the long run, it is the economic factor which proposes or disposes. ... There are very few individuals who are prepared to allow that income or any single factor determines class structure.[20]

Most respondents agree with the assumption that: 'loss of capital investment is synonymous with loss of cultural standards and political influence'. All dismiss the suggestion that money might soon become the sole determiner of class, yet (not expressed in so many words) make it plain that they practise forms of 'elegant economy' as a conscious defence against conjectured threats of moneyed-class intrusion. The real threats, if any, were seldom characterised by malice, and middle-class bulwarks of financial constraint were, as always, futile. Few working-class or moneyed-class people as yet deliberately prioritised upward social mobility.

Contemporary economist Clare Griffin observes that 'the worker doesn't feel poor ... he has more money than before and his job is more secure'. True as this often was, neither more money nor a more secure job was able to exorcise the mindset of permanent financial deficiency.[21] Even if he had more money the worker clearly still felt poor, otherwise there would have been no re-emergence of a buoyant market in check trading and devious loan schemes. Since the war illegal or barely legal exploitation of the poorest classes had been allowed to cause serious problems for small retailers and their customers in working-class areas. While banking and hire-purchase facilities remained strictly regulated, shopkeepers found their business increasingly handicapped by the 'easy credit' promoted by unscrupulous profiteers. Following de-rationing in March 1949, this problem was of particular concern to the cheap clothing trade.

A spirited article exposing the impact of the situation published in the *Draper's Record* of October that year, somehow came to the attention of the mandarins of the Board of Trade. Its author W.C.H. Johnson, in championing the clothing retailers, asserted that 'something approaching a panic exists'. Small traders, he claims, were unable to sustain check club 'discounts' of between 7½ and 15 per cent of sale price eating away at their profit margins. Among other ills, Johnson identifies the excesses practised by the club agents; often unsavoury characters who effectually blackmailed struggling shopkeepers to extract unwarranted concessions and if denied would, as he so discreetly puts it, 'create difficulties'.[22] The traders dared not abandon the clubs for fear of loss of turnover and goodwill and were legally restricted from reflecting the discount in the price of Utility clothing, (controlled until 1952). Not only were the shopkeepers being cheated, but their customers too got a raw deal from the clubs that deducted more than the official maximum 5 per cent 'poundage' on sale of the checks. In addition, customers irrecoverably lost any unspent balance – ranging 'from a few pence to as much as twenty shillings'.[23] The true cost of anything bought with a check thus always proved disproportionately higher than its cash price.

As a direct result of Johnson's article, the Board of Trade kept check trading under intense surveillance for almost four years. Initially, although sympathetic to the retailers and censuring the 'socially deplorable consequences of the tally business', it considered the matter 'inappropriate to state intervention' and took no action.[24] The Board's contention was that it fell outside the scope of price control legislation and that further controls 'would come very near to prescribing minimum prices receivable by the shopkeeper'.[25] In December 1950 Labour MP Austen Alba took up the cudgels on behalf of the retailers and raised the question in the House of Commons. Ensuing enquiries reported that the Board had investigated the situation further and, in something of a surprising change of heart, concluded that the check traders' charges were justified by their overhead expenses.

F.G. Richardson of the London Local Price Regulation Committee refused to let the matter drop, pleading through subsequent correspondence that customers 'seldom complain because only rarely do they know what they are actually being charged'. The well-briefed Richardson wrote:

> There is also a certain amount of intimidation by collectors, who often are not loath to make harsh use of the knowledge that many of their customers are buying 'on tick' without their husband's knowledge. This element of what might be called a form of blackmail adopted by certain collectors is perhaps the gravest feature of tally trading … They [the 'tally houses'] are in a particularly sheltered position by reason of the nature of their business; yet they are the very businesses from which, in our view, the winds of enforcement should not be tempered.[26]

For all Richardson's determined eloquence the Board of Trade remained unmoved and no legislative amendment transpired. Tally and check traders were permitted to continue their unrestrained exploitation of the urban poor until post-war price regulation ended and accessible bank and hire-purchase finance resumed.

Meanwhile, whether or not impaired by these and similar exploiters, the British people were growing weary of living in an animated labyrinth of regulation. They were even growing weary of saving, but still they saved. Harold Mackintosh was not a man to allow his National Savings publicity machine to lose momentum simply because the war was over. To support the export drive and rearmament programmes, with undiminished dynamism and with austerity as his greatest ally, he marketed thrift and moderation to rich and poor alike. In March 1948, the Treasury eased his task by tightening its grip on the banks' already limited freedom to lend. The British Bankers' Association, as 'a gesture to the Chancellor of the Exchequer' (Sir Stafford Cripps) asked its members to cut their advertising by 18 per cent for twelve months.[27] The building societies, perhaps as a gesture to the banks, seized the opportunity to intensify their advertising to attract greater deposits, with considerable success. New accounts were opened and savings bolstered in anticipation of favour when houses and mortgage finance became accessible, although building society advertisements always studiously eschewed any such promise. Nine months later the *Building Societies Gazette* continued to bemoan that 'years would elapse after the war before any tangible progress would be made even towards a preliminary state in reconstruction [in the private sector]'.[28] Until that tangible progress was made in reconstruction, saving was destined to continue to dominate personal finance.

In particular families continued to inflict 'forced saving' upon themselves by religiously paying the premiums on the life policies they believed an impenetrable shield against all misfortune. The insurance companies' 'ambassadors of thrift' returned to their pre-war strength and wasted no time in regrouping to assault the consciences of the security seeking majority. The annual reports of the Prudential Group reveal not only accelerating sales in every department but reflect a now forgotten accelerating evolution in working-class attitudes to personal finance. In 1945 the Prudential's income from *ordinary* life assurance premiums was £17.8 million or 59 per cent of the £30.2 million collected from holders of small and fruitless *industrial* policies. Five years on, in 1950, ordinary business premiums yielded £32.5 million, now over 80 per cent of the £40 million still being paid by traditionalists and the poorest in the land, who addictively handed over their weekly few coppers to their reassuring ambassador. In 1956 individuals paid £51.6 million for the more realistic protection of the ordinary policy, finally overtaking the still far from insignificant £49.9 million in industrial premiums and thereafter the income from ordinary business continually extended its lead until, by the mid-1960s, it had driven its bargain basement rival to unmourned extinction.[29]

Investors in the false security of the industrial policy included many of the small depositors, who kept the faith with the similarly lacklustre Trustee Savings Banks (TSB). The conservative ambience of the post-war era could not have been more conducive to the business of the TSB's eighty-four autonomous banks, with over a thousand branches, thick on the ground in Scotland and northern England. All fostered a single creed – the virtue of thrift for its own sake. This alone was sufficient to beguile hundreds of thousands of almost exclusively working-class savers to deposit the rewards of the full employment they assumed to be at best temporary and at worst capable of instant self-destruction. In 1949–1950 alone the TSB opened 378,000 new accounts and was administering almost five million by the end of that financial year, the majority in areas considered among the most deprived in the land. These savers, many employed in newly nationalised industries, were less than optimistic about the future of their employers. They could sense that Britain's once great sources of wealth – cotton textiles, ship building, coal mining, agriculture and other industries – would not survive the competition of regenerated international markets. Thus the TSBs were able to attract savers with minimal proactive marketing and compete with National Savings (with which they were loosely affiliated) with comparatively colourless publicity. They never attempted to better the 2½ per cent interest paid by the POSB or even offer an incentive of appreciable value to win market share. Evidently their best, and possibly only, specific promotional offer was the 'useful concession' permitting withdrawal of up to fifty pounds on demand at the depositor's own branch.

By 1950, despite their consistent and seemingly passive success, the TSBs' management expressed concern that the changing social structure might result in an ongoing loss of business. The free monthly journal *National Savings* mused:

> The considerable redistribution of income which has taken place in the last decade has not been accompanied by a parallel spread of the middle-class tradition of saving. The lessened propensity to save for the community as a whole may be one of the major problems of the next decade.[30]

This report, predominately chronicling and extolling TSB achievements since the war, claims that it was 'attacking this problem [the fear of withdrawals] at its root – the savings habits of the weekly wage earner'.[31] 'Attacking' might be thought an intention to improve services, provide enhanced depositor facilities, intensify advertising, or even offer incentives. For the TSB 'attacking' involved none of these: it had its own distinctive and, it has to be said, highly effective public relations methodology.

Induction into the philosophy of the TSB could not start too young. Earnest representatives toured the country setting up 'thrift clubs' in every school that would let them through its door. In November 1947 the minutes of the Scottish 'Youth and Adolescents Coordinating Committee' (YACC – a possibly apt sounding acronym) for the Fife area recorded: 'Council courses in [local] secondary schools will soon include instruction in Thrift in the first three years of the course'.[32] The following month James Campbell, the chairman of YACC, visited London 'to confer with the Standing Committee of National Youth Organisations', and apparently achieved considerable success. The minutes record: 'They agreed that the [school] teaching of personal finance, (an expression which he preferred to the word "thrift") was in the country's interest and would be prepared to publish an article on the subject in their monthly journal'.[33] Campbell had also persuaded the BBC to allocate air time for him to explain to the nation the importance of teaching personal finance in secondary schools. The minutes do not disclose the reaction to his broadcast or clarify if any school in Fife or elsewhere added Personal Finance (or Thrift) to its curriculum. Other YACC minutes do, however, detail the progress of TSB representatives in promoting national training schemes for youth club leaders, and an impressive succession of accomplishments in instructing YMCA, YWCA, Boys Brigade, Boy Scouts, Girl Guides and Church youth organisations on the administration of savings groups for young people of school age and beyond.[34]

Neither the Victorian culture of thrift and self-help, tinged with Christian ethics congenial to the TSB, nor the friendly societies, savings banks, industrial insurers and similar predominantly working-class financial institutions were conducive to personal ambition or the spirit of enterprise. Both were critical to Britain's post-war recovery and the encouragement of saving simply for its own sake would prove a short-sighted strategy. That so many people, especially young people, were easily convinced of the rectitude of sterile thrift and saving to support a depleted economy can be seen as a rather sad manifestation of the dispiritedness of the times. As Callum Brown observes:

> It was an age of economic retrenchment in Britain's old basic industries, marked by widespread nationalisation and concern with the fiscal health of a nation that had borrowed heavily during and at the end of the war. The mood of the country seemed dour, unexciting and intensively conservative. Even the rhetoric of the bold, new welfare state was resonant with Victorian religious philanthropy in its talk of educating the working-class girl and preventing juvenile delinquency.[35]

An age of economic retrenchment might have seemed to its contemporaries more an age of economic turmoil, and 'the bold, new welfare state' came with a price tag attached, which its potential beneficiaries would have no choice but to pay. From 5th July 1948 every employee with more than minimal income was required to purchase a weekly National Insurance stamp from the post office. The initial rate for an employed man was 9s 1d, (now about £20) with an employer's contribution of 4s 2d. A woman paid 3s 10d towards her stamp, priced at a lesser 7s.1d, to acknowledge her invariably lower wage. There were reduced rates for under eighteen-year-olds, while the self-employed paid the fixed price of 6s 2d. The stamps were affixed to a card to be forwarded when filled to the Ministry of National Insurance for its value to be credited to the individual – in theory. This charade was transparent from the outset. The welfare state could not operate like a profit orientated insurance company. Stamp revenue would never be sufficient to pay all its benefits and claims, and the deficit would always have to be made up from other tax revenue, reserves, or borrowing. Those who neither required nor received immediate benefits soon came to regard their contributions as the supplementary income tax they really were, and indeed remain.[iii] The welcome for 'the bold, new welfare state' was not one of universal joy. Those who put their hands in their pockets do not throw their hats in the air.

Thus most people's first practical experience of the realisation of William Beveridge's visionary 1942 report on *Social Insurance and Allied Services* was that of having to pay for it – one more financial imposition and one more facet to the penance of austerity. Yet the flawed implementation of the only government publication for which the British public ever queued in their thousands to buy, was to be the seed of profound and enduring changes in attitudes to personal finance.

National insurance and having to pay for it were not new in 1948. The 1911 National Insurance Act had entitled a worker earning less than £2 per week to join a rudimentary sickness and accident benefit scheme, whereby he paid a weekly contribution of 4d, his employer 3d, and the state added a further 2d. This 9d covered the costs of so-called 'panel' doctors, hospital charges and medicines, as well as seven shillings per week for up to fifteen weeks absence from work. The benefits did not extend to the unemployed, the non-employed or to the contributors'

[iii]   National insurances contributions did not then vary with income.

wives, children or any other dependants.[36] This money was not enough to support a single man, let alone a family: all that can be said is that it was better than nothing. Only a tiny minority of enlightened employers provided sick pay or accident compensation. A man unable to work simply lost his job and a redundancy payment was as yet an unknown phenomenon. Unless, as was seldom the case, covered by adequate private insurance, a worker had to supplement the state benefit from his savings, beg, borrow, steal or resort to charity to support his family.

Even employed workers, often earning barely sufficient to support their families, were unable or unwilling to pay for private medicine or medical insurance, but rather than resort to state welfare would choose to smile through their pain, in some cases until relieved by an early grave. Medical historian Geoffrey Rivett describes in graphic detail how impossibly high numbers were treated in appalling conditions by overworked interwar general practitioners. Patients would have to wait for hours to be called by one of perhaps four or five panel doctors who could afford no more than a minute or two to carry out an arbitrary diagnosis and write out a not necessarily free prescription. In such conditions, needless to say, few people received proper care and attention. As Rivett explains:

> Working-class people did not expect to be comfortable. Most went hungry and their undernourished children showed evidence of rickets until vitamin D supplements, provided by welfare clinics, controlled it … Successful treatment by the doctor was accepted with gratitude and the many failures were tolerated without rancour or recrimination. Patients' expectations were not high.[37]

Hospitals funded by local authorities, philanthropists, charities or public subscription provided free admission, operations and medicines, although they were often limited by charter or constitution to the treatment of specific ailments. Two-thirds were built in the nineteenth century and, due to decades of underfunding most were in severe need of maintenance, ill-equipped and unhygienic. They were mainly poorly staffed and the quality of care such that anyone in a position to do so would dig deep to pay for a private hospital or nursing home. For a fortunate few, more dignified treatment was accessible without direct payment or insurance cover. General practitioners would often work on a Robin Hood basis: overcharging richer patients and, at their own discretion, caring for the poor free or for whatever they could pay. Others organised voluntary regular contribution schemes, entitling their patients to free consultation but usually not medicines or hospitalisation.

All this was brought to an end by the National Health Service Act 1946, the most ambitious component of the welfare state. From 5th July 1948, never again would the sick or injured have to worry about money or the social stigma of asking for charity. And never again would anyone have no choice but to pay for a doctor's time, prescribed medicines or a stay in hospital. No conditions whatsoever applied to the National Health Service (NHS). Its entire range of facilities, practitioners, consultants and specialists in every branch of medicine were free to all, regardless of social status or financial situation. It was not even necessary to have ever bought a single National Insurance stamp. The state even refunded all expenses to a patient and a companion, if required, who had to travel receive specialist treatment. The Ministry of National Insurance advised the public that it was 'all for 4s 11d out of your weekly pay-packet'[38] with the inevitable result that, as John Benson puts it, 'The establishment of the NHS unleashed a torrent of pent-up demand for medical care'.[39] Here was an investment from which dividends could be drawn down from day one – and they were. Returns were taken in cosmetic surgery, wigs, prescribed spectacles, prosthetic dentistry, handmade therapeutic footwear and many more previously unthinkable luxuries. Aneurin Bevan, whose impenetrable mental armour, untiring efforts and immutable ideology had turned Beveridge's vision into reality, saw nothing of this. He believed that 'If you succeeded in Britain in establishing the correct social climate, where people valued things on the basis of need rather than sordid profitability, then expenditure on the NHS would progressively moderate'.[40]

In today's lights this seems a naïve judgement. Having been given unlimited free access to the finest medical attention for simply being a citizen, why would anyone forego the maintenance of their most valuable asset, their own body, in order to progressively moderate expenditure on the NHS? 'The correct social climate', where people valued things on any basis other than their own interests was, and would remain, at best an illusion.

Arthur Marwick, among others, claims that due to the rationed diet, 'the nation as a whole was healthier and fitter than it had ever been before'.[41] If that were true, it is arguable that the NHS came at a time when it was least needed. It was not true. No branch of the NHS would want for employment. Britain's towns were smoke-polluted and its factories and workplaces squalid and accident prone. The war had left more than bombed-out buildings in need of restoration. Its death toll in Britain was mercifully comparatively light, but no one counted the survivors unable or unwilling to afford treatment for their long neglected war-inflicted injuries, ailments and traumatic disorders. Abused, under-resourced and an administrative nightmare from the start, for its new patients the NHS was and would remain a godsend. By 1950 it had caused infant mortality to fall for the first time below 30 per 1,000. It reduced the 65,000 cases of diphtheria in 1938 to just 53 in 1956, and cases of pneumonia to half their pre-war level. Before and during the war there had been long waiting lists for sanatoria to treat respiratory tuberculosis: by the early 1960s the disease had been eradicated.[42]

In theory, the money the rich and prudent had previously earmarked for medical treatment, health and accident insurance or their doctor's surgery scheme, was now free to be spent as they saw fit. In practice, the rich and prudent were in no hurry to throw caution to the wind and entrust the care of their and their family's precious health to the nation. It was no coincidence that in anticipation of the formation of the NHS, the newly founded British United Provident Association (BUPA) proclaimed its mission to 'preserve freedom of choice in health care'. Nor was it a coincidence that a clutch of new private medical insurance companies aiming to meet the demands of those wishing to opt out of the NHS followed hard on its heels, and that they had no difficulty attracting people prepared to add the cost to the taxes and national insurance contributions they were legally obliged to pay. Established insurance companies too found their clients increasingly prioritising health cover: the Prudential, for example, more than trebled its comparatively small sickness and accident business between 1948 and 1956.[43] Since the formation of the NHS, a significant proportion of British people with the means to do so, and more than a few without, has opted to pay twice.

Those who 'go private' defend their decision by claiming that the state service has too often fallen short of their expectancies as consumers. They take no account of the undeniable truth that for over sixty years, three hundred and sixty-five days per annum, twenty-four hours per day, in every corner of the land, the NHS has served every sector of the community in accord with Bevan's doctrine to neither favour the rich nor preclude the poor. Nor do they accept that the negligible percentage of cases of demonstrable professional failure is no higher than in private or 'alternative' medicine. Private healthcare consumers have always been aware that their money could not buy greater assurance of a cure or a successful operation than the NHS provided free, but still they wish to buy the emotional expectancies of convenience and personal attention. Now (in 2011) some 14 per cent of the population invest in private health insurance schemes and many more pay directly for medical care.

The simultaneous introduction of a variety of other social security legislation similarly caused mixed emotions in matters of personal finance. Like the NHS, the new system of welfare benefits was free for all, or as was suggested at the time, a free-for-all manipulated with ease by opportunists seeking to enhance their already adequate income. The National Insurance Act 1946 entitled the unemployed to a basic 26s per week plus supplements for wives, children and dependants, while the National Assistance Act 1948 provided additional amounts in cases of severe hardship. These, and sickness or accident benefits, were intended to provide no more than a cushion against the worst onslaughts of privation or misfortune, but in practice often added up to more than the take-home pay of a poorly paid worker. To draw these benefits there was no compulsion to demonstrate job-seeking, nor was there a formal time limit. For the work-shy it must have seemed a dream come true – free cash handouts forever. Some indeed would never work again. But for others, it would take many years to exorcise the stigma of being seen at the 'labour exchange', even if now designated the office of the Ministry of National Insurance. Potent memories of the indignities of the pre-war dole queue and the draconian means test, left many men too proud or too inhibited by social conscience to claim even the rightful entitlements for which they and their fellow workers had fought long and hard, and for which they themselves were now paying.

Richard Hoggart points out that the post-war welfare state did not immediately expunge the working-class tradition of treating government generosity with grave suspicion. Some mothers, he writes, 'would not go near the [National Health] clinic, not even for their orange juice: they mistrust anything authority provides and prefer to go to the chemists, even though it is more expensive'.[44] While these mothers might have believed it unethical to accept things they could afford to pay for, it is less likely that they viewed *cash* provided by 'government generosity' in quite the same light. It is improbable that many refused the £4 maternity grant and the 30s for thirteen weeks after giving birth, or the extra 5s per week conceded in 1945 for second and subsequent children.[iv] No widow, regardless of age or financial status, would have refused the £20 death grant, now a realistic contribution to funeral expenses, let alone the pension for the rest of her days, starting at 36s per week. Nor would anyone refuse to draw the pension of 26s per week or 42s for a married couple from age sixty-five (women from age sixty), to which the disabled were similarly entitled regardless of age. Still all these and the many other benefits paid by the welfare state to victims of misfortune were far from sufficient to satisfy the entire spectrum of people in need, if for no other reason than a universal policy requiring them to also be paid to people *not* in need.

Even long accustomed philanthropists and dedicated charitable donors started to become apathetic. It was not always easy for them to grasp that, however vast the sums poured into state welfare, they would never be enough. According to historian David Owen, in post-war Britain charity was 'no longer newsworthy' and the voluntary sector a 'junior partner in the welfare firm'.[45] More and more people were becoming disillusioned with the virtue in gratuitously giving of their time or money. They had been led to believe that their National Insurance stamp would buy social security for all, from the cradle to the grave. Why care for the cared for? To compound such negative attitudes, the media in exposing and sensationalising cases of alleged reckless abuse, made no distinction between the presumed unlimited resources of the welfare state and the depleted resources of the voluntary sector. Frank Prochaska explains:

> A major problem for charitable societies in the welfare field was how to adapt
> to the complex and compromising world of state social provision without
> distorting their objectives or losing their way ... Fundraising emerged as the
> most immediate concern, for people often now assumed that as governmental
> benefits were comprehensive charitable donations were unnecessary or
> inconsequential.[46]

Fortunately, to counter those who made that assumption or subscribed to the post-war anti-charity views cited in the previous chapter, there remained enough humanitarians, philanthropists, small donors and voluntary workers who understood that the war on want was far from won. When confronted by genuine misfortune, the British public always managed to find a coin or two, and often

---

[iv] By the time the family allowance, repeatedly called for in the 1930s, found its way into a mother's purse it was too little to make an appreciable difference to her spending pattern, but was nevertheless considered a breakthrough for women's financial independence.

much more, if only to alleviate their conscience when they had surplus money in the bank. Some of the nation's finest charitable institutions owe their foundation to such post-war emotions and the shortcomings of the welfare state, among them, MIND (originally the National Association for Mental Health), War on Want and The Samaritans which all overcame early set-backs to continue their invaluable work – always dependent on voluntary private donation.[47]

The commitment to the ever-escalating costs of the NHS and social security thwarted any ambitions of the Attlee governments, and indeed their successors of both parties, to appreciably extend the range of essential welfare services. Even medical research remained largely at the mercy of public generosity. The many charities and good causes the state has never financed owe their survival, above all else, to the wartime and post-war technological and artistic development of mass communication. The cinema and radio inspired empathy and compassion at levels beyond the dreams of the preachers, orators and writers, whose words at best reached a usually converted audience of a few hundred. The mass media could now reach a few million and open their eyes to suffering and troubles beyond their personal knowledge and experience. Over time, broadcast appeals and disaster funds, as well as sponsored entertainment and sporting events, would never fail to move rich and poor alike to part with their money. These donors have expected and received nothing in return other than a modicum of psychological gratification and, in general, have been happy to remain anonymous. Today a computer generates the words 'thank you' and instantly loses even the feel-good factor in a billion electronic impulses but it is surely true that, since 1948, the growth of generosity with neither tangible nor intangible incentive has been a beneficial social advance of no less significance than the mixed blessings of state welfare.

Responsible individuals have always found the concept of dependence on either charity or the state abhorrent. Rather than trust in a remote knighted civil servant to see fit to don his or her shining armour and gallop to their aid at moments of distress, when possible, they found it more pragmatic to attempt to defend themselves and their most effective shield has always been their own capital. Historian H. Oliver Home noted in 1947: 'There can be no disputing the revolution in the ownership of capital which took place in [the] war ... It might be a safe guess that the insured population more than doubled their capital in the six years'.[48] The wartime revolution in the possession of capital of the 'insured population' was inspired far more by self-defence than by greed to amass riches for their own sake, but socialist ideologists could not accept the concept of the individual as a capitalist or even a minor capitalist. Contributions to the common cause, directly through voluntary donation or indirectly through commercial enterprise, job creation and taxation were all pronounced sins of the moneyed classes – vulgar capitalists and still more vulgar *new* capitalists.

Adherents to the plain-living-high-thinking culture of austerity and state control lost few opportunities to censure their fellow Britons for alleged misuse of their own money. No one was more persistent and influential in this school of thought than the writer and broadcaster J.B. Priestley. The popularity of his novel, play and film *The Good Companions*, romanticising the time-honoured precept that happiness and personal fulfilment are worthy only in the absence of money or luxury, enabled Priestley to enjoy a prolific lifestyle divided between his manor house on the Isle of Wight, his Georgian townhouse in Hampstead and extensive travel.[49] This much-admired, self-proclaimed socialist and uninhibited self-publicist resumed his pre-war crusade against his self-coined epithet – 'admass'. To Priestley advertising to the masses was destructive of all that was admirable in the English (never British) character, culture and tradition. Much like Orwell, he laboured his aversion to Americanisation, celebrating a sentimental fantasy of a tranquil classless England – and was rewarded with mass advertisement and mass sales on both sides of the Atlantic.

By 1948 everyone in Britain knew that the USA was the only nation to have significantly strengthened its economy through the war years and it was widely assumed that the wealth of all its citizens was automatically boosted simultaneously. American cinema, in particular, did little to dispel this image. Its films innocently portrayed characters in all walks of life seeming to lavish money on things the British considered inconsequential trivia. An audience with no personal experience of America saw a land where everyone had more money than sense, where everyone lived in a house too big for their needs, where everyone had central heating and instant hot water which they used with inconceivable extravagance to take a shower *every day*, where everyone had a refrigerator stuffed with more unrationed food than they could possibly eat, where everyone watched television all day, where everyone poured torrents of unrationed petrol into enormous streamlined motor cars, and where everyone was dressed in the unrationed clothes of their choice. This demi-paradise was a million miles from reality and thousands of miles from an England accepting the honeyed words of a wealthy traveller denouncing the vulgarity and ostentation of American commerce as inferior to British austerity. Possibly Priestley envisaged an English reader conditioned to the virtues of 'elegant economy' and fostering Gaskell's genteel 'sour grapeism' when he wrote of:

> A battle being fought in the minds of the English between 'admass ... and
> Englishness, ailing and impoverished, in no position to receive vast subsidies of
> dollars, francs, deutschmarks and the rest, for public relations and advertising
> campaigns.[50]

He admits that 'admass is better than starvation due to unemployment' but adds 'you have to be half-witted or half-drunk to endure it'. Did Priestley really believe that sober English people in their right minds were unable to *endure* the commercial advertising that had been peripheral to their daily lives since birth? Why was a novelist and playwright, an artist himself, unable to appreciate that creative publicity aims to evoke the popular imagination by precisely the same means as his novels and plays? Did he really not understand that the only difference is that the creativity in an advertisement is bounded by positivity and truth, since a consumer gives no quarter if the reality fails to satisfy his or her expectancy? Mackintosh's National Savings movement and hence the British (or English) economy was dependent on advertising campaigns every bit as emotive as those of competing commercial interests. They were indispensible to the unrelenting efforts of 'Englishness' to repay the 'vast subsidies of dollars, francs, deutschmarks and the rest' borrowed during and since the war, to enrich the nation with its people's money. The self-styled people's champion would deny them the free pleasure they took in the wit, wisdom and art of commercial publicity. If nothing else it brought a touch of colour to the drab austerity Britain that Sir Stafford Cripps, of whom Churchill famously remarked; 'There, but by the grace of God, goes God', seemingly wished to perpetuate in his own image.

Cripps took office on 13th November 1947 after Dalton was given no choice but to resign having leaked some insignificant details of the previous day's Budget to the press. The new Chancellor of the Exchequer, like Priestley, made it clear from the outset that he was averse to the vulgarity and ostentation of conspicuous consumption. He too saw commerce as an enemy to the moral fabric of British society. He too was a rich socialist (although far from a 'champagne' socialist) ashamed of Britain's dependency on American aid. But there the similarities end. Not entirely devoid of hypocrisy, Cripps had a fine intellect, maintained a deep religious faith and was sincere to his political convictions. To associate him with the sentimental excesses purveyed by Priestley would be a grievous misjudgement of Cripps's invariably well-intentioned, if often naïve and sometimes misguided, record of public service.

Stafford Cripps was born in 1889 to a 'wealthy old family', benefited from a public-school and Oxford education and thereafter abandoned a brief career in research chemistry to qualify as a barrister, deliberately choosing patent and compensation claims as the most lucrative branch of the profession.[51] At the age of twenty-one he entered in his private diary: 'I frankly admit that I am ambitious to make money and as such it is wrong, but surely you would not call a man a good man if he did not want any of these things'.[52] Having achieved his ambition to make money, he left the bar for left-wing politics – presumably in order to become a good man. An abstemious workaholic, Cripps was generally respected, although never greatly liked by his fellow Labour members of parliament. Attlee appointed him by dint of his single-minded commitment to his vocation but not before expressing doubts about his Chancellor's ability to communicate with ordinary people – and with good reason. Cripps, for example, on one occasion tried to urge the trade unions to greater wage restraint by arguing:

> I don't agree to the men having extra money in their pay packets. I think if a man puts up a good performance on the shop floor and you found he was doing a good job, then he should be given a medal. Then everyone else would try to emulate him to have the medal.[53]

Dedicated socialist as he was, Cripps seemed neither to have nor wish to have any appreciation of ordinary people's attitude to money. He struggled even to understand or justify his own wealth, forwarding the incredible hypothesis: 'I am in the middle class of wealth ... if the money of all those richer than myself were given to all those poorer, I should be a normal man'.[54] (This theory, it should be observed, does not involve giving *his own* money to 'all those poorer'.) His biographer, Peter Clarke, asks 'Did Stafford really think that he was just in the top five out of ten incomes, when in fact he was in the top five out of ten thousand?', and comments that 'his concept of a normal man ... is beyond ridicule'. Clarke later concedes that 'his peculiar unworldliness licensed him to prosper from manoeuvres that in any other politician would naturally have been attributed to ruthless ambition'.[55]

The making of austerity cannot be laid at the door of the peculiarly unworldly, though not unambitious, Stafford Cripps. He inherited its structure in part from the war chancellors and in part from his immediate predecessor.

Hugh Dalton had hastily drafted the emergency plan announced by Attlee after the succession of natural and economic catastrophes of 1947 into his last Budget. He had arrived at the despatch box with nothing to offer the consumer or taxpayer and, desperate to attract revenue, doubled the purchase tax on all non-Utility goods, raising its top band to 125 per cent, and in a move he had previously shunned increased the levies on football pools and gambling. He had also won muted applause for reducing the income-tax relief on advertising by 50 per cent to curb business expenditure – because it was 'a serious waste of money, labour and materials'.[56] Even the ostensibly non-commercially minded Cripps saw the folly of this imposition on businesses crucial to economic recovery and reversed it shortly after taking office.[57]

On the eve of Dalton's ill-fated November Budget, a fully tax-relieved advertisement for Johnnie Walker whisky had proved itself a step ahead of the surprisingly philosophical press support for the outgoing Chancellor's dispiriting measures. It proposed a toast, reflecting the thought the country hardly dare speak: 'Today may be austere, but it won't last. Here's looking forward to the age of plenty!'[58]

By the time Cripps replaced Dalton the British people were in no mood to join their frowning new Chancellor in poring over the grim reading of the economic statistics. Heedless, he burned the midnight oil and dutifully reported back that he could find not a glimmer of hope for an early end to austerity. The ration books, the controls, the regulations and, the anything but fair, 'fair shares' policy were entrenched for and beyond the foreseeable future.

Leading contemporary economist, Roy Harrod, in a generally constructive criticism of the Dalton-Cripps economic policies demanded the immediate cessation of rationing, on the grounds that:

A mood of great despondency has descended upon the people ... They are
downcast in regard to both our immediate troubles and to the more distant future
... People began to take a pleasure in showing the logical impossibility of better
times coming.[59]

Harrod, and like-minded purveyors of pessimism, took no account of the herculean
efforts being made by the people themselves to overcome the mood of great
despondency and their immediate troubles. Far from believing them a 'logical
impossibility' these same people were impatiently awaiting better times coming,
and if rationing and controls had to accompany their wait, they could be better
disregarded through moods of pleasure than through moods of despondency.
However restrained in the realm of material consumption, the British people were
free to indulge in their fair share, or more than their fair share, of all that was
brightest in the realm of ethereal consumption. Culture, entertainment and sport
were no longer inhibited by war or decimated by rationing. Few needed to even
encroach on their savings to delight in the more than ample choice of diversions
that escaped the net of control and regulation.

The worn-out seats of pre-war cinemas showing two feature films, a newsreel
and occasionally adding live music on the Wurlitzer organ were filled to capacity.
Local repertory companies found the resources to captivate their audience with a
new production each week. Variety shows, where the stars of radio could be seen
as well as heard, enjoyed a golden age in patched-up theatres throughout the land.
Parading elephants, horses and artists through provincial towns ensured travelling
circuses sold every seat and thousands flocked to Bertram Mills' spectacular winter
shows at London's Olympia. The commercial illuminations of Piccadilly Circus,
ablaze with replaced light bulbs, attracted thousands more each night, perhaps to
also enjoy a meal, for less than the five-shilling limit, in the fading grandeur of the
art-deco dining halls of one of the four great Lyons Corner Houses.[v] In crowded
dancehalls everywhere, young people foxtrotted and jitterbugged to live bands
or vocalists emanating from crackling shellac gramophone records eroding crude
steel needles. Decaying smoke-filled pubs, devoid of wine, food, jukeboxes or
drugs, thronged with social drinkers sobered by short licensing hours. Full seasons
of football matches were again being played at shabby local grounds. At shabbier
and dangerous tracks speedway became Britain's second most popular spectator
sport, with thirty-three teams competing in the three divisions of the National
League. In 1949, ninety-three thousand spectators packed Wembley Stadium to
watch England win the first three places in the World Final, a feat never before

---

[v]   Minister of Food, Lord Woolton introduced the five shilling limit on 1st June
1942, as a temporary measure 'to prevent any feeling that those able to pay high prices for
restaurant meals might be able to obtain more food than others'. It was not withdrawn until
1950, and only then because it was thought 'one of the greatest irritants to tourists [and] the
tourist and catering industries will now be able to make a bigger contribution to our dollar
balance of payments' (*The Times*, 2nd May 1950).

achieved nor since repeated – like a later historic English sporting victory at the same venue. In summer, cricket could again be watched for a fortnight on makeshift county grounds, with changing tents to separate amateur gentlemen from professional players (until 1962). Record numbers took day excursions to hastily renovated attractions around the coast, perhaps to stay on to admire the dated animated illuminations resurrected on the Blackpool and Southend promenades in the autumn season. Nobody took home anything but emotion from these events but neither did anyone resent the expense.

A unique opportunity to buy an emotional respite from the 'mood of great despondency' arose when London hosted first post-war Olympic Games in 1948. It was of no concern to the buyers that the event is remembered, with good reason, as the 'Austerity Games'. Britain's depleted economy did not run to the building of dedicated venues: competitors and officials were expected, like their hosts, to make do with hastily mended facilities and spartan accommodation. The American team politely declined the additional rations conceded to the athletes: they preferred to fly in their own steaks, orange juice and coffee. Political overtones too were hardly conducive to the convivial atmosphere of an international sporting festival: Stalin's USSR spurned its invitation, even though Britain had not similarly honoured Germany or Japan. Low-budget publicity resulted in Wembley Stadium being half empty for the opening ceremony and it was only after media coverage drummed up patriotic fervour that spectators begin arriving in their thousands to cheer on the British athletes. BBC Television staged its most ambitious outside broadcast to date, received by a tiny audience straining its eyes to make out inch-high moving images of athletes flickering among snowflakes on their ten-inch black and white screens.[60] To see the events clearly, share the excitement and sense the occasion involved an expensive outing: bus or train fares, purchase of entrance tickets, refreshments, programmes and almost obligatory souvenirs. Great Britain's performance could be described as undistinguished at best, but the emotive expectances of those who incurred the cost were all fulfilled.

As with all sporting and newsworthy events, highlights of the Olympic Games were shown a week or two later in black and white on the big-screen newsreels that no one came specifically to see. There was a more compelling reason for British people to spend their weekly few shillings at the cinema. Within its warm dark tranquillity they were transported to faraway places of prosperity and plenty, aware that when they left the bright lights of the foyer their purchased illusion would be shattered by a dark and dingy place of cold Crippsian austerity. Less and less did these people, with money in their pockets, in their savings banks and in their insurance policies, understand why this was still the place where they lived, and less and less did they care.

The enjoyment of a taste as opposed to a vision of prosperity and plenty was, nonetheless, possible for those insensitive to the legislation and social conscience, and willing to pay. Regardless of rationing and import controls there were ample opportunities to revive some of the pleasures of the pre-war table. The main obstacle was the five-shilling per head limit for a restaurant meal. Hotels and restaurants employed a variety of questionable devices to enable their customers to enjoy as much food and drink as they could afford. In a probable understatement, Zweiniger-Bargielowska describes 'false returns by catering establishments on meals served, which formed the basis of allocations of rationed foods [as] a persistent problem'. Some restaurants exceeded the price limit by adding disproportionate charges for drinks and service, while others asked their diners to pay for one course, leave the restaurant and immediately return to another table for the rest of their meal to be charged on a second bill.[61] These inconveniences and the necessity to violate the law or regulations, as has been seen in the previous chapter, could be avoided simply by crossing the English Channel.

It had not escaped Dalton's notice that people were attracted to Europe less by its culture, history, tree-lined boulevards and alpine scenery, than for a holiday from consumption constrained Britain. Convinced that extended stays abroad were a serious drain on the economy, in 1946 he had introduced a really quite generous £100 per head currency limit (now over £4,000). When this failed to discourage foreign travel, he had reduced the allowance to £75, then briefly to £50 before suspending it altogether. Apparently in a rare moment of undisguised compassion for the middle classes, Cripps restored it at £35 in 1948 and the following year back to £50. These undulating limits possibly encouraged some cash-rich individuals to spend their holiday money at home but more often led to abuse of the far more generous allocations for business travel. Most violations went undetected since the Treasury lacked sufficient resources to undertake the near to impossible task of identifying tourists masquerading as businessmen. Conviction and penalties were thus avoided with comparative ease. The *Manchester Guardian* reported in March 1948 that a fine of £100 imposed on a 'fifty-one year old company director' for attempting to take cash of £65 and $40 out of the country had been quashed on acceptance of the barely credible defence that he 'put the bundle of notes in his pocket while in London and had forgotten it'.[62] For many years Britain's best known tourists, the flamboyant millionaire Sir Bernard Docker and his glamorous wife Norah blatantly flaunted the currency restrictions while courting publicity aboard their 212-foot luxury yacht *Shemara* (built for Docker in 1938), accommodating up to fourteen guests and a crew of thirty-two. Despite regular press exposure since the war, the heir to the BSA motorcycle and Daimler motor car fortunes was not prosecuted until February 1955, and only then due to the direct intervention of the Chancellor of the Exchequer, R.A. Butler.[63]

It was unnecessary to follow the extravagant adventures of the Dockers or invest in a visit to France, Belgium, Holland or Germany to be aware that the economic recovery of these, and other European states was outpacing Britain. The press constantly carried detailed accounts and photographs produced by journalists on all-expenses-paid business travel. Almost all shone a negative light on contemporary British life and served only to exacerbate frustration with Sir Stafford Cripps inability to take austerity out of the equation. Every move he made was denounced, if not in the press, then in the pubs, in the shops and in the ubiquitous queues, as another unnecessary imposition or undeserved penance.

Cripps cannot be accused of deliberately prolonging austerity but neither can he be exonerated from intensifying it and its debilitating effects. His whole demeanour and obsession with driving productivity with disseminating 'pep-talk leaflets' and 'putting-you-in-the-picture' adverts and posters increasingly grated with Britain's consumers. They supposed victory and peace synonymous with personal freedom and found his intrusions into their familiar lifestyles and financial affairs annoying and unacceptable. Housewives, straining their culinary skills to produce an appetising meal from the family rations, did not wish to be told that 'by cooking two courses in the oven at the same time you can increase productivity in the home'.[64] Under Cripps' tutelage people soon learned that, however high the thinking, plain living can quickly become extremely tiresome and boring.

Little by little, material comforts did begin to reappear in the shop windows. In March 1948, an advertisement in the *Manchester Guardian* for the gentlemen's outfitters Austin Reed proclaimed encouragingly that 'it is years since we had such a fine selection for you'. Perhaps it was as well that more clothes were available, since in a juxtaposed announcement the government asked householders to observe strict economies in their usage of fuel, advising 'Watch Your Meters – Danger Hours for Electricity 8 am to 10 am and 4 pm to 6 pm'. And to shame the extravagant, it added: 'a two bar electric fire needlessly switched on for only twenty minutes robs the country of one pound of coal urgently needed to bring recovery to all of us'.[65] The majority again exercised voluntary restraint, though not entirely in the same spirit as in the treacherous winter of the previous year when they had acquiesced to far more rigorous bans. As with so many of Cripps' well-intended efforts to control inefficiency, waste and breach of the law, appeals to the public conscience incited as much distain as compliance.

According to Hopkins, 'Probably never before in modern Britain had a single individual in time of peace exerted a direct effect on such a diversity of individuals'.[66] That might well have been true but it is less probable that the direct effect he exerted was always as Cripps intended. The simultaneous nadir of austerity and zenith of the criminal black market during the three-year term of the irreproachable Chancellor cannot be divorced. Both were within his sphere of influence and many of the effects he exerted were neither beneficial nor defensible.

In defiance of his dispassionate reputation, Cripps introduced his first Budget on 6th April 1948 by declaring an affinity with cultural consumerism and easing the duty on tickets for the theatre and all live entertainment. Apart from that, a small reduction in the purchase tax on a few luxury items was the only semblance of encouragement he had to offer the British consumer. He increased the prices of many basic necessities in greatest demand, including clothing and non-Utility furniture, and went so far as to propose a 33⅓ per cent purchase tax on children's clothes.[67] A week later he reinstated their full exemption because, according to the *Manchester Guardian*, 'as a grandfather he had little sympathy for the tax'.[68] Extending his grandfatherly concern to the nation's moral welfare, he boosted alcohol taxes to near prohibitive levels and doubled the betting duty. In a nation unrecovered from the tensions and traumas of war and with a cult of gambling at its apogee, Cripps' endeavour to tax human weakness did less to restrain drinking and betting than to further the interests of its black-market traders and off-course bookmakers.

His discouragement of material consumption naturally assured the Chancellor of a supportive press. *The Times* headline read 'A Budget to Counter Inflation' and congratulated him on achieving a substantial surplus, but a perceptive letter to the *Manchester Guardian* presented a rather different view. Its former leader writer, lawyer and businessman Harry Sacher, criticised Cripps for failing to match income to expenditure and for creating his substantial surplus only by means of taxation:

> Taking excess taxes is just as inflationary as leaving money in the pockets of taxpayers. High prices due to the high cost of imported food and raw materials, excessive profits of industry and inefficient production: for none of these is taxation a remedy.[69]

This neatly worded reflection of the opinion of the ordinary consumer and taxpayer might have caused greater comment had not the Budget contained a far more controversial measure, a retrospective 'once only special contribution'. *The Times* suggested that panic in the face of economic downturn and pressure to strengthen military resources had driven the Chancellor to resort to this extraordinary addition to income tax. Whether or not the unflappable Cripps was capable of panic, the special contribution was clearly ill-considered, since not only did it undermine the spirit of the law and damage his reputation but would prove a poor tax gatherer. The negligible percentage of taxpayers who had declared total income of £2,000 or more in the previous year, 1947/48, would pay two shillings in the pound (10 per cent) on investment income exceeding £250, rising to 10 shillings (50 per cent) payable by the even smaller percentage who declared £3,000 or more. Nonetheless, when added to the 95 per cent aggregate top rate of income-tax and surtax, the highest imposition was now 145 per cent.[70] Later Conservatives often reminded Labour opponents of the apparent brutality of this unpredictable blow, but it is unlikely that the maximum appeared on more than a handful of tax assessments, and possibly on none at all. It is even less probable that the special contribution resulted in hardship or appreciable capital encroachment. Conceivably recognising the small impact of the tax itself, in the post-budget debate the Opposition concentrated its attack on the inequity of legislation that moved the previous year's goalposts. Conservative Member of Parliament Toby Low described the 'capital levy', as he chose to deprecate the special contribution as, 'A great danger to the incentive to save ... The Chancellor, in bowing to demands from Labour members that there should be a smack at the so-called rich classes, has done himself a great disservice'.[71] It was nonsense to suggest that the special contribution or 'capital levy' put the incentive to save in great danger and the smack at the so-called rich classes was quite painless, but in exasperating the national mood of financial despondency Cripps had indeed done himself a great disservice. He had ensured that his name would be forever linked to austerity.

On 6th April 1949, the precise anniversary of his first Budget, Cripps returned to the House of Commons to play the same old tune, if in a slightly lower key. Not until exports bought Britain's independence would he begin to address the personal financial concerns of its people. He would not raise direct taxes but leave them close to their record levels. Again the ordinary consumer would bear the brunt of his attack on the economic deficit. The shops would continue to stock only minimal essential imports and the home produced goods that foreigners refused to buy. The controlled prices of basic foodstuffs, including meat, cheese and butter would be increased. The subsidies that maintained the price of tea, sugar and other basic commodities would be reduced. Even postage stamps and telephone calls would cost more. And in an apparently eccentric attempt to discourage smoking without further raising the already exorbitant tobacco duties, Cripps, a heavy smoker himself, introduced a tax on matches and cigarette lighters. The one consolation for the consumer was a reduction in wine and spirit duties, too small to be toasted by those who could afford to swallow the Budget's array of additional liabilities with their still excessively expensive glass of whisky, gin, brandy or Beaujolais.

Cripps also used his budget speech to announce that all social security benefits were exempt from income tax. Most people had by then assumed this to be the case and were aware that it was of no help to those recipients whose income was below the tax threshold and that pensions, grants and allowances were seldom sufficient to bring them into the lowest tax bracket. Cripps had done himself another disservice by adding this unnecessary announcement to his smacks at the 'so-called *poor* classes', the interests of whom his party claimed to prioritise.

The Chancellor had proposed no obvious concessions to the 'so-called rich classes', yet in the House of Commons his Labour colleagues condemned him for presenting a 'Tory Budget'.[72] This seemingly uncalled for reaction was clarified on publication of the detailed Finance Bill, incorporating a clause that no doubt brought a smile to the face of every investor and speculator in the land – not all of whom voted Tory in 1945. Cripps had yielded to the pressure from the City, always resisted by Dalton, and lifted the ban on free bonus share issues.[73] Within weeks, announcements of capital distributions had begun to reappear in the financial columns of the national press. For sixteen more years equity investors could go on passively expanding their share portfolios and retaining their capital gains without incurring a penny piece in personal taxation on the proceeds.

The *Financial Times* again praised Cripps for his discouragement of consumerism, maintenance of high taxation and determination to sustain the export drive. The editorial concurred with the general press verdict that state welfare, social services and defence commitments, although an enormous strain on the economy, had to be prioritised in the current conditions.[74] It was, however, unique in observing that these were matters of little interest to people whose personal financial situation was proportionately stronger than the national economy.

The same issue of the *Financial Times* carried the headline, 'Full Employment in Bolton'.[vi] According to this pertinent report, there were now three or four job vacancies for every worker in the area and although a 'cotton town [was] less vulnerable than it appears' due to a diversity of buoyant local employers. It undoubtedly intended to send a message to the Chancellor that the wages of the fully-employed workers of Bolton and similar towns could buy them little to enhance their lifestyle and they demanded an end to rationing and controls. Cripps, oblivious to all such entreaties, made it abundantly clear that his order of priority was set in stone: 'Exports first, capital investment second and the needs, comforts and amenities of ordinary consumers last'.[75]

Through his final year in office, undaunted by his failing health, the penultimate Chancellor of the post-war Labour administration lost none of his left-wing single-mindedness. Just as his resolute efforts at last looked as if they were beginning to pay off despite the 'orthodox prejudices' of the cabinet, the City and the Treasury, a weakening of the American economy through the summer months forced him, on 18th September 1949, to yield to the devaluation of the pound from $4.03 to $2.80.[76] Initially, the devalued currency brought down the price of British goods to American importers and increased the price of American goods to British importers, and resulted in a positive effect on the balance of payments. Although encouraging, Cripps was rightly sceptical that this mirage of headway held small promise for his statesmanlike objective that Britain 'cease to live on American charity, with all that this freedom implies for national self-respect and for our independent position in the world'.[77]

His contemporary Britons would have echoed that sentiment but those who convinced themselves that national self-respect and an independent position in the world were imminent possibilities were to be soon disillusioned. Amidst mounting calls for remission from austerity from all sides of the House, on 18th April 1950 Cripps rose to deliver his final budget speech. Again unmoved in his convictions and again disregarding his deteriorating health,[vii] he again turned his back on the demands of ordinary people and presented a meticulously planned, if, as *The Times* judged it, 'barren' statement. Again he would offer nothing but nugatory tax concessions. And again he resorted to retrospective legislation to close a technical loophole that had permitted avoidance of surtax on cash 'gifts' to highly paid executives through restrictive covenants.

Cripps' naivety never deserted him. A few months earlier, in the face of the exuberant welcome and enormous demand for Christian Dior's 'New Look', he persuaded the British Guild of Creative Designers to 'save materials and help the national effort considerably by co-operating in keeping the short skirt popular

---

[vi]   Before the war Mass-Observation had selected Bolton for a photographically illustrated survey of conditions and deprivation caused by unemployment in a typical northern industrial 'Worktown'.

[vii]   Cripps was suffering bone-marrow cancer which caused his resignation in October 1950 and death in Switzerland on 21st April 1952, aged sixty-three.

in Britain'.[78] Now he confidently told bus and coach commuters that the 33⅓ per cent he added to the purchase tax on commercial fuel 'should not lead to many additional applications for increases in fares'. Private motorists heard that they too were to suffer an additional 9d on the price of a gallon of petrol and might well have concluded that when Cripps simultaneously doubled their petrol ration that it was a cynical attempt to avoid a net loss of revenue should they reduce their mileage. Four weeks later, following a reciprocal trade agreement with leading American oil companies, he silenced his critics by bringing fuel rationing to an abrupt end.[79] In doing so he also put an end to the petrol black market, although not to exploitation of the demand for spare parts and maintenance components still in desperately short supply due to the tardiness of the revival of the motor industry. Cripps had done little to benefit the private motorist. He had made petrol prohibitively expensive, failed to ease credit restrictions, and provided no direct incentive to acceleration of motor car production for the home market. Would-be car buyers, like other would-be material consumers, went on hopefully depositing their money in National Savings.

Cripps used his last budget speech to announce two further measures destined to remain crucial factors in personal finance for decades after his death. The most far-reaching was a guarantee of funding to support Aneurin Bevan's plans to build 200,000 rent-subsidised council houses per annum for the next three years. When the Conservatives came to power in 1951 they endorsed the continuation of large scale public-sector construction by giving full rein to Harold Macmillan's ambitious programmes, the effects of which will be discussed in Chapter 7. In a similarly farsighted initiative, Cripps convened a committee to be led by King's Counsel, Millard Tucker, 'to consider the wider question of the proper scope for income-tax relief in relation to saving for old age or retirement or to provide for widows and dependants after death'. Personal pensions were still comparatively rare in the private sector and employees were generally unenthusiastic about them, as their employers' contributions were taxable as additional income and their own only relieved at the two-fifths life assurance rate if paid to an approved scheme.[80] Endowment life policies remained the most favoured method of saving for old age, since they could be surrendered for cash if need be and their lump sum proceeds were tax-free, whereas retirement annuities were paid subject to income tax. Also a life policy could be used to accumulate a mortgage repayment when a pension scheme could not. The findings of the Tucker committee, published a month before Labour left power, were to prove seminal in the progression of taxation incentives and developments in insurance provision and pension-scheme backed mortgages which, by the 1970s, had transformed the nation's attitude to personal pension planning, home-purchase finance and investment.

Endeavouring to instil greater fairness into the system of assessment and collection of direct taxation was always near the top of Cripps' agenda. If for nothing else, he deserves to be remembered for his endeavours to limit income-tax relief to expenses wholly, exclusively and *necessarily* incurred in carrying out the duties of an employment. This straightforward rule has always proved remarkably difficult to grasp and evidently misunderstood or misinterpreted by expense claimants large and small – not least by Members of Parliament themselves. Had Cripps survived, his legacy might have been a simplification of the task of restraining tax avoidance and evasion, if not with a completely lucid statute book, then possibly with one of fewer inequities.

Throughout the 1940s and 1950s the law of taxation remained punctured with loopholes. In addition to the tax free benefits in kind detailed in Chapter 3, an employee might receive a heavily discounted or interest-free mortgage or even a rent-free house in lieu of remuneration without incurring liability. Income-tax law also as yet made no distinction between 'business entertainment' and 'advertising and publicity'. The Inland Revenue might accept anything from a packet of cigarettes to a country house as having been purchased wholly and exclusively for commercial promotion, (*necessarily* cannot be applied to business expenditure). In practice the cigarettes, more often than not, were all smoked by the individual who bought them and the house acquired as an investment or second home for the claimant company director and seldom, if ever, used for business entertainment. Controlling directors were not classed as employees, bought the cheaper flat-rate self-employed stamp and paid tax on the remuneration they 'voted' to themselves retrospectively. This was usually the sum of the amounts drawn as and when required during the financial year, (often in unpoliceable violation of company law) and retrospectively 'grossed up' by adding the tax that should have been paid earlier. 'Pay As You Earn' might have more correctly have been named 'Pay As and When You Are Paid' as that was its intention from the outset. Had Cripps had his way, he would have thwarted a vast amount of exploitation but for all his and his successor chancellors' sincerest endeavours, legislative reform remained hesitant, intermittent, based on pre-war convention and subservient to the financially privileged.

Cripps' reputation as the perpetuator of austerity and his unprepossessing manner would always overshadow his attempts to encourage just and proportionate contribution to the common cause, yet, albeit unwittingly, he was equally responsible for the progression of personal consumerism. Merchant banker Walter Salomon's *One Man's View*, a rhetorical assault on Crippsian ideology, argues that what he refers to as 'restraint' (apparently akin to 'elegant economy') as a defence against inflation is:

> ... futile because it has an apparent basis of morality and has been the attempt to govern by exhortation, homily and sermon ... The attempt to insinuate a sense of sin among the people for not working harder or for not wanting more pay falls flat because it ignores human psychology. It has about as much chance of succeeding as there is of persuading a hungry man not to eat a large meal put before him ... [The] wage freeze engineered by Sir Stafford Cripps, noble as its inspiration was, must be counted as the failure of 'restraint'. It did not last. It was unjust between those who had earned increases and those who did not'. The 'price freeze' was even shorter lived and even more futile.[81]

With reference the Chancellor's attempts at 'budgeting for surplus' Salomon claims:

> Some of the money sucked into the coffers of the Exchequer may have
> represented private spending, but a large part merely eroded private saving,
> whilst the crippling level of tax imposed to yield the surplus, ensured that an
> adequate level of private saving was impossible.[82]

Doubtless Salomon had many supporters for his view of the effects of Cripps'
attitude to the financial position of ordinary people, but it fails to reflect the
reality. The 'unjust' wage freeze, contrary to contemporary trade unionist
pronouncements, was generally accepted by the workers themselves and, as has
been demonstrated, private saving far from being 'impossible' consistently rose
while Cripps was in office. After his ultimately fatal cancer forced his resignation
on 19th October 1950 Sir Stafford Cripps left 'restraint' alive if beginning to
kick. He left austerity growing stale with the smell of an unpleasant past and a
people wilfully camouflaging it with the fragrance of a richer future. With the
purchase of every ticket for the cinema, theatre, dance-hall or sporting event,
every gramophone record and every excursion to the seaside, so the confidence
of the British people strengthened a fraction. They were still employed; they still
had their savings and the security of their paid-up insurance policies, but just as
their hopefully redundant ration books were being made ready to fuel the 'bonfire
of controls' that the youthful President of the Board of Trade, Harold Wilson, had
promised a year earlier, the progress of economic recovery was again waylaid,
this time by the politics of a remote corner of the globe of which few Britons had
previously heard.

When in June 1950 war broke out between the states of North and South
Korea, Britain honoured its commitment to support American endeavours to halt
the march of Communism and defend the South. Once again non-combatants took
to arms at their post office counters and National Savings soared to record levels.
The Prime Minister reluctantly admitted that 'the relief we had all been waiting
for might not now appear'.[83] The rearmament programme cost the nation an
unaffordable £3.4 billion over the next three years.[84] As a result, inflation jumped
by almost 7 per cent – but the cinemas, the dance halls, the sports stadiums and
the seaside resorts were still packed to capacity and the profits of Butlin's Holiday
Camps went on rising.

Against this paradoxical backdrop, Hugh Gaitskell, a socialist intellectual,
literally of the same school (Winchester College) as Cripps, entered the scene.
The last Chancellor of the Attlee administration needed no rehearsal to pick up the
script precisely where his predecessor left the stage. A new actor did not mean a
new play and 'the relief the British people had been waiting for' did not make an
appearance.

One week before Gaitskell's only Budget on 10th April 1951, the Federation
of British Industry put forward a 'formidable case against purchase tax and
Utility schemes'. 'After a detailed study', it had concluded that both were serious

obstacles to the continued need to expand export markets. The public, it said, were unable to afford prices inflated by excessive levels of purchase tax and had no wish to buy unimaginative Utility products.[85] However convincingly argued, like Cripps, Gaitskell chose to ignore all entreaties for greater attention to the demands of the home market. And like Cripps, he would concede little or nothing to the consumer, the saver, the taxpayer, the importer or even the exporter. His budget speech contained a compendium of proposals that reads like a manifesto intentionally drawn up to lose the popular vote. Gaitskell made his objective plain enough: 'to ensure a swift and smooth transfer of resources from providing for consumption to providing for defence and exports'.

The future Labour leader doubled purchase tax to 66⅔ per cent on motor cars, wireless sets, television sets and a number of domestic electric appliances – all dismissed as 'gadgets'. He increased taxes on petrol, cinema tickets and greyhound racing. He lightened workers' pay packets by adding 6d to the three lower tiers of income tax and raised the standard rate to 9s 6d (47½ per cent) – just 2½ per cent below the peak imposed in the depths of war by Sir Kingsley Wood.[86] All Gaitskell had to give were small purchase-tax reductions on a few 'necessary' items and a tiny rise in the old-age pension. He even discouraged businesses from capital investment by suspending the initial allowances on acquisitions of plant, machinery and industrial buildings, and increasing the profits tax from 30 to 50 per cent.[viii] *The Times* responded to the Chancellor's claim to be in favour of the profit motive by saying it was: 'hypocritical ... in an economy three-quarters of which is run by private enterprise'.[87] This and similar allegations of stifling personal initiative might have resulted in greater press and parliamentary debate had not such turbulence, especially on the government's own benches, been aroused by his proposal to bring in charges to meet the mounting costs of the NHS. The half-scale fee for dentures and spectacles and one shilling per medical prescription were comfortably affordable by all but the poorest, but asking patients to pay over and above their National Insurance stamp was judged by true socialists to be a crime against the high principles of the welfare state. Aneurin Bevan and Harold Wilson resigned in protest. Their display of disunity ensured Labour's loss of the general election six months later.

Gaitskell's demand that the British saver, consumer and taxpayer meet the cost of a strategic war of no personal significance to them inevitably received press and parliamentary approbation. Churchill, as leader of the Opposition, conceded that the Budget made an 'honest attempt to solve the problems'. The *Daily Mirror* described the post-budget broadcast as 'the clearest and most straightforward explanation any Chancellor has given the country'.[88] These were not opinions shared by British savers, consumers and taxpayers: to them Gaitskell was another austerity chancellor and another opponent of modernity.

[viii] The profits tax was a supplementary tax on profits of corporate bodies, introduced by Dalton in January 1947 at 25 per cent, and increased by Cripps to 30 per cent in October 1949.

Modernity in itself presented a dilemma to the British saver, consumer and taxpayer. Its implication of conspicuous consumption remained condemned as symptomatic of the supposed destructive American influence on all held holy in British pre-war culture. Yet as had been made abundantly clear by the visitors to the *Britain Can Make It* exhibition, the desires of the British people were for those things that best reflected their expectancy of a vibrant future for their nation. In 1951 patriotism and optimism again dominated the reaction to the *Festival of Britain*, the swansong of the Labour administration. The spectacular array of colour that had grown from the gloom and squalor of London's bomb sites evoked no hint of American or foreign influence or of the ills for which they were so often blamed. This great celebration of British productivity, above all else, inspired the revival of personal confidence and consumer expectancy. The festival gave its ten million and more visitors their first true perspective on post-war affluence: British affluence – an affluence blending the best of the nation's arts, sciences, technology and industry. It marked the beginning of the end of the age of austerity. Visitors left enthused by the ethereal value they received for the cost of their day's outing. Their money had been well spent. It had bought the certain knowledge that Britain could still make it – and this time Britain was determined to have it.

Much of *it* was still nowhere to be had. As forecast at the Victoria and Albert Museum five years earlier, the return of readily available British-made goods to the high-street shops was to be a slow and protracted process. Glimpses of light at the end of the tunnel would occasionally appear. Controls were revoked and coupons for clothing and certain foodstuffs were cut from the ration books and joyfully binned. But the main pillars of austerity stood firm. Consumer choice continued to yield to the priorities of the economy and in the disbursement of personal finance the material continued to yield to the ethereal.

Signs had also begun to appear that attitudes to consumption were easing. The compulsion to save was lessening. Near full employment and personal solvency were being maintained. Commercial enterprise was being revitalised both by burgeoning entrepreneurs and established businesses, and there was a discernable increase in the affordable home-produced and imported products they could offer for sale. In the six years of Attlee's two governments inflation had risen by a manageable 35 per cent.[89] People were feeling the practical benefits of the welfare state. The housing lists were a little shorter. The inhibitions of money spending were fading a little. The change was slow and agonising but the shadow of 'conspicuous consumption' was clearly visible and advancing over the sphere of 'elegant economy' towards the first quartile of its eclipse.

Endnotes

1   Goldthorpe, John H., *Social Mobility and Class Structure in Modern Britain*, 1980 (1987), 176.

2   Marquand, David, 'Sir Stafford Cripps' in Sissons and French (1963), 246.

3   Morgan (1992), 17.

4   McKibbin (2000), 270.

5   Todd, Judith, *The Conjurers: Wealth and Welfare in the Upper Income Brackets* (1966), 21.

6   Richards, Jeffrey, *Happiest Days: The Public Schools in English Fiction* (1988), 1.

7   McKibbin (2000), 270.

8   Kitson Clark, G.S.R., *The English Inheritance: An Historical Essay* (1950), 141.

9   *The Spectator*, 3rd and 9th September 1948 (letter from Sir E. Graham-Little MP).

10 Barbara Young, personal interview.

11 Sandbrook (2005), 395–396.

12 Barnett (1986), 279.

13 Ibid., 286–287.

14 Hopkins (1964), 488.

15 McKibbin (2000), citing 'Managers: A Study of their Careers in Industry' (1958), 90.

16 Thompson, Paul, 'The Pyrrhic Victory of Gentlemanly Capitalism: The Financial Elite of the City of London, 1945–1990, Part 2', in *Journal of Contemporary History*, vol. 32, No. 4 (1997), 431.

17 Ibid., 432.

18 Kynaston, David, *The Financial Times: A Century of History* (1988), 213.

19 MO: FR 3073, 'Middle Class – Why?'.

20 Ibid.

21 Black, Lawrence and Pemberton, Hugh (eds), *An Affluent Society? Britain's Post-War 'Golden Age'*, citing Clare Griffin (2004), 2.

22 NA, PRO, BT/94/471, 'Check Trading, Hire Purchase, Long-term Credit Sales etc'; *Draper's Record*, 22nd October 1949, 33–34.

23 Ibid.

24 Ibid., Correspondence culminating in letter of 20th March 1951 from Richardson, Local Price Regulation Committee (London) to Marwick, Central Price Regulation Committee.

25 Ibid., Bean, Board of Trade to Marwick, 9th January 1951.

26 Ibid., Richardson to Marwick, 20th March 1951.

27 LTSB: 1678: HO/GM/Adv/2, 'Advertising 1931–1970, Memorandum for the Board from Advertising Committee', 25th March 1948.

28 *Building Societies Gazette*, January 1949, 35.

29 PGA: Box 273, 'Annual Reports 1931–1956'.

30 NSI: *National Savings*, vol. 7, No. 6. 1950, 12–13.

31 Ibid.

32 LTSB: TSB/A/2/3, Fife TSB Minutes, entry 19th November 1947.

33 Ibid., entry 5th December 1947.

[34] Ibid., entry 25th November 1948.

[35] Brown (2001), 17.

[36] Thane (1982), 190–193.

[37] Rivett (1998), 1–2.

[38] Hopkins (1964), 125.

[39] Benson, John, *Affluence and Authority: A Social History of 20th Century Britain* (2005), 56.

[40] Addison (1985), 110.

[41] Marwick (2003), 49.

[42] Hopkins (1964), 138.

[43] PGA: Box 273, 'Annual Reports', Boxes 279, 280, 286 'Board of Trade Returns'.

[44] Hoggart (1992), 76.

[45] Owen, David, *English Philanthropy 1660–1960* (1965), 1.

[46] Prochaska, F., *Royal Bounty: The Making of Welfare Monarchy* (1995), 244.

[47] Idem, *The Voluntary Impulse: Philanthropy in Modern Britain* (1988), 2.

[48] Home (1947), 362.

[49] British Library Sound Archives, F9728–F9729 (Sylvia Goaman, daughter of J.B. Priestley, 15th August 2001).

[50] Priestley, J.B., *The English* (1973), 217.

[51] Marquand in Sissons and French (1963), 172.

[52] Clarke, Peter, *The Cripps Version: The Life of Sir Stafford Cripps, 1889–1952* (2002), diary entry 27th July 1910, 6.

[53] Hennessy (1992), 341.

[54] Clarke (2002), 6.

[55] Ibid., 6, 481.

[56] *Financial Times*, 13th November 1947.

[57] Ibid., 4th December 1947.

[58] Ibid., 10th November 1947.

[59] Harrod, Roy, *Are These Hardships Really Necessary?* (1947), 11, 149.

[60] Richards (1997), 148.

[61] Zweiniger-Bargielowska (2004), 167.

[62] *Manchester Guardian*, 8th March 1948.

[63] NA, PRO, PREM/11/411.

[64] Hopkins (1964), 88.

[65] *Manchester Guardian*, 5th March 1948.

[66] Hopkins (1985), 85.

[67] *The Times*, 7th April 1948.

[68] *Manchester Guardian*, 14th April 1948.

[69] *The Times*, 9th April 1948; *Manchester Guardian*, 12th April 1948.

[70] *Daily Mail Income Tax Guide 1949/50*.

[71] *The Times*, 9th April 1948.

[72] Ibid., 9th April 1949.

[73] Ibid., 5th May 1949; 17th May 1947.

[74] *Financial Times*, 7th April 1949.

75   *Oxford Dictionary of National Biography*, 'Sir (Richard) Stafford Cripps (1889–1951)'.

76   Marquand in Sissons and French (1963), 187.

77   Clarke (2002), 512.

78   Pearson, P., 'The New Look' in Sissons and French (1963), 141.

79   *The Times*, 19th April 1950.

80   Blake (2003), 38–39.

81   Salomon, Walter, *One Man's View* (1973), 10.

82   Ibid., 41.

83   Hopkins (1964), 260–262.

84   Cairncross (1995), 4.

85   *The Times*, 5th April 1951.

86   Ibid., 8th April 1941.

87   *The Times*, 13th April 1951.

88   Ibid., 11th April 1951; *Daily Mirror*, 11th April 1951.

89   Cairncross (1995), 61.

Chapter 6

Dividend-Seeking 'Socialists'
(*The Co-operative Movement*)

'You talk almost as though you believed in socialism'.

'Oh I do, with all my heart. And every day I thank my stars that others don't and allow people like you and me to live in such extraordinary privilege'.

Joseph Heller[1]

This chapter makes a brief diversion from chronological order to consider the role played by 'co-operation' in the transformation of British attitudes to the disbursement of personal finance caused by the Second World War.

The post-war environment of austerity had few redeeming features but to the Co-operative movement it was the gateway to a golden age. And to its members it was the gateway to a golden opportunity to go shopping, to spend, to save, to enhance investments and to return home confident of having acted within the spirit and the letter of the law. By the early 1950s, almost a third of the adult population, some thirteen million people of all social classes, had been persuaded to sign up and become 'co-operators'. The majority were and for a few years continued to be regular Co-op[i] customers and as such part owners of the most prodigious and comprehensive private-sector business in the land. At their disposal were over 30,000 service and retail outlets, supplied by their own Co-operative Wholesale Society (CWS), that managed their farms, their factories and their warehouses in every part of the British Isles. All were consistently expanding and returning profits but, as is the way of commerce, unbridled success does not last forever.

By the early 1960s Co-op retail units were among the first victims of social evolution and changed attitudes to personal finance. By 1971, members' share and loan capital had fallen from a peak of £302 million in 1950 to £170 million, and official membership was down from 12.9 million to 11.3 million.[2] The drop in business activity was greater than these figures imply, but a surprisingly large core membership remained faithful to the assurance that their Co-op would not surrender to its *capitalist* competitors (as it's press invariably referred to them) and would always return a share of its albeit diminishing profits.

---

[i]   The development of this multi-faceted organisation produced a complex and confusing structure and nomenclature; 'The Co-operative Wholesale Retail Society', for example. Hence the universally understood contraction 'Co-op' is employed throughout this chapter.

Founded on the most worthy of socialist principles, by the first half of the twentieth century the Co-operative movement had evolved into a force for capitalism. As the capitalist disbursed money to yield money, so the co-operator disbursed money to yield money in the form of a dividend credited to him or her each quarter. Every purchase was an investment in a local society controlling a diversity of enterprises, all motivated by profit. The more affluent co-operator might leave his or her dividend undrawn and accelerate the accumulation of capital in an investment as sound as National Savings and, for a while, a great deal more productive.

Dividend rates varied with the trading performance of the individual society but through the war and early post-war years nearly all returned an annual surplus (the Co-op did not like the word profit). In 1947, for example, every co-operator could confidently expect more than a shilling (5 per cent) back from every pound disbursed whether on material things or ethereal services. Most English societies paid between 1s 6d and 2s 6d, while the 'divi' paid by the Scottish societies was almost everywhere above 2s 6d and in some places exceeded 3s. The highest dividends tended to be declared in smaller and more remote areas, such as Falkirk Bo'ness (Scotland) where members received as much as 3s 7½d (over 18 per cent).[3] The prospect of high and seemingly sustainable tax-free unearned income would prove a magnet to middle-class and aspiring middle-class customers, who under normal circumstances would never be seen to set foot on Co-op premises.

Even price regulation helped boost the dividends. Where retail prices were controlled wholesale prices were not, and as its own wholesaler and often its own producer too, the movement had a head start over most of its competitors. They could seldom better its shops on price, choice, quality, convenience, and sometimes service. The middle and moneyed classes need feel no qualms about openly shopping at the local Co-op, and demonstrating their compliance with the principle of 'fair shares' and perhaps their superiority over neighbours allegedly infringing the regulations. The Co-op would never allow itself to be seen exploiting trading opportunities created by ubiquitous shortages. It existed to promote a socially conscious ideology with a long and proud history, a little of which must first be explored to appreciate the attitudes of the movement and its members in the age of austerity.

The self-made industrialist and philanthropist, Robert Owen (1771–1858) has been described as a man predominately concerned with the welfare of others, who 'never cared for the wealth he knew so well how to make'. His outstanding achievements in the ruthless world of commerce proved no barrier to his conception of a belief in the ethical superiority of co-operation over competition, and his fervent dedication to that conviction was to be the seed from which the Co-operative movement was to grow and flourish.[4] In 1844, Owen's work inspired Dr William King to found 'a self-supporting home colony of united interests' to be achieved through 'self-employment and retail trade'. It was King's idea to distribute dividends, after paying fixed-rate interest on accrued capital, in proportion to the money spent at his co-operative store.[5] The broader altruistic ideology was introduced in 1879 by the economist and social reformer Arnold Toynbee, who together with a group of colleagues advocated education as 'life's necessity for co-operation' and exhorted the burgeoning societies to educate their members 'generally, in their own principles and in those of economic science'.[6] It is indisputable that Owen, King, Toynbee and other Victorian pioneers of co-operation were motivated by commendable ambitions to relieve the plight of a severely oppressed working class. They sincerely believed that its financial lot would be enhanced by active participation in mutual benefit societies and did all within their power to promote them. Yet by the turn of the twentieth century their high principles seemed to have soon gone by the board. As Pat Thane explains:

> The Co-operative Movement was a form of mutual aid with a wider working-class appeal, although it largely excluded the poorest. ... Co-operative stores ... were rarely situated in poorer districts, required a membership fee of up to £1, which the poorest could not afford, and did not allow 'tick' (credit) or sales in the very small quantities of foodstuffs (½ oz tea, two rashers of bacon, etc) which the poor were forced by low or uncertain incomes to buy.[7]

It would seem improbable that the movement largely excluded the poorest after the First World War, as this would suggest a general increase in spending power at a time of widespread unemployment. But by the mid-1930s the retail and service Co-operative societies were as quick as their capitalist competitors to perceive and fulfil consumer expectancies in areas of rising affluence. After the Second World War, they were quicker than their capitalist competitors to exploit constrained consumer expectancies at a time of almost full employment, and did so with a vigour that might have astonished, and probably disappointed, their socially conscious founders.

The CWS demonstrated remarkable business skills in adapting to emerging demand. It employed the latest technology and management methods to expand the huge production and distribution infrastructure it used in the war for its invaluable, though often forgotten, contribution to keeping the nation fed, watered, clothed and supplied with necessities. After the war it regenerated at an astonishing pace, opening as many as thirty-six major new manufacturing units between May 1945 and November 1946, and would have opened more had not the Board of Trade rejected its development plans in areas of full employment.[8] The choice and, in some products, quality of mainly own-label branded products the CWS supplied exclusively to the retail societies could seldom be matched by its capitalist competitors, who restricted by price controls, were unable to offer even the incentive of a discount to counter the Co-op divi.

In 1944, precisely a century after King established his seminal co-operative store, an expanded movement engaged in a diversity of commercial enterprise beyond his dreams still held his egalitarian principles sacred, while its press proclaimed:

> In a moneyed sense at all events, British people are far from being impoverished.
> All the figures show that – whether they relate to Saving Certificates, Defence
> Bonds or the like, or to bank deposits – very substantial increases have taken
> place.[9]

It is true that the year before the Nazi surrender the British people were not
impoverished in the manner of their Victorian forebears, but as has been seen,
until (and beyond) the advent of the welfare state, they continued to number those
in genuine need, whose plight should not have been completely overlooked and
the compassionate spirit of the founders of co-operation not completely forgotten.
Paul Johnson was right to say quite bluntly that before the war: 'The mass of the
members were more interested in money than in social development; it was the
dividend, and the use to which it could be put in managing a family's finances
that was the real inducement to co-operate'.[10] After the war, the mass of members
indeed had money to occupy their interest and to use in managing their family
finances. They were not interested in the Rochdale Pioneers Society's set of
'rules' composed to invest the poor with the high-minded virtues of self-help, self-
responsibility, democracy, equality and solidarity. Cautious and thrifty as post-war
Britons were, the familiarity of such dated platitudes had begun to breed contempt.

In July 1947 *The Producer: The Co-operative TJournal*, told its readers that:

> In modern industry there are no oppressed slaves living on the border line of
> destitution. The 'middle-classes' are now the new poor, and the accumulation of
> the 'divi' now often means more to them than to the comparatively prosperous
> artisan ... If expansion cannot depend on the dividend appeal, the alternative can
> only be *better service*.

This editorial goes on to contend that the 'submerged tenth no longer exists [and
that] most Co-operative societies already offer the discriminating shopper the best
value for money and the most efficient service in their locality'.[11] A month later
a Mass-Observation survey carried out in four socially mixed areas of London,
reported that members generally agreed that the Co-op's primary attraction was
'good and fair service', second came the dividend, and the 'available' choice of
goods third. As one shopper clarified, unlike their competitors 'all their stuff is
displayed, not under the counter'. The overall satisfaction level was described
as 'striking', 67 per cent saying their dividends were 'good' and that shopping
at the Co-op was economical and helped them save.[12] Just 9 per cent claimed
to subscribe to its 'non-trading' organisations, 'all of which were financially
orientated': the clothing club, coal club, insurance club, provident club, sick club,
and so on. Indeed, the observers claimed to have experienced difficulty in finding
anyone at all actively involved in an educational, social, political or cultural group
affiliated to any society.[13]

It did not follow that all Co-op customers were so easily pleased. The original
file notes of the observers (most of which do not appear in the final report) include

a number of less than flattering comments on prices and value for money. One such comment; 'They always charge more [where] there's no fixed price', apparently contained a seed of truth, at least as far as price-controlled foods were concerned. That is until 24th April 1948, on which date the *Co-operative News* headline heralded 'Price Cut Zero Hour, when hundreds of Co-ops will reduce prices below those set by the Ministry of Food – The first large-scale voluntary campaign of action against inflation'.[14] Triumphant as this sounds, it begs the question why did a movement dedicated to helping the poorer classes not sooner join the vanguard of voluntary inflation fighters? The most probable answer is that the price cuts were not made to fight inflation or in the interests of members but out of fear of losing market share to emerging competitors. Tesco, for example, was expanding fast across the country: it had recently become a public company and its celebrated 'pile 'em high and sell 'em cheap' stratagem was enticing customers away from food retailers of every kind.

Overt competitiveness was naturally alien to a socialist movement, but this was of no interest to consumers primarily concerned with obtaining goods in short supply. More than 97 per cent of the London sample showed not the slightest concept of the Co-operative movement's political aspiration even though, after the trade unions, it was the Labour Party's most powerful supporter and sponsor of many of its parliamentary candidates and MPs currently on the government benches. Co-op shoppers were found to be overwhelmingly 'financially motivated'. The few who claimed to support the movement politically were still mindful of their dividend; as one socialist professing shareholder declared in its praise: 'You see some of the profit that's what I like ... Why should the *owners* get it all?'[15]

Those owners actively involved in the Co-op's management were quite aware of the lack of enthusiasm or support for their wider objectives. Time and again their press drew attention to the dangers of abandoning the basic tenet of member control. *Co-operative News* attributed the lack of interest to the Co-operative Union[ii] having become simply too big and unwieldy, the 'National President of the Men's Guild' writing that the 'educational committees [are] our greatest asset in fighting apathy'. This zealous official cited 'the provision of education' as one of the 'eight principles of the Rochdale Pioneers', evidently intending to convey the impression that a thriving educational programme was at the disposal of every co-operator.[16] It is true that the original principles laid down by the pioneers in 1844 had included the 'provision of education', but a century later it was provided to precious few co-operators.

What the Co-op called education tended to be thinly disguised indoctrination into its ideology through 'short lecture courses' teaching dated precepts. Official guidelines urged local societies to impress upon members that 'a class in co-operation is more important than choral or dramatic activities' and dismissed non-ideological education as 'cultural' – seemingly used as a derogatory term. Of the

---

[ii]   The Co-operative Union then embraced the CWS, all Co-op affiliated bodies, the financial arms, and 1,070 local societies.

cultural activities, that included sport, music, arts and crafts, and so on, the choirs and amateur dramatics were naturally among the most popular. In 1950–1951, of a membership in the region of twelve million, educational enrolments across the country totalled 38,906. Of these 13,706 were full-time employees (out of about 300,000), whose education consisted of work-related evening or day release classes and training programmes; 6,796 were members of the cultural activity groups while the rest, presumably, were keen to devote their free time to the study of the principles of co-operation and economic science.[17]

Seven years later, there was still less evidence that members were enthused by ideology. Of 204 members interviewed in 1958 only one said that he had 'joined for political reasons'.[18] They could see no evidence of a truly democratic Co-op. The dictum that it was 'run for and by ordinary people for whom all customers can vote' had effactually deteriorated to a farce.[19] As Lawrence Black explains:

> Local management was largely inbred, boards of directors elected from (and by) a 'restricted circle' of employees, guildswomen and socialists, much less the average shopper-member. Less than half a per cent of members attended society meetings, 1.41 per cent voted in board elections in 1960 – by all accounts the 'lowest extremity of member apathy'.[20]

Almost two decades of expansion and sustained success had left the Co-op complacent and over-confident. Meanwhile, capitalist competitors had turned on their bright lights, dressed their windows with innovation and colour, and directly challenged the dividend with trading stamps promising beguiling 'gifts' instead of money. These, together with seasonable discount sales and special promotions were to the now affluent shopper more desirable, more fun and more economical than the shrinking divi. Attitudes to money-spending had moved on from the heyday of austerity. Then, the British housewife battling to manage her household budget through the mass of legislative inequity had found her most reliable ally at the local Co-op. It had welcomed her to the safest haven from black marketeers and violators of the retail regulations, and guaranteed of some of her money back. She had had good reason to join millions who flocked to the Co-op during and after the war.

In January 1946, beneath the banner headline 'The Rush of Christmas Shoppers had to be Regulated', *Co-operative News* reported the hardly sensational news that 'Portsea Island's fashion store had to be closed for short periods to regulate traffic'. The record trading figures (not the restoration of peace) evidently showed that 'goodwill has returned to the world'.[21] It would have been more newsworthy if the Co-op or indeed any other retailer at last able to offer a marginally wider choice to their making-do-and-mending customers had not been pleased with the seasonable trade. It was, after all, the first peacetime Christmas. But to the Co-op, the 'rush' (where possible to replace necessities rather than to buy festive frivolities) was conclusive evidence that the British people would never again have cause to spend their money elsewhere. Buying from the capitalists would never be in their best interests or those of the nation. The paper immediately published an 'An open letter to Mr Attlee' demanding that the Co-op be taken into public ownership: 'Surely a nationalised Co-operative movement would either be a more formidable opponent of all other forms of trading or it would be a public monopoly, like a public utility'. The Prime Minister's response, if any, might not have been published but it is safe to presume that his rejection was couched in characteristically minimalist terms.

As post-war business grew more buoyant and lucrative, the ethics of the profit motive became a frequent question of debate among 'those choice men and women who have the Owen outlook and temperament', as one publicist described his fellow co-operators. The writer, D.W. Stewart, took 'pride in the pioneers' but reluctantly admitted that 'vitality and punch did not develop until the individual member found that co-operation returned him a profit'.[22] Adjacent to his article in praise of the co-operative 'non-profit motive', above a montage of photographs celebrating the opening of new department stores, cinemas, holiday centres, etc., established or acquired in 1945, the headline reads 'A Notable Year in Pictures'.[23] Not one image of the notable year (in which the Second World War ended) is of a non-commercial nature.

Again in 1948, in an advertisement appearing in the *Manchester Guardian*, the movement boasted its commercial success by announcing that 'Co-operative trading cuts the cost of living … in 1947 nearly £35 million was returned to … nine million members in their quest for savings[iii] … tangible evidence of the non-profit motive'.[24] This unconvincing reconciliation of the non-profit motive with dividends paid out of what anyone else would call profit, might more truthfully have been described as tangible evidence of exploitation of market opportunities. In its endeavours to raise profitability Co-op trading had entered an unprecedented phase of competitive dynamism. A speaker at a weekend school in April 1947 impressed upon managerial trainees the necessity to 'Copy the capitalists and introduce greater specialisation, standardisation and co-ordination between production and distribution … Forty years ago 7 per cent of a working-class budget was spent other than on basic necessities, now it has grown to 60 per cent'.[25] For the next decade Co-op retail management followed that advice, not satisfied to simply copy the capitalists, but stay ahead of them and attract a great deal of that 60 per cent of the working-class budget into its socialist tills.

For all its high principles there were surely occasions when Co-op employees or officials were tempted to put their hands into their socialist tills, filled predominantly with cash. Yet there can be found few published reports of wrongdoing or criticism of employee conduct at the Co-operative National Archives or in its press. Extant literature is the work of employees, professional writers, and commissioned specialists who invariably extol their paymasters.

[iii]   The advertisement is perhaps not as boastful as it appears. Since all other sources put the membership at around twelve million, it might imply that three million members were *not* returned a dividend.

In January 1948 *Co-operative News* did, however, print some 'angry criticism'. A report had appeared in the previous issue describing how the sales representative of a large soap and detergent group had placed one hundred £1 notes (now over £4,000) on a grocery manager's desk as a 'bonus' for exceeding the target set by his 'background boys ... No receipt was given or asked for'. The 'angry criticism' was not directed at the buyer's acceptance of a substantial bribe but an attack on the paper's editorial for 'the considerable harm that it had caused to Co-op grocery managers and buyers' by daring to publish the unembellished facts.[26]

Notwithstanding the probability of covered-up corruption and the hypocrisy of some officials, there is no reason to question the Co-op's general reputation for honesty. Pioneering managerial methods and proficiency in meeting consumer demand, in some cases years ahead of their time, played a far more significant role in its post-war triumph than any form of deceptive practice. As early as 1941, the newly created CWS Film Unit produced a retail training documentary of exceptional quality to promote an honest and innovative approach. Using a professional director and actors, *Behind the Counter* contrasts with considerable wit, the outdated practices of the traditional British family grocer with the procedures now followed in the modern Co-op store.[27] In addition to commending the novel concept of the importance of food hygiene (without over-stressing it) the modern manager urges his staff to keep physically fit, to take a pride in their appearance, practice good manners, speak clearly, and build up customer goodwill through courtesy and 'very good humour'. He carefully explains and demonstrates a primitive stock control system, seemingly something of a breakthrough in retail management. He ensures that his staff have a thorough knowledge of all the products, encourages them to take advantage of opportunities to visit CWS factories and farms, and teaches salesmanship 'from the customer's angle', with tips such as 'sell the largest sizes – they are nearly always accepted'.

The film makes no mention of the experimental self-service stores that had already been introduced by a few societies in the 1930s. On the contrary, it emphasises that co-operators have the right to expect personal and practical service from helpful sales assistants. The manager explains that regular customers value their rapport, trust the experience and advice of the professional grocer, expect free home delivery, and are accustomed to having the value of their business properly acknowledged.

Soon after the war the Co-op took the bold decision to dispense with the personal touches and proficient salesmanship advocated so convincingly in *Behind the Counter*. Urban customers suddenly discovered their local grocery store had been completely transformed. Gone were the white-coated salesmen, the delivery boys, and even the counter itself. Instead they were confronted by banks of shelving and display units, from which they were told they must select their purchases unaided, carry them to the till, and then transport them home themselves. Remarkably few complained: the new method proved an unqualified success and by 1950 the movement was operating more than six hundred or 90 per cent of the country's self-service stores.[iv] In 1959 The Co-op still owned 4,500 of Britain's 6,400 self-service outlets.[28] Capitalist competitors remained surprisingly wary, refusing to copy the socialists until supermarket shopping was proven wholly acceptable to their customers. It was the Co-op, and not Tesco's Jack Cohen, who first recognised that people are convinced by the illusion of cheapness where products are piled high on the self-service shelves, even if their prices do not always reflect the full economy of bulk buying and staff saving. Tesco did not open its first full self-service supermarket until 1956.

After the war purpose-built and renovated Co-op department stores began to appear so frequently that the prophecy of the movement's press that they would devour all the great names of the British high street seemed almost credible. The new outlets were often as imaginatively designed, efficiently managed, and well-stocked as the best of their competitors and aimed to attract people of all classes. Twelve per cent of the members interviewed in 1949 described themselves as middle class, while others made it plain that they were new-moneyed class. All praised the Co-op for being practical and economical as well as enabling them to accumulate dividends and enhance their investment. As one middle-class housewife revealed: 'Since we are members of CWS[v] we receive a dividend of 2s 2d in the pound on anything lying there ... each quarter'. In other words, she was being repaid almost 11 per cent of her total shopping bill and, by not drawing her dividends, also receiving quarterly compound interest on her accumulating investment – all tax free.[29]

It is improbable that this comfortably-off and money-minded lady retained her enthusiasm for Co-op shopping for long after the dividends began to fall away. By the end of the 1950s hardly any societies could manage a shilling, let alone 2s 2d. Once the requirement for customer registration with a named retailer had ceased with the abolition of food rationing in 1954, co-operators were no longer under any legal obligation to remain loyal to the movement which claimed him or her as its part owner. The middle and moneyed classes now patronised businesses whose names offered an incentive of greater value than the largest divi. Money paled into insignificance where the affluent consumer's conventional expectancies of ambience, prestige or social cachet were fulfilled. The Co-op could not entirely come to terms with this reality.

By 1958, although official membership numbers remained close to their peak, there had clearly been a substantial contraction in business. The number

---

[iv]   According to its published figures, in the same period the total number of Co-op employees fell from 327,962 to 277,099. Staff reduction resulting from retail reorganisation no doubt contributed to this extraordinary fall, but considering the concurrent overall expansion, it was more probably mainly attributable to greater efficiency in CWS production and savings in other divisions rather than self-service (NCA: *Annual Co-operative Statistics*, 1958).

[v]   CWS *per se* did not have members or pay dividends; the interviewee was presumably referring to her local society.

of societies was down to 918, and of these 57 per cent had less than 5,000 names on their registers of members.[30] Many Co-op stores were looking shabby and superfluous against the new temples to capitalist consumption transforming the retail landscape: Tesco's and Sainsbury's American-style supermarkets, Woolworth's all-embracing bazaars, Marks and Spencer's affordable all-British quality. These and a plethora of enterprising newcomers were seducing the masses from a Co-op showing symptoms of exhaustion from self-inflicted over-exertion. The turnover of many outlets was not keeping pace with their rising overheads and maintenance costs. Innovative and dynamic as the Co-op's retail management had been just a few years before, now it was misreading all the market indicators.

Even in the heady post-war years, its unnecessary newspaper advertisements reveal a lack of perception of the social aspirations of a moneyed working class. Those offering soft furnishings and (rationed) clothing, for example, continue to extol the genteel lifestyle with fine-line drawings of manifestly middle-class people in characteristically comfortable surroundings. Small print apologies for 'short supply' accompany assurance of the 'highest quality' with no connotation of price competitiveness. The Co-op or its publicity advisors assume that the new worker-consumer possesses an innate desire to emulate traditional British social standards. In practice, his or her desires were more subtle. Like all consumers, they looked forward not back, with expectancies coloured by the evolution of post-war convention, media romanticism, and emotional aspiration.

To compound its commercial myopia the movement's extensive press unreservedly forwarded left-wing socialism, sometimes bordering on the extreme. In January 1946 *Co-operative News* keenly endorsed the more controversial of the Labour government's policies, 'particularly those proposals which will establish public ownership'.[31] *The Producer*, the Co-operative trade journal, put the case for 'worker-co-operative power', permanent price controls, and even the long-term maintenance of rationing.[32] In the ethereal realm of co-operative ideology, post-war Britain was misjudged as permanently peopled by impoverished workers downtrodden by the upper classes they hated, while in the material realm of co-operative commerce post-war Britain was equally misjudged as permanently peopled by moneyed workers desiring to spend in emulation of the upper classes they revered. A *Co-operative News* report in January 1946 informed austerity-suffering co-operators that their holiday provider Travco Hotels[vi] had acquired several properties including:

> The eighty-bedroom country house, Lincombe Hall Hotel, Torquay [then probably Britain's most fashionable seaside resort] set in five acres with suites, ballrooms, central heating, a palm court, tennis courts, and so on ... The newly acquired luxury retreat will open all year round [and] be one of the most popular

---

[vi]   Travco Hotels (formed 1939) controlled jointly by CWS and the Workers Travel Association was formed to provide non-profit-making holidays but after the war acquired resort hotels of various grades to operate commercially.

... demand within the movement is by no means restricted to the cheaper kind of hotel.[33]

Two weeks later Travco announced another facility for the middle-class aspiring co-operator: the purchase of the one hundred and twentyroomed Grand Hotel, Glasgow, to be refurbished 'on post modern lines'.[34] In March *The Producer* reported that 'a large number of requests for registration for accommodation in ships going to many parts of the world are being received by the Co-operative Travel Service operated by CWS ... reservations can now be taken for Australia, New Zealand, Canada and the USA subject to a few simple conditions'.[35] There was of course no reason for the announcement to identify the source of the requests, but the countries mentioned were all enjoying a higher standard of living than Britain and attracting emigration. The requests might have been from emigrants, middle-class tourists unable to book elsewhere amidst the rush for austerity respite, socially aspirant *nouveaux riches* or, less probably, business travellers. Whoever they were, they were not typical of the British working class. The Co-op's inroad into the luxury travel market was destined to be short lived.[vii] Even those able to afford them seldom coveted the staid pleasures of a five-star hotel or an elegant cruise to exotic shores; they had other priorities for their money.[36]

The Co-op could hardly attribute its failure to read the changing markets to ignorance of its members' patterns of consumer expenditure and disbursement of personal finance. All the evidence and data it needed was, or should have been, at its fingertips. If nothing else it had the analysed sales records of its numerous and diverse retail and service divisions around the country. It also had three major financial arms: the Co-operative Bank, the Co-operative Permanent Building Society (CPBS) and the Co-operative Insurance Company (CIS), which, without breach of confidentially, might have provided invaluable statistical information. The objective of these organisations, however, was to promote saving not spending, and while their internal commercial support was generally constructive, it was also the cause of serious and enduring tensions. Hence to appreciate the impact of the Second World War on the attitudes of the movement and its members, it is necessary to explore something of the history of their main purveyors of personal financial services.

The Co-operative Bank was founded in 1872 with no greater objective than to act as deposit taker for the movement's then comparatively small business activities but inevitably early expansion was accompanied by a requirement for wider banking services and credit facilities. The small private bank had neither the capital resources nor customer base to provide either until about 1912 when it attracted its first external customers of significance. Newly formed trade unions closely empathised with the aims of the Co-op and felt it congruous to employ its bank: the establishment and expansion of CWS manufacturing and agricultural

---

[vii] Co-operative Travel, which offers mainly competitively priced popular tours, is among the most successful of the movement's enduring businesses.

divisions brought in additional business, and as local authorities began to fall under Labour control they too began to transfer their allegiance. By 1924 the Co-operative Bank was operating 18,700 accounts. Of these the largest numerical category was said to be local society officials.[37] Evidently working for the Co-op was better remunerated than might be imagined: a personal bank account was an almost unknown phenomenon for anyone without high income or substantial capital.

Through the interwar years the Co-operative Bank remained largely dependent on the fortunes of the greater movement and affiliated organisations. It provided basic and essential services, seemingly not unduly concerned with attracting outside customers but like all British banks it rapidly boosted both its deposits and capital through the Second World War. Growing membership, CWS wartime production and supply, saving for post-war recession, investment, and compliance with war loan obligations all contributed to raising the bank's reserves from £114 million in 1939 to £259 million in 1946.[38] The advent of peace found the bank strongly funded, unburdened by the costs of a network of branches, and well placed to equal or better the services of the 'big five' and other larger competitors. It responded to the unique post-war situation with the same regenerated energy as the retail Co-op and rapidly attracted new customers. Over a hundred Labour led local councils transferred their accounts and, according to CWS biographer Sir William Richardson: 'so favourable were the terms and facilities offered by the Co-operative Bank that in some places it even received Conservative support'.[39] All the customers questioned in a 1947 survey said that they had consciously chosen the bank in preference to its competitors, while just 4 per cent claimed that they used it as a matter of principle or because they sympathised with the Co-op's ideological or political aims.[40] Now providing a fully comprehensive service, the bank established a sound reputation for efficiency and integrity, and by the time it became independent of the Co-operative Union in 1971 was operating over 200,000 accounts.[41]

Having resolved to proactively attract private business, the bank's post-war advertisements, if similarly bland in appearance, were ahead of their larger competitors in that their message left no one in doubt as to whom it was addressed – that is, *not* to the impoverished. They made it clear in so many words that the Co-operative Bank was interested only in customers with money to deposit, invest or spend. An announcement appearing regularly through 1948 in *The Producer*, (editorially, nothing if not the champion of the underprivileged), informs co-operators that:

> [A bank account] would relieve you of the trouble of paying insurance premiums, subscriptions, school fees, building society and other payments. ... Services include banker's orders, safe custody, travellers' cheques [and] buying and selling marketable securities. ... The co-operative practice of distributing profits amongst customers makes a current account with the CWS Bank an attractive proposition.[42]

Another advertisement in *Co-operative News* explains:

> The increasing preoccupation of the state with the individual in the field of
> taxation, deferred pay and family allowances makes a banking account more
> than ever desirable.[43]

The down-to-earth tone of Co-op's copy distinguishes it from the 'big five' whose
armorial crests continued to adorn the quality press and discreetly remind its
moneyed readers of the banks' status as steadfast pillars of British tradition. These
symbols of security, occasionally surmounting a tombstone cliché or two, preach
to the converted that a bank is the guardian of the rich or, preferably, the very rich.
Co-operative Bank adverts, perhaps a little too patronisingly, inform those unfamiliar
with the mysteries of credit that 'with a cheque book one needs no longer to carry
large sums of money'.[44] The Co-operative Bank also undertakes stock market
dealings with 'advice freely given'.[45] It will be another decade or more before the
'big five' see fit to address prospective customers in such pragmatic terms.

Post-war CPBS advertisements were even more pragmatic than those of the
Co-operative Bank: 'Invest your money with the Co-operative Permanent Building
Society: complete security: ease of withdrawal when necessary: good interest, free
of income tax'.[46] Its resourceful president, Harry Score, aware that the future of
the society was by no means certain, was desperate to attract deposits by whatever
means at his disposal. As a Co-op official he was also obliged to endorse his
employer's socialist principles and support the Labour government, but his vision
of 'full liaison between state, local authorities and building societies' did not match
Aneurin Bevan's vision of state-subsidised housing for the working classes. Score's
entreaties made no impression on the Health Minister who, as has been seen, had
nothing but contempt for building societies, regardless of political affiliation. To
Bevan they were all 'part of a Conservative plot to hinder socialist tendencies' and
the immutable Co-op support for the Labour party did not make its building society
an exception.[47] Nevertheless, in early 1946 Score took the initiative of cutting the
standard interest rate from 5 to 4 per cent for all new mortgages and to 4½ per cent
for those currently in force. All other building societies immediately followed suit,
but the more attractive rates failed to produce any discernable easing in the housing
market and were not altered again for the next six years.[48]

Score went on marketing the CPBS as robustly as he could, but attracting
depositors proved as much a minefield as being seen to encourage members to
invest in private-sector homes. Many of the movement's officials sympathised with
Bevan. They saw Score's initiatives as an incentive to co-operators to divert their
saved dividends and shareholdings into building society accounts, and a conflict
of interest which caused feelings to run high. If he was promising to prioritise the
mortgage applications of loyal members that too would have had a hollow ring in
a half-dead housing market. Yet the CPBS survived and flourished. In every town
private houses of the pre-war boom were there in abundance for all to see and
be reminded of the benefits and pleasures of owner-occupation. As for all other

Britons, 'bricks and mortar' retained their irresistible magnetism for co-operators. They experienced no feelings of guilt in foregoing their loyalty to take a step in the direction of a home they could call their own. Nor did they always choose the CPBS. They had plenty of choice. Whether or not it had the resources to meet their future mortgage demands, every building society welcomed their savings with a smile. Competition thus combined with internal prejudices against his supposed capitalist policies, to present Score and, as it transpired, his successors with a formidable challenge.

Commerce and co-operative ideology clashed here as nowhere else. The flow of funds away from Co-operative investment culminated in a rift between the CPBS and the general movement. The rift was to be permanent. Time and again, Score employed his formidable persuasive talents to assuage the situation. He invited representatives from diverse Co-op divisions to join the society's board. Some accepted, but the arguments raged on. For all his good intentions there followed 'twenty years of suspicion, doubts and fears' until eventually, as its biographer Michael Cassell puts it, 'the very roots from which the society had grown were to be chopped away'.[49]

The very roots from which the society had grown can be traced back to 1884, when the eight-man committee of the London Guild of Co-operators, appalled by the condition of members' rented homes, founded the CPBS with unequivocal faith in the social benefits of owner-occupation.[50] The conflict between co-operation and accumulation of private capital, even in the cause of self-help, was evident from the outset but would not be allowed to impede the society from becoming commercially competitive – aggressively so. The CPBS was among the forerunners in assisting wage earners to become first-time buyers: concentrating on smaller loans and if necessary encouraging the secondary security of the later denigrated 'builder's pool' (see Chapter 2). In 1931 it spent £28,000 on a promotional campaign on a scale rarely, if ever, preceded by any building society and as a direct result advanced more than £3.5 million to over 6,000 home buyers. Among the novel incentives it offered was a loan over and above an existing mortgage for 'maintenance, modernisation and improvements'.[51] It meant greater indebtedness but owners enthusiastically took advantage of the 'second mortgage' to release equity and refurbish or extend their homes. In the second half of the twentieth century, the second mortgage would enhance the lifestyle of millions. It would also to be subjected to unscrupulous abuse and the cause of negative equity and repossession.

By 1938 the CPBS had expanded to thirty-two branches and that year made advances of over £7 million to house buyers of all classes (compared to £180,605 in 1919).[52] After the war, growing exposure to the benefits and pleasures of home ownership and high levels of employment again persuaded potential buyers to move their savings to the building societies. But both the societies and their growing membership were to remain frustrated by credit restrictions, lack of private-sector building, and the small number of houses coming onto the market. For the CPBS, the Labour government years resulted in only modest and intermittent progress, hampered by struggles not only with austerity, but still with internal dissent and now socialism itself. Though it made little headway, it fared no worse than other building societies. In 1950 there were 1,508,000 active building-society mortgages in Britain, just 5,000 more than at the beginning of the war.[53]

In 1951 the CPBS did not distinguish itself from its capitalist competitors by hiding its delight at the election of a Conservative government with policies favourable to owner-occupation and property investment.[54] Although the new Minister of Housing, Harold Macmillan, relaxed the building licence controls he concentrated the bulk of his efforts on the expansion of local authority stocks. Even in 1953 when the total completions exceeded his most optimistic forecast and approached 320,000, no more than 20 per cent were for sale.[55] Under the Conservatives the private house market did soften a little and mortgages become more accessible, but still for Britain's prospective home buyers, progress remained all too slow and painful.

Despite internal differences, working in close association with the general movement through its most prosperous years had contributed to the strong expansion of the CPBS in the 1950s[viii] but mutual support was quickly put aside when it became essential to attract funds by appealing to external sources. As the retail Co-op lost market share and its public image became tarnished, the CPBS loosened its bonds and endeavoured to portray itself in the image of its competitors. It was to prove a successful strategy. In 1958 mortgage advances reached a record £30.2 million and thereafter the society never looked back. The house market became more active, the demand for finance grew, and the CPBS became more profitable. Regardless, the movement remained openly opposed to private property investment and the accelerated expansion only intensified internal friction. The building society, trying to present a modern face to the nation and retain public confidence, viewed the attitude of its parent body as retrospective, unrealistic and unsustainable. By the 1960s the very word 'Co-operative' in its name had become so embarrassing that branch managers were instructed to deny all links to the movement.[ix] After a spate of mergers and acquisitions, to everyone's relief, the CPBS renamed itself the Nationwide Building Society and formally announced its independence in 1970. Safely divorced from the Co-op, by the turn of the twenty-first century the Nationwide was promoting itself as the 'largest building society in the world'.

There was no similar cutting of apron strings by the Co-operative Insurance Society (CIS). Unlike the bank and building society it remained, from its inception in 1918, a steadfast ally of the wider movement. Its comparatively late entry into the insurance market was primarily aimed at alleviating financial hardship through the economic downturn which followed the First World War. Thereafter

---

[viii] The CPBS' assets reached £100 million in 1954 (Cassell, 1984, 72).

[ix] A former CPBS manager confirmed to me that in the 1960s he was instructed to tell members (untruthfully) that the society no longer had any connection with the Co-operative movement (Personal interview: non-disclosure of name requested).

working-class demand for all forms of insurance grew extensively, and with it the interwar fortunes of the CIS. During the Second World War fears of post-war unemployment, physical dangers, uncertainty, and the emotional need for a shield of financial security were particularly conducive to working-class business. As has been seen, almost everyone in the land effected or maintained one or more policies and, together with the rest of the industry, the CIS grew dramatically. In 1947 it would describe itself as the 'third largest of the British offices transacting industrial and ordinary life assurance, with premium income of £19,430,000'.[56] This was something of an exaggeration, as it was still in the shadow of giants like the Prudential, Sun Life, Norwich Union and UK Provident, but CIS had clearly made its mark and emerged from the war a market leader.[57]

Ignoring the Co-operative movement's support for public ownership, in 1949 the CIS allied with the other insurance market leaders to win a hard-fought battle against the Attlee government and escape nationalisation. Having been freed from the threat of state control, the CIS chose to remain under the aegis of the socialist Co-operative Union and to strengthen its support. In practice, it became all but autonomous, but the maintenance of an inter-dependent relationship proved an effective defence against the ideological disputes that dogged the movement's other financially orientated arms. Left-wing officials and employees trod carefully: they could not afford to incur the displeasure of the provider of their free or discounted private insurances, life policies and pension plans.

In the post-war era the CIS cast its net wider; increasingly promoting its services in the capitalist markets. In 1958 premium revenues reached £47.7 million enabling it to embark on central Manchester's most ambitious commercial building development to date. The contemporary skyscraper opened in 1961 with the letters *C I S* prominent on its façade, still symbolically as well as physically, dwarfs its next-door neighbour, the Victorian offices of its seemingly poor relation, the Co-operative Union.[58]

In common with all the great names in British insurance, the bulk of the CIS's capital came from the millions of penny premiums faithfully poured into industrial policies (see Chapters 3 and 5). Its industrial life department acquired a reputation for 'fixed premiums, air of stability, apparent efficiency of operation and professional collecting services unadulterated with social embellishments'.[59] This, at best, was a myth and, at worst, a moral crime against the working classes. Having been examined by several pre-war parliamentary committees of inquiry, all providers of industrial assurance came to be vilified by the press and politicians of every persuasion, if not for downright dishonesty then for social injustice. The CIS of course subscribed to the doctrine of social justice but, like its capitalist competitors, chose to turn a blind eye to the transparent defects in their lucrative product. In his 1946 annual report the CIS chairman Aneurin Davis, enthusiastically welcoming the Labour government's new social security programme, commented: 'I consider the new scheme rather than hindering workers from taking out life insurance policies, will enable them to enter into contracts with greater confidence'. He then announced the traditional worthless annual bonus for the industrial section that had earned £3.4 million of the CIS's £7.75 million surplus.[60]

Co-operative News, also welcoming the death grants, old-age and widows's pension provisions in the Social Security Bill, negated Davis's perspective on personal finance by expressing the hope that 'the public will be sensible enough to take the surrender values on millions of superfluous policies'. The editorial goes on to strongly condemn industrial insurance and demand that agents be 'compensated to keep them off the doorstep'.[61] As has been seen, neither this nor any amount of exposure of its shortcomings could quickly separate the working class from the industrial policy. According to CIS biographer, R.G. Garnet, in the early 1950s people were still blindly paying their 6d a week not even knowing the name of the company underwriting their policy, let alone what they might expect for their money: 'All they knew was that they were in Mr Jones's club'.[62] By the end of the 1950s, again like its capitalist competitors, the CIS had abandoned most of its industrial business in favour of the more beneficial and rewarding ordinary life policies: exploiting the evolution in attitudes to personal finance as keenly as they – and profiting as they.

Had the CIS not seized the opportunities to move with the times many more Co-op retail outlets and divisions of the CWS would not have survived the 1960s. While they had prospered in the post-war ambience it had willingly financed their expansion projects, but once it became clear that their market share was unsustainable it changed its tack. Pumping money into failing businesses was commercially unsound.[63] Indecisiveness and again internal wrangling had resulted in critical deterioration in the standards of management. The retail Co-op had not moved with the times or kept pace with consumer demand. Former regular customers now saw it as a dowdy remnant of a past they were anxious to forget. Its shops were stocked with uninteresting and poor quality products – reminders of austerity.[64] Older premises and even some built since the war were showing signs of neglect and inadequate reinvestment. Societies struggling to maintain dividends could not always sustain competitive prices. The 1958 report of a three-year commission, headed by Labour MP and socialist theorist Richard Crossman, implies that the Co-op retained hardly an attractive feature. Amidst heavy criticism of its 'strong institutional resistance' to modernisation, it argues that 'its difficulties were self-inflicted rather than the result of social change' and calls 'the buildings, the atmosphere and ... managers ... dreary and uninspiring' in some areas.[65]

Even before publication of the Crossman report *The Co-operative Official* had recommended the closure of 'smaller and older branches where trade cannot justify the wages bill', warning societies that had overreached themselves by opening 'new emporiums' that they 'may find themselves early candidates for the [metaphorical] CRS ambulance service'.[66] The exemplary retail innovator that had recently operated 90 per cent of the nation's self-service stores was down to less than 25 per cent by 1968. Capitalist retailers were embracing professional management, offering better value for money, and attracting consumers to modern environments. The moneyed and middle classes had never really liked the idea of shopping at the Co-op when they had done so out of expediency.[67] Now a younger working-class generation with new romantic and emotional expectancies and wider aspiration to social mobility found little in its shops to interest them.

New romantic and emotional expectancies irreconcilable with the Co-op's confusion of ideology and commerce caused a particular problem for its ailing retail outlets trying to drum up business by offering hire purchase or extended terms. Store managers could not maintain the Co-op's traditional 'no credit' policy and hope to keep their working-class customers.[68] Hire purchase was one of the more persuasive factors in their nostalgia for the pre-war life. It had brought benefits and pleasures beyond the dreams of their parents and grandparents but the potency of the Aladdin's lamp made no impression on the Co-operative stalwart. The attitude of this post-war idealist still echoed the sentiments of the nineteenth-century co-operator who argued that 'the credit system in this country is only second in its demoralising effect to the drinking customs of the people'.[69] But the proponents of 'no credit' could not hold out for long. By the mid-1950s the Co-op had started to lead its members into the bureaucracy infested and, to many, uncharted waters of hire purchase. As Co-operative historian Arnold Bonner writes: 'Many co-operators came to believe that if consumers were intent on credit trade it would be better if undertaken by their own organisations and so under their own control and *free from profit making and consequent exploitation*' [my italics].[70] In July 1947, in early anticipation of a reversion to pre-war attitudes, *The Producer* put a discrete case for the introduction of *planned* hire purchase. (Can there be such a thing as unplanned hire purchase?):

> The Co-operative member, who is in general a decent sort, should not be penalised by his own society if he prefers furnishing his home by means of hire purchase instead of cash down. … Credit trading is an established custom in Britain today … The furnishing manager generally is a man of experience and can sense 'a good risk' as opposed to the other type. His judgment should be trusted.[71]

The introduction of hire purchase, whether or not 'planned' or 'free from profit making and consequent exploitation', involved more problems than knowing a good risk from the other type. Correspondence at the National Archives between the Co-operative Union and the Board of Trade commencing in 1950, highlights not only practical complications but the almost incredible small-mindedness of contemporary Co-op officials, civil servants, and the rules and regulations they were expected to follow. For reasons doubtless long drowned in a sea of paperwork, the Board divided hire-purchase goods into three classes: 'service charge prohibited', 'regulated charge', and 'unregulated charge'. Goods of more than one class could not be included in a single agreement, so if a customer bought 'mixed goods' two or three separate agreements had to be drawn up.[72] This (surely in few cases) involved extra work and created a problem for Co-op department stores which offered a small discount on their service charges for settlement without arrears. The Union complained that 'service charge prohibited' agreements lost this incentive, ignoring the fact that to the hirer no service charge was obviously better than a conditionally discounted one. Further, term contracts for sales above five pounds were required to be affixed with a sixpenny postage stamp, penalising buyers of 'mixed' goods, who had to incur the expense of two or three. The Board of Trade, it must be presumed with good reason, declined all representations (including those from capitalist retailers) to change the system.[73] Traditionalist co-operative officials added this nonsense to their case for distancing themselves from credit – and went on losing irreplaceable business until, with the renaissance of hire purchase in 1954, a specially commissioned internal report concluded with the predictable recommendation that 'societies which have not so far provided such facilities should take steps [to do so]'.[74] Whether they all immediately acquiesced is uncertain, but the Co-op had at least formally acknowledged the redundancy of 'cash only'.

This and other once justifiable Co-op policies were clearly out of place in a capitalistic society of growing affluence, but it seems not quite everyone agreed. Among the more extraordinary examples of clinging to the fantasy that every co-operator was a resolute socialist, was a small monthly called *Co-operative Home Magazine*. As do all women's magazines of the time, it accepts and approves of conventional British middle-class tastes and aspirations. It carries articles on 'how to grow pelargoniums' and 'how to choose furniture', cookery recipes, knitting patterns, romantic short stories and travel features – while its July 1954 editorial, next to a whole-page advertisement for CWS own-brand fish and meat pastes, reminds its housewife readers that:

> The analytical student of world affairs will discover … many of the conflicts which we are passing through today are the outward sign of the fundamental yearning of the human spirit, searching for a higher way of life.[75]

Neither such edifying offerings, nor the image of an untroubled Co-op painted and published by its wider press could mask the reality. By the end of the 1950s, though aware of its shortcomings and stagnation, the movement was too deeply immersed in internal controversy to meet the challenges of evolving society. Almost every retail and service division, including some remaining commercially viable, cut back its operations. The strategy worked: the foundations of the Co-operative movement were too solid to buckle beneath the pressures of changing attitudes to personal finance. The thousand-plus societies time and again regrouped and amalgamated until in 1982 they were just twenty-five. These larger and more autonomous bodies, adapted to consumer demand, streamlined their operations, survived and flourished. The remodelled Co-op is still among the market leaders in agriculture, pharmacies, undertakers, travel agents and grocery supermarkets, while the principles of co-operation attract large and active followings around the globe.

Britain's followers of the principles of co-operation had held the culture of austerity close to their hearts. 'The Musings of a Retired Official', which appeared in *The Co-operative Official* in January1958, is a paradigm of a certain post-war attitude to personal finance that would not be eclipsed by conspicuous consumption. Reiterating the advice of 'several years back' from another 'well-known official', on how to accumulate 'a tidy sum', the author explains that:

> The choice of wife is most important, for women are notorious money spenders,
> if not checked. Don't do anything so extravagantly foolish as to own a car unless
> you can put its running and maintenance on the firm's expense account. Live
> simply, look twice at every penny, spend nothing unnecessarily and do not
> frequent places where there is temptation to do so. Invest wisely and pay much
> attention to this, and learn, or get to know from someone how to avoid, not evade
> – an important distinction – income tax.[76]

This was not intended to put the usual argument for thrift and self-help, but in a familiar style in places attempting to imitate a North Country accent, laments the failure of redistribution of income:

> Yet if, as some would aver, the 'poor' are now rich and the rich poor (or much
> poorer) there would seem to be quite a lot of rich people left in the country. ... If
> you are made that way you can do it [make money]; if not, you can't.

The retired author is particularly annoyed with the Oxford Institute of Statistics for having had the audacity to class among the rich Co-operative officials earning between £1,000 and £2,000 per annum. Without revealing if he himself is 'among the rich', he implies that his honest service has been its own reward. He is an initiate into what Bonner describes as 'the subtle power of the Co-operative faith in which we discover the secret of that administrative success of the British Co-operative movement, which perplexes the ordinary man of the world'.[77] How could the ordinary man of the world, concerned with making and spending money, be other than perplexed by such *subtle power*?

In the latter years of the retired official's career millions of co-operators had frequented places where there was 'every temptation to spend' – places they were told that they themselves owned. They had indeed 'looked twice at every penny' but most stopped looking twice at every penny with the advent of growing affluence. They had never taken account of the merits of capitalism, socialism, or the 'Co-operative faith' when deciding where, when, and how to spend or save their own money. The nineteenth-century theories of the Christian socialists Ruskin, Maurice, Kingsley and others, opposing the 'iron law of competition', were far too remote from the thinking of the ordinary twentieth-century Briton.[78] The Co-op's esoteric 'secret of administrative success' that had defied the iron laws of austerity floundered in the soft culture of affluence. The self-induced iron laws of 'elegant economy' had endowed dividend-seeking socialists with respectability but 'conspicuous consumption' held no such subtle power.

Endnotes

1   Joseph Heller, *Good as Gold*, 1976 (1985), 272.
2   NSI: Page Report (1973), 267.
3   NCA: *Report of the 79th Annual Co-operative Congress: 3rd–6th May 1948* (1948), 461 et seq.
4   Richardson, Sir William, *The CWS in War and Peace: 1938–1976* (1977), 27.
5   Ibid., 37.
6   Bonner, Arnold, *British Co-operation: The History, Principles and Organisation of the British Co-operative Movement* (1961), 119.
7   Thane, *Foundations of the Welfare State* (1982), 31.
8   Richardson (1977), 177.
9   NCA, *The Producer: The Co-operative Trade Journal*, Tyldesley, S., 'Bigger Taxes, Yet we Save more Money', May 1944, 10–11.
10   Johnson (1985), 127.
11   *The Producer*, July 1947, 1.
12   MO: FR 2510/2460: 'People and the Co-op', August 1947, 4.
13   MO: FR 2510/2460, 10–11.
14   *Co-operative News*, 24th April 1948.
15   MO: FR 2510/2460: 4.
16   *Co-operative News*, 18th December 1948, 3, 11.
17   Bonner (1961), 289.
18   MO: FR 2510/2460.
19   NCA: S 22, 'It's All Yours' (1955).
20   Black and Pemberton (2004), 96.
21   NCA: *Co-operative News*, 19th January 1946.
22   Ibid., Stewart D.W., 'What is Left if the Dividend Goes?', 2.
23   Ibid., 26th January 1946.
24   *Manchester Guardian*, 3rd March 1948.
25   NCA: *The Co-operative Official*, May 1947, 97.
26   *Co-operative News*, 18th January 1948.
27   NCA: S24: *Behind the Counter*, George Wynn, director and producer (1941).
28   Bonner (1961), 248–249.
29   MO: TC/57/1/A: (1949c).
30   NCA: *Co-operative Statistics* (1958).
31   *Co-operative News*, 5th January 1946.
32   *The Producer*, 13th July 1946.
33   *Co-operative News*, 19th January 1946.
34   Ibid., 2nd February 1946.
35   *The Producer*, March 1946.
36   Hoggart (1992), 62.
37   NCA: 334.2 COO: 'The Story of the CWS Bank' (1963).
38   Ibid.
39   Richardson (1977), 178.

[40] MO: FR 2510/2460: August 1947, 8.
[41] Fairlamb, David and Ireland, Jenny, *Savings and Co-operative Banking* (1981), 201.
[42] NCA: *The Producer*, 1948.
[43] NCA: *Co-operative News*, Advertisement from 5th January 1946.
[44] Ibid., 13th July 1946.
[45] Ibid., 6th July 1946.
[46] Ibid., 12th October 1946 et seq.
[47] Cassell, Michael, *Inside Nationwide: Hundred Years of Co-operation* (1984), 64.
[48] Ashworth, Herbert, *The Building Society Story* (1980), 129.
[49] Cassell (1984), 63–66.
[50] Ibid., 10.
[51] Ibid., 45–46.
[52] Ibid., 52, 140.
[53] Boleat, Mark, *The Building Society Industry*, 1982 (1986), 4–5.
[54] Cassell (1984), 69.
[55] Ibid., 69–72.
[56] NCA: *The Co-operative Congress Report 1948* advertisement.
[57] *The Banker*, March 1947.
[58] Bonner (1961), 262.
[59] Garnet, R.G., *A Century of Co-operative Insurance* (1968), 6, 232.
[60] *The Producer*, vol. 26, No. 23, 1946, 32.
[61] *Co-operative News*, Twigg, J.H., 'Paying for Social Security', 2nd February 1946.
[62] Garnet (1968), 293.
[63] Ibid., 292.
[64] Black and Pemberton (2004), 97.
[65] Ibid., 96.
[66] *Co-operative Official*, Jan 1958, 11.
[67] MO: FR 2510/2460: 2, 5.
[68] McKibbin (1990), 117.
[69] Johnson (1985), citing Acland and Jones, *Working Men Co-operators* (1884), 131.
[70] Bonner (1961), 248.
[71] *The Producer*, July 1947, 3.
[72] NA, PRO, BT/94/152: Board of Trade to Local Price Control Committee, 15th March 1948.
[73] NA, PRO, BT/64/565: 'Hire Purchase and Credit Sale Orders – Discussions and Correspondence with Co-operative Union and other Co-operative Branches'.
[74] *Hire Purchase Journal*, January 1954.
[75] *Co-operative Home Magazine*, July 1954.
[76] *Co-operative Official*, Jones, Frank, 'Musings of a Retired Official', January 1958.
[77] Bonner (1961), 317.
[78] Kitson Clark (1950), 155.

Chapter 7

Spreading Shadow
(*1951 to 1957*)

In general the second half of the twentieth century has been characterised by social peace and by a prevailing affluence which, though not universally enjoyed, would have left earlier generations awestruck.

Dilwyn Porter[1]

Among the many historians who have taken a negative view of the rise of conspicuous consumption, E.P. Thompson characterises the 1950s as 'the slavery of the human soul to material trivia'.[2] Commentary of this type has always been an overreaction to what was no more than a predicable post-war liberation in attitudes to personal finance, a hesitant emergence of the age of affluence spreading slowly into following decade. In Dominic Sandbrook's view, 'Far from being a period of "unprecedented intensity", as one account has it, or of staggering and unexpected change, the Sixties revealed a fundamental continuity with older periods of British history'.[3] When British people recall the Fifties, they do not use terms like 'staggering', 'unexpected change' or 'of unprecedented intensity': they more often comment that if anyone 'never had it so good' it was certainly not them or anyone they knew.

This chapter will consider the evolution of attitudes to personal finance from the election of Churchill's government on 25th October 1951 until Harold Macmillan's celebrated speech at Bedford on 20th July 1957. During those six years of Conservative rule memories of the privations of war slowly began to fade while austerity was laid to rest at a similarly, and perhaps appropriately, funereal pace. Media images simultaneously romanticising pre-war nostalgia and post-war ambition gradually began to stimulate greater demand for products, services, homes, and for the facilities to pay for them. Where these new or revived consumer expectancies cut across social barriers class distinction might lose a modicum of its rigidity. Widening access to the trappings of modernity progressively transformed attitudes to money, possessions and status. For the middle and aspiring middle classes the nightmare loomed ever larger that their cherished and expensively acquired emblems of superiority might soon lose their potency. They sensed an antagonistic dry rot eating into the prestige value of their King's English, their country casuals, their account at the 'right' bank, their membership of the 'right' golf club, their all-mod-cons suburban villa and their modest career advancements. Some feared that their status had been eroded to the point where they felt compelled to retaliate against what they now recognised as a moneyed working class. For this futile struggle they continued to employ their two intangible weapons – criticism of conspicuous consumption and overt self-denial – to preach the virtues of resisting 'the slavery of the human soul to material trivia'. For such exertions these dreamers of a Britain that never was, addicts to the culture of austerity and unmitigated snobs were justly destined to received little or no reward.

Still in 1951 private financial strength accumulated or enhanced in the previous decade remained camouflaged by public dereliction. Neglected bomb sites survived as constant reminders of the nation's debt and the costly war that caused every consumerist decision to be influenced or restricted by the host of rules and regulations long condemned as unacceptable in peacetime. The disillusioned of all classes increasingly yielded to the vulgar and ostentatious temptations of conspicuous consumption, but still they were the minority. The majority remained more concerned with the practicalities of their household budget.

Ninety-eight per cent of homes were continued to be heated by open coal or other solid fuel fires (see Chapter 4).[4] Though dirty, laborious and expensive, they remained conventionally indispensible. Not only the rich found it expedient to pay a charwoman to clear away the depressing cold ash and re-lay the grates in the morning. The chimney-sweep, belying legend, a decidedly unromantic figure, also had to be paid for his literally black art. Before his periodic visit, all the furniture had to be covered in advance with old newspapers, and after he left the soot which polluted the air and found its way into every crevice had to be cleaned away, dirty and unpleasant jobs it was well worth paying someone else to do. Despite such unmistakeable affirmation that they were more economical and hygienic, many people who could well afford smokeless fuel stoves or central heating postponed their installation until compelled by law to extinguish their open fires. The day of the domestic servant had not yet passed.

The 1951 national census revealed that 1.2 per cent of private households supported *resident* domestic staff.[5] This significant proportion of the middle class continued to nurture the illusion that it had a duty to provide employment for the servant classes, to preserve a traditional lifestyle and defend it from the threat of modernity.[6] But now the servant classes opened fewer doors for traditional employers than modern employers opened for them, doors that led to better pay and working conditions in commerce or industry.

The responses to a 1949 Mass-Observation's survey 'The Middle-class Housewife and her Housekeeping Expenditure', including questions on attitudes to expenditure on domestic servants, were described by the surveyors as having 'a hollow ring'. Typically, 'a stockbroker's wife' retorted, 'I pay a woman two-and-six per hour and do the work myself', while another middle-class housewife added, 'Now you have to beg and pray before you can get a girl and when she condescends to do anything she expects a day off for it'. One family was so desperate that it was paying 'an ex-serviceman – daily help – four shillings an hour because he had to walk to the top of a steep hill to reach their house'. Just 13 per cent of these women said they needed a vacuum cleaner. Nine out of ten used laundries they criticised for high prices and inefficiency but only 23 per cent expressed any desire for a washing machine.[7] Most chose to do as their neighbours and spend their valuable time writing out the weekly laundry list, packing the box provided, waiting for the deliveryman to collect it, and on his return checking each item against the list and bill before paying in cash. In the 1950s such attitudes to domestic priorities would be slow to change, delayed partly by blind convention and partly by more practical obstacles.

Had modern domestic appliances been readily available, trusted and considered economical, putting them to work would not always have been straightforward. Many houses still lacked appropriate or safe electrical wiring and older dwellings were often without mains power at all. Some were served only with DC electricity, requiring the purchase of (not always obtainable) adapters to accommodate post-war AC-only appliances. Power sockets were few and far between and came in a variety of shapes and sizes. A vacuum cleaner was indeed less efficient than a broom or mechanical carpet sweeper in a room with no power socket or one that did not fit. During daylight hours it was possible to plug a vacuum cleaner or perhaps an electric iron into an overhead light fitting – at the risk of destruction and injury by a sudden fuse. Before giving serious thought to more tangible modernisation homeowners often had no option but to invest in rewiring. This too often had to be postponed until skilled labour and materials became affordable and accessible. Meanwhile house-proud women vigorously defended the merits of manual domestic chores. The war-time blackout curtains might have been torn into cleaning rags but they had not reached the end of their useful lives.

If, as Sandbrook claims, daily life in 1956 was 'a struggle against three foes: darkness, cold and dirt', how much more arduous had that struggle been five years earlier?[8] Then, in 1951, only a solitary star shone a promise of a brighter, warmer and cleaner future. Of all that was finest in British technology, design, and culture on display at the Festival of Britain, surely the most conducive to emotive consumer expectancy were the providers of light, heat and cleanliness to combat the darkness, cold and dirt. There was no need to venture far from the South Bank conclave to witness that this was among the most urgent of the economic and social challenges to be faced that autumn by a Conservative government elected with a minority popular mandate and a parliamentary majority of just seventeen.[9]

The dark, cold and dirty scene could not have failed to escape the eyes of Winston Churchill as he returned to Downing Street through the smoke-blackened streets of London. Cultural changes too would not have been lost on a man so perceptive. Driving through the West End he would have seen well-dressed people of indistinguishable class seeking to buy the expensive luxuries now reappearing in its emporia of consumption. Clothing was no longer rationed and the new and colourful fashions would have contrasted with their old and drab surroundings. In some measure Churchill owed his electoral victory to the advent of the *nouveau riche* conspicuous consumer, the alleged paradigm of decline in working-class moral culture, to which the Labour party ascribed much of its waning support.

Though he possibly never admitted it in so many words, the Prime Minister himself undoubtedly empathised with conspicuous consumption. Unlike most of his contemporary Labour leaders and despite his aristocratic heritage, Churchill was no stranger to the vacillations of personal finance. Lifelong habits of self-indulgence had led to generous friends rescuing him from bankruptcy on more than one occasion.[10] His depleted inheritance had compelled him to finance his political ambitions through writing and journalism and taught him the potential rewards of flaunting wealth – real or apparent. He had bought the grand estate at Chartwell in Kent with privately borrowed money, less as a home than as an appropriate setting in which to entertain leading figures of the day.[i] His career thereafter must rank among the most persuasive exemplars of the maxim: 'nothing succeeds like success'. None of Churchill's multifarious talents matched his ability to enjoy his money to the full. Not for him misgivings about the moral rectitude of conspicuous consumption: 'elegant economy' was not his personal taste and austerity was not his political policy.

Before Attlee had yet vacated Downing Street, Churchill summoned a surprised R.A. Butler to his London home and offered him the post of Chancellor of the Exchequer.[11] Butler could not have left that meeting in any doubt that the appointment carried with it the onerous responsibility to dismantle the substantial remnant of austerity. Over the next four years he not only carried out his task conclusively but changed the British people's attitudes to personal finance across the social divide. He was destined to receive no thanks for either and little of the recognition he richly deserved.

While the country was suffering the most acute balance of payments crisis since the war Churchill and Butler harboured no illusions that their new brooms could quickly sweep clean the remaining emergency measures, rationing and controls. Economic consensus, immortalised by the mythical 'Mr Butskell', was hardly a matter of choice. For the time being, Butler would have to assume Gaitskell's mantle. Former Labour minister Edmund Dell's later résumé explains that 'Retaining power with such a small majority left the new government with little room for radical change or for radical disturbance of the existing policy'.[12] The cost of Labour's welfare state, its economic reforms, and its defence policy, including development of the nuclear deterrent of which Churchill approved, also left little room to ease the lot of the consumer or taxpayer. The nation's wealth producers were in regression and international competitors were forging ahead.[13] The spindles and looms of the Lancashire cotton mills were falling idle.[14] The Treasury simply could not afford to support these and other tired, and soon to be redundant industries, or the many workers of the industrial north dependent upon them for their livelihood. For the time being austerity would be tolerated, a clinging parasite sucking the life blood from the money in the British pocket.

On 11th March 1952, against a background of a tightened credit squeeze, high inflation, and an electorate becoming daily less enamoured with seemingly endless

---

[i]   Churchill's widowed mother had squandered most of his father's fortune. His wife, Clementine, whose parents' acrimonious divorce effectually disinherited her, is reputed to have hated Chartwell.

consumer restraint, Richard Austin (Rab) Butler presented his first spring Budget. Its objective, said the *Manchester Guardian*, was to 'restore a sense of reality to our personal as well as to our national accounts'.[15] The Chancellor chose to engineer this restoration with a diverse set of proposals which, rather than restore a sense of reality, assured most people that their sense of the grim realities of austerity was in no need of restoration.

He caused an immediate rise in food prices by withdrawing the subsidies he claimed were 'no longer justified'. He added a further substantial 7½d to the price of a gallon of petrol. He imposed an additional tax on sports tickets. He left income-tax and surtax rates close to their record high and proposed no easing of credit restrictions. All he could offer in consolation were some small increases in social security benefits and minimal tax concessions.

Shortly after taking office Butler had added ½ per cent to the bank rate. Now he raised it by a further 1½ per cent to 4 per cent – double the 'cheap money' rate sustained for the previous twelve years. On the first occasion the building societies had made no move to increase their interest rates but now they were unable to absorb so steep a rise. Mortgagers would have to pay more. A spokesman for the hire-purchase industry, hit hard by new restrictions a month earlier, stoically or unrealistically claimed that the higher rate would have 'only a small effect'.[16] Although the Budget had proposed nothing to help consumers, three days later they would receive at least some reparation with the repeal of one hundred and eighteen control orders, notably the final abandonment of the unloved Utility scheme. The iconic double C was to be replaced by the quality 'kite mark' of the British Standards Institution. It was too little, too late. The stock market had already fallen sharply.[17] Yet given the severity of the inherited economic deficit people were, in Dell's phrase, 'let off lightly'.[18] As his appropriately sympathetic press reflected, Butler had done his best to raise confidence and encourage cautious optimism. Apart from the *Daily Herald*, voicing ongoing TUC fears of a return to unemployment and labelling his effort a 'bad and unjust Budget',[19] every national newspaper echoed the *Daily Mail* headline: 'A Brilliant Budget'.[20]

Thirteen months later, these seemingly overstated accolades proved well founded. Butler's 'incentive Budget', as he named it, of 14th April 1953 was not simply hailed as brilliant but as 'A Triumph'.[21] Assisted by the unforeseen end to the costly Korean War, his unyielding retrenchment policy was seen to be working. There had been a substantial improvement in the balance of payments which had helped bring down inflation. The Chancellor could now reduce each band of income tax by sixpence in the pound and win the approval of Britain's ever-growing legion of lower-earning taxpayers. He could withdraw the excess profits levy and cause an immediate rise in the stock market. But Butler's most acclaimed proposal was to cut 25 per cent from all purchase-tax rates and reduce the prices of material commodities across the board – a special gift to the many waiting to buy their first new post-war motor car.

'Thank You Mr Butler' read the banner headline in an advertisement for Lancaster Daimler motor cars targeting the privileged few rich enough to buy a vicarious link to a great British engineering tradition – now possible for £353 less than before. The *Daily Telegraph* published a post-table showing the saving on every current model from the top Bentley, down by £431 to £4,392, to the Ford Anglia, the most popular car of the day, cut by £44 to £445.[22] In the previous year, production for the home market had been restricted to just sixty thousand private vehicles.[23] Soon patient buyers would be asked to pay delivery charges on new cars for which they had been waiting years to be delivered.

Seldom had a Budget been better received. Even the organ of the Labour Party, the *Daily Herald*, could find no more critical comment than an uncharitable 'Election Budget', though the next general election was two years away.[24] From the Opposition front bench, former Deputy Prime Minister, Herbert Morrison was heard to congratulate Butler as many as three times. The *News Chronicle* enthused, 'He simply oozed optimism'.[25] Only residents of the Scilly Isles had cause for complaint: no longer were they living in a tax haven. The *Glasgow Herald* picked up that the Chancellor had omitted to explain his demand that 'private enterprise must play a bigger part [in housing] and relieve the Exchequer'.[26] Possibly, as the paper suggests, he was intending to help landlords with the maintenance of their rent-controlled properties (a serious problem in Glasgow), but it is more probable that Butler was dropping a none too subtle hint to Harold Macmillan, his rival for the premiership, that his record-breaking house building programme was putting too great a strain on the public purse.[27]

In the House of Commons Aneurin Bevan brought up the by now rather stale issue of dependence on American aid, describing it as 'humiliating'. The *Daily Mail* reported that the Chancellor responded to his left-wing opponent by 'caustically' reminding him that Gaitskell had accepted three times as much.[28] Bevan, who was seldom other than caustic, ignored the put-down and raised a laugh by commenting on another of Butler's concessions: he had allowed authors the privilege of mitigating their income-tax liabilities by spreading lump-sum advances back over two years and subsequent royalties over three. That, said Bevan, might well benefit highly-paid writers like Churchill but not those like himself whose publications, to say the least, failed to attract a mass readership.[29] Surprisingly, he missed the opportunity for caustic comment on another new tax concession whereby, under certain conditions, chattels of importance to the nation's heritage would be accepted in lieu of estate duty. That similarly would have been of greater value to the heirs of prominent Conservatives than to the beneficiaries of Bevan's comparatively modest estate.

For ordinary people, concerned neither with the income tax on book royalties nor the preservation of inherited treasures, Butler's second Budget was nonetheless to mark the prelude to crucial changes in attitude to personal finance. His speech was the first since the outbreak of war to lay greater emphasis on the encouragement of spending than on saving and investment. Consumers began to speculate that the days of the ration book were numbered. Inspired by signs of stabilisation in the economy and growth in commercial enterprise, consumer confidence was escalating in every sphere and inflation was falling fast: before the end of 1954 it would be down to just 1.9 per cent.

Butler's policy of maintaining interest rates at a comparatively high level had, in fact, proved a little short-sighted and obstructive to full economic recovery. He had failed to wholly appreciate that the easing of austerity would reopen the floodgates of demand and throw down such a formidable gauntlet to commerce and industry. In fairness, it would have been surprising if he, or anyone else, had wholly anticipated the extent of the change in the pattern of consumer attitudes which was soon to begin.

Meanwhile, still ruled by upper-middle and upper-class luminaries including Attlee, Gaitskell, Churchill, Macmillan and Butler himself, Britain was a land where social perspective changed only at a sedate pace and the rise of the new-moneyed class was observed only from a decent distance. In her *Study of Banbury*, Margaret Stacey reveals that within the town class divisions were clear-cut and obvious to all, but largely unspoken or acknowledged. In Banbury, she writes, 'it [was] even doubtful that there [was] a sense of community among all of those who were born and brought up in the town'.[30] As in most provincial towns there was a diversity of communities, aware of each other's existence, but who studiously kept themselves well apart. Near neighbours observed one another's daily movements, perhaps knew their names and occupations, but lived in separate private worlds.

Stacey writes of adverse and sometimes sharp reactions to her questions about religious belief. It was simply 'not done' to ask. Professing membership of a faith, she was told, was not considered a social necessity and questioning it was irrelevant to serious research.[31] Perhaps because she thought it equally 'not done', Stacey's otherwise painstaking account omits in-depth exploration of personal finance – unquestionably a social necessity and relevant to serious research. She might have taken it for granted that traditional English reserve and modesty would prohibit open discourse, but had she persevered she might have been rewarded with unique information about contemporary financial attitudes. Charles Madge, as has been seen, had no qualms in the 1940s about asking direct money-related questions to people of all classes and, although he expressed doubts about the accuracy of the answers, his findings added invaluable insight into attitudes to a broad range of social issues.[32]

Stacey does make at least one direct reference to money. 'Factors like occupation and income are important' but being accepted within a 'set', she claims, is the all important factor: 'You must know or learn the language and current private passwords'.[33] This seemingly farfetched assertion was close to the truth. Adherents to exclusive 'county' sets were distinguishable by their near uniformity of dress, manners, tastes, speech, educational background, and political persuasion. It was unthinkable that they might vote other than Conservative. In practice, the occasional deficiency in one or more of these conventions was far less a hindrance to acceptance by a 'set' than the inability or failure to 'pay your way'. By the late 1950s the selective show of affluence had reverted to a prerequisite of status. 'You are what you own' (or do not own), which had prevailed since possession of a fine horse had defined a knight of chivalry until the intervention of the Second World War, again defined *your* place on the social scale.

The realignment of attitudes to material culture and overt usage of money that affected all classes and cultures can be ascribed to the chivalrous events of a single day. On 2nd June 1953, less than three months after Butler's optimistic Budget, the nation celebrated the coronation of Queen Elizabeth II. The fairy-tale picture of a youthful royal court heralding the spirit of a new Elizabethan age captured the public imagination as nothing before. In that single day all the romanticism of millennia of history, folklore and literature was imposed upon the private domain. The BBC television coverage conveyed 'live' black-and-white images of this most colourful of spectacles into the homes of 56 per cent of the adult population. Almost twenty-eight million people did little else but sit with curtains drawn gazing at the tiny images.[34] As many as possible crowded into every room furnished with one of the nation's approximately six million television sets.[ii] A special Bank Holiday silenced commerce and industry. No traffic stirred. No interference was permitted to obscure Britain's first televised coronation. The gentle unimpassioned voice of Richard Dimbleby transformed every viewer into a true patriot, certain that the sovereign realms of Great Britain and the Commonwealth were, and would forever remain alive, well, and at peace. In their minds, everyone and anyone knew that now they could buy a share of this great romance for their own private realm. No commercial publicist, however creative or persuasive, could have inspired consumer expectancy on such a scale.

And nothing captured the imagination of the consumer as much as the television set itself. To all but the most sceptical the coronation broadcast was an unmistakeable foretaste of its infinite benefits and pleasures. No longer would the occasional retrospective cinema newsreel be the only means to visually experience the momentous events of the world. They would be transmitted every day of the year to every private home, packaged with continuous entertainment to suit every taste – all for just a £2 licence fee. Four years earlier the British people had overwhelmingly rejected television as worthless: now it was their cherished symbol of entry into the age of affluence.[35]

Although ethereal surrogates for conspicuous consumption ceased to be the most active markets after basic necessities, it is an oversimplification to state that the rising consumer boom of the mid-to-late 1950s involved only television sets, motor cars, domestic appliances and similar material products. All ethereal markets, including saving and investment, flourished in tandem. Accelerating development of the mass media, now led by television broadcasting, intensified every type of consumer expectancy, while the maintenance of near full employment translated into greater consumer confidence.[iii] Lawrence Black concisely summarises the evolution:

[ii]   At the end of 1952 there were estimated to be 5.25 million televisions and 8.16 million a year later (Emmett, B.P., *The Television Audience in the United Kingdom*, 1956).

[iii]   Unemployment fell to its lowest level since the war in 1955 – 232,200 (Mitchell and Jones, 1971).

'In the 1950s affluence began to break down and liberalise Victorian social norms, expand popular choice and encourage a degree of individualism'.[36] At the end of the decade the social norms of Stacey's *Banbury* remained outwardly unbroken by the liberalising effects of affluence, which perhaps implies an underlying middle-class acceptance of the inevitability of independence and individualism emerging from the working classes. American historian, W.D. Rubinstein, writing on *Wealth and Inequality in Britain* goes further:

> [With] the end of austerity … it might be expected that some reversion in income distribution towards greater inequality might be apparent from the available statistics. In fact, the data which is available shows nothing of the sort, only a steady continuation, perhaps at a slower pace of the general trend towards income equality.[37]

However Rubinstein interpreted 'the data which is available', a narrowing gap between the income of the richest and poorest in Britain was as much a myth in the 1950s as it always had been and would largely remain. The 'general trend' was simply an illusion created by a novel situation where people of every walk of life faced more daily decisions in the usage of their money than ever before – a social change so profound that even the BBC could not ignore it.

In May 1950 the predominant popularity of the daily radio saga *Mrs Dale's Diary*, portraying the conventions demonstrated by Stacey as the authentic domestic lifestyle of the middle-class minority, found itself challenged by *The Archers*. The new programme broke the mould by telling the tale of a socially mixed rural community and scratching its conventional surface to confront the practical issues common to all. Every day topical information and advice, not all of it agricultural, was embedded in the plot: the protagonists moved with the times and took personal financial decisions like everyone else. On budget day 1952, it was reported that the script had been hastily rewritten to illustrate the practical effects of Butler's measures.[38] In 1953, it can be safely presumed that the scriptwriters again returned to the studio to weave the more far-reaching changes into the fictional life of Ambridge – but it is improbable that they made many revisions the following year.

When Rab Butler presented his third Budget on 6th April 1954 his demeanour was not as it was on the two prior occasions. There was no beaming smile to hide the awesome responsibilities he faced. Severely restrained by a series of inflationary wage settlements, the Chancellor could muster little or nothing to please either the taxpayer or the consumer.[39] His sole compromise, a belated speeding up of the repayment of post-war credits, was accompanied by the vain hope that the handful of recipients would 'not spend it unless their need is really urgent, but put it into National Savings'. *The Times'* leader rephrased the sentiment more emphatically: 'He would give nothing to those who were in any way likely to spend what they were given'.[40] It was, as the Chancellor himself named it, a 'carry on' Budget.

Building societies carried on increasing the number of loans to private home buyers, insurance companies carried on making record sales of life polices, and consumption carried on becoming more conspicuous. Three months after the Budget, on 4th July 1954, the last ration books and their redundant coupons for butter, cooking fats, cheese, meat and bacon were at last thrown on the open fires that carried on blackening Britain's towns and cities for another decade and longer.[iv]

Attitudes to personal finance carried on becoming more liberal. It was time to liquidate some of the capital earning precious little interest in war savings or to venture through the recently unlocked gates of hire purchase, perhaps to acquire the coveted, but still expensive television set. Since the Coronation the BBC's audience had expanded beyond its most optimistic imaginings. The eighty thousand primitive boxes that had received the blurred images of the 1948 Olympic Games in a few select areas had by 1955 engendered 14,925,000 screens disseminated throughout the land, while almost every household could also boast a radio.[41] This was as well, since when a twenty-six day print workers' strike brought all press coverage to a halt that spring, viewing or listening remained the only ways to follow the unfolding political events. The nation learnt from BBC television and radio that Churchill had resigned as Prime Minister on the 5th April and that his successor, Anthony Eden had called a general election for 26th May.[42]

The British public also saw or heard reports and commentary on Butler's penultimate Budget of 19th April 1955, but would have to wait another few days to read his exact words and the Opposition response.[v] Either way, it learnt that there had been a cut in purchase tax on household textiles by 25 per cent; helpful to consumers but insufficient to alleviate the plight of the ailing Lancashire and Northern Ireland cotton mills. Taxpayers had been given another 6d reduction in the standard rate and encouraged by a range of other concessions. The Chancellor had confidently predicted a healthy surplus and with a flurry of optimism to conceal the personal tragedy of the recent death of his wife and misgivings about his future under Eden, concluded by telling the country that he had presented a 'Budget for Liberation'.[43] The Labour Opposition alleged that he chose the title to support the new election slogan 'Conservative Freedom Works', but it would be more characteristic of Butler to have sensed and endorsed a growing liberation in attitudes to private spending and saving. Whatever his thinking, as soon as it could, the press unanimously condemned his speech as a crude exercise in electioneering.

Butler's Budget had put money in the pockets of British people and inspired them to spend it at the very moment when they sensed the demise of austerity, yet

---

[iv]   City-centre smokeless zones were introduced from 1950 and legislation followed in December 1952 with the first Clean Air Act. The Beaver Report (November 1954) urged universal use of smokeless fuels but these were often considered uneconomical and open coal fires remained common until the late 1960s (NA, PRO, POWE/14/487).

[v]   Direct broadcasting of parliamentary procedures was prohibited from radio until 1975 and from television until 1990.

the only positive reports were of a brief stock market 'boomlet'.[44] All the tributes to his past performances disintegrated. Dell boiled the press verdict down to 'totally inappropriate to the economic circumstances'.[45] If, improbably, Butler had intentionally presented an electioneering Budget, he achieved that aim. A month later Eden was returned victorious, with the Conservative overall majority increased to sixty. The Chancellor's contribution received scant recognition from the press or parliament, and less still from the new Prime Minister who was particularly scathing of the supposed failure to restore the international reputation of sterling.

The Labour party naturally had no sympathy to offer the hapless Butler, especially after he had inadvertently employed some colourful rhetoric he would live to regret. At the Lord Mayor's banquet a few days prior to his final budget speech, he declared: 'We must not drop back into easy evenings with port wine and over-ripe pheasant'.[46] His intended plea for greater 'restraint at home' had presented the invariably anti-conspicuous consumption socialist Opposition and press with an unwitting gift.[47] Removing Butler's remark from context, both, as always, flattered the British people with extraordinary innate virtues of restraint and condemned upper-class over-indulgence in the most extravagant language. The Chancellor's private life was far from over-indulgent.

On 26th October 1955 an exhausted and disappointed R.A. Butler rose to deliver an emergency Budget to an unreceptive House of Commons. It was to be his last. The economy was beset with problems. There were urgent needs to support sterling in a weakening market, to reduce inflation, to avert industrial unrest, to assuage wage claims, to reduce imports, and to increase exports. To address them all simultaneously the Chancellor confessed to having no option but to curb 'increased spending on both consumption and investment'.[48] To curb consumption he added 20 per cent to purchase tax and to curb investment he added 5 per cent to the tax on company distributed profits. He left direct taxation unchanged but withdrew housing subsidies and imposed more stringent controls on local authority expenditure, particularly in the emotive area of council house subsidies. The media again reviled Butler's speech, voicing outrage at his insensitivity in raising prices on the eve of the festive season. Parliamentary reaction too could not have been more scathing. Two Conservative members turned their backs and voted against the purchase-tax rises. On 20th December 1955 Eden moved Butler to the prestigious sounding but effectually impotent positions of Leader of the House of Commons and Lord Privy Seal. His new Chancellor of the Exchequer would be Harold Macmillan.

Macmillan had been Foreign Secretary for only nine months when he accepted the Treasury. He did so without great enthusiasm. His heart remained in foreign affairs, to which he continued to devote as much or more of his time as to the nation's economic tribulations. His one budget speech on 17th April 1956 seemed at first to hold little of promise for the individual taxpayer, investor, consumer, or the economy itself. The additional revenue he aimed to collect was a trivial £28 million, exceeding his concessions by only £8 million, but Macmillan's unique sense of the theatrical ensured that his performance would be on everyone's lips for weeks, months, and indeed years to come.

No one seemed to notice the move which would have the most enduring effect on attitudes to personal finance. Six years had passed since the Tucker Committee instigated by Cripps to investigate income-tax incentives for retirement provision had published its report, but only now did Macmillan take a preliminary step towards its implementation. The self-employed, including partners and controlling directors, would qualify for income-tax and surtax relief on certain premiums to secure pensions and annuities. Macmillan's almost unnoticed proposals had in fact kick-started the progression of legislative development which would dominate personal financial planning and private investment until the close of the century. Soon the private pension plan would surpass the endowment life policy as the most popular means of provision for old age and mortgage repayment,[vi] but for the moment, Macmillan had other things to capture the British imagination.

In accord with his bland title, 'A Savings Budget', he informed savings-bank depositors that the first fifteen pounds of their annual interest would be free of income tax, a concession Harold (now Lord) Mackintosh and others had been advocating since the war to encourage working-class thrift. Although it was now too little to be of consequence as a saving incentive *The Times* reported that its announcement was greeted with a 'crescendo of cheers'. If that were the case, the crescendo was as nothing compared to the immediate and ongoing reaction to Macmillan's proposal to promote National Savings on a scale grander than any since the war. His nondescript statement suddenly erupted into high drama. As *The Times* put it, 'he could not have wished for a greater flutter of mingled astonishment, delight and shocked uneasiness with his announcement about introducing a premium bond'.[49] Macmillan had dared offer an investment that would pay cash prizes instead of interest. The top monthly prize would be £1,000: hardly excessive when compared to the football pools paying lucky winners the £75,000 legal maximum but this would prove no barrier to the shadow Chancellor, Harold Wilson, further sensationalising the occasion with his legendary response: 'Now Britain's strength, freedom and solvency apparently depend on the proceeds of a squalid little raffle'.[50]

The premium bond was another brainchild of the devoutly Methodist Mackintosh, adding a touch of irony to the mass of protest and moral disparagement emanating almost exclusively from Church sources. Macmillan was told personally by Dr Donald Coggan, then Bishop of Bradford, 'Already in England betting is a major curse. What the country needs is not an incentive to the spirit of gambling

---

[vi]   Hopkins writes: 'By 1957 nearly half the nation's male workers were in line for "private occupational pensions"' (Hopkins, 1964, 341). The true proportion was almost certainly considerably less: 'in line' usually meant a waiting period usually of up to a full year of continuous full-time service and being subjected to stringent conditions before being permitted entry into an employer scheme for salaried executives only.

but an incentive to honest hard work'. In similar vein, a letter to *The Times* signed by a group of Sheffield churchmen preached:

> The Christian believes that the principle of 'something for nothing' is of the nature of sin. The distribution of wealth by chance without regard to need or merit is socially unjust. The appeal to men's acquisitive instinct without relation to effort cannot but undermine the country's moral and social well-being. In fact, we believe that condonation of such a principle by the state will be a moral disaster of far-reaching consequence.[51]

Publicly, Macmillan defended what was to become the most popular and enduring savings scheme of all time against allegations of abject gambling, on the grounds that the investment would never be lost. Privately, perhaps reacting to a letter from the general secretary of the National Sunday School Union, advising him that 'a state-sponsored system of gambling must set the seal of approval to an evil which makes for moral slackness',[52] the reluctant Chancellor confided some pertinent lines to his diary:

> Oh that there might in England be
> A duty on Hypocrisy!
> A tax on Humbug; an excise
> On solemn plausibilities!
> Henry Luttrel[53]

Possibly apprehensive of the magnitude of his own assessment, Macmillan made no attempt to introduce such potentially lucrative tax gatherers before leaving the Treasury to fill the office of Prime Minister vacated by Eden on 10th January 1957. He could hardly have chosen a better moment in terms of a softening in British attitudes to personal finance. When his first Chancellor, Peter Thorneycroft, introduced the spring Budget on 9th April it was amidst an unmistakable mood of confidence in both the economy and personal prosperity. The new Chancellor would be the first since the war to address a nation of growing affluence.

Encouraging as it was, the economic climate was not without its problems. Among them, a so-called 'brain drain' was causing widespread concern. Trained professionals were migrating to take advantage of more financially rewarding opportunities abroad. A scientist in Canada, for example, might expect to earn two and a half times more than his British counterpart and be left, after tax, with four times as much to spend or save.[54] Fortunately the outflow transpired less r than anticipated and British commerce and industry capable of absorbing its effects. More often than not qualified and ambitious people took their chances on perseverance at home and the Chancellor mindfully endeavoured to make life more affordable for them. Among other moves, he cut purchase tax on all furniture and household goods, reduced the price of a gallon of petrol by one shilling and, to promote vocational training, extended child allowances until completion of full-time higher education.

Labour opponents complained that Thorneycroft had presented a 'middle-class Budget' but one of its measures – the overdue removal of duty on live entertainment and sports tickets – was soon to transcend the class divide to an extent that neither he nor his critics could possibly have foreseen.[55] Television was becoming a serious threat to the theatre, concert performances and spectator sport. The cost of an outing to such an event for one person, even without travelling expenses, might exceed the cost of the annual broadcasting licence. Hence affordability played an essential, if rarely acknowledged, role in the rise of the pop music, political satire and provocative drama which characterised the 'swinging sixties'. The press increasingly devoted its space to comment on the transformation of youth culture: some positive, some negative, and some totally absurd. William Stannard, Bishop of Woolwich, famously wrote on the unhallowed subject of 'Rock 'n Roll': 'The hypnotic rhythm and the wild gestures have a maddening effect on a rhythm-loving age-group and the result of its impact is the relaxing of self-control'.[56] The only possible effect of this and similar unworldly dictates, was to add to the incentive (or even maddening effect) of the free samples on the miniature screen to purchase a personal experience of the new popular culture. This emotional expectancy produced a new consumer market effectually disseminating an old class convention to the masses. For centuries the upper classes had paid for the ethereal benefits of 'being there and being seen there' – at the theatre, the opera, the grand ball, the hunt, the race meeting. Now a post-war generation, less sensitive to class convention, again paid for the ethereal benefits of 'being there and being seen there' – at the pop concert, the night club, the discotheque, the coffee bar, the football ground. In the same spirit as its predecessors, it too invested in the enhancement of its own image, dressed in emulation of popular idols and judged the experience itself value for money, whether or not pleasure or benefit had been honestly derived from the culture paid for.

Allegations of a direct link between popular culture and reckless hedonism or criminality were never sustainable. Nor was there sustainable evidence to suggest that the millions spent on gramophone records and innovative clothing per se had any adverse effect on morality or religious observance. Falling church attendances were more attributable to receding memories of the horrors of war than to liberation in attitudes to money spending. Where once those stricken by the anxieties of war might have been comforted by overt religion and morality, now those stricken by the anxieties of affluence, might be comforted by overt, if secular, benevolence.

Britain's profit-orientated banks, uninspired by religion, morality or benevolence, continued to regard proactive commercialism as demeaning to their professional integrity. Only with the utmost caution did they revise their approach. Among their first departures was to offer direct incentives (free banking, small cash additions to new accounts, etc.) to university students, whom they presumed to be well educated and future money spinners requiring no instruction in financial affairs. To the presumed uneducated public at large, the banks felt it necessary to offer some simplistic instruction. The Lloyds Bank advertisement *On 'Filling up' Financially* (*c.*1955), for example, commences:

> You would not begin a journey across Britain by loading your car with enough petrol for the whole trip. The same applies to your cash requirements. The experienced traveller knows that *Lloyds Bank Travellers' Cheques* enable him to 'fill up' financially as he goes.

It is hard to appreciate how Lloyds Bank thought promoting travellers' cheques, cashable where and as required, could be associated with making completely unnecessary refuelling stops on a long journey. The risks involved in carrying significant sums of cash when abroad were and remain considerable but there was never a realistic probability of a tank of petrol being lost or stolen when driving across Britain. Perhaps some motorists still bought petrol in small quantities from habits formed in the days of coupon economy, but petrol rationing had been scrapped some five years before the advertisement appeared.[57] The learner's L-plate drawn close to the petrol cap as a £ sign seems to indicate that the post-war banker saw his function akin to that a of primary-school teacher using simplistic symbols to explain basic money management. He feels no obligation to answer to his innocent pupils for his rationale or lack thereof. His advice is unassailable – he *knows* and they do not.

The banks had also begun to show awareness that a married woman might have need of a current account in her own name. This should hardly have come as a revelation: a high-street banker need only step out of his front door to observe that women were not simply out shopping for food and practical necessities; they were controlling an entire family budget. A working-class housewife of the 1950s had to be particularly adroit in the management of money. While her husband was at work, it was she who queued at the Gas, Electricity, and Water Board offices, at the coal merchants, and at the town hall Rating Office to settle the bills and possibly waited her turn at the Co-op office to collect some of the necessary cash from the family dividend. It was she too, who on her front doorstep paid out cash to the baker and the milkman and for the weekly rent, the hire-purchase and credit instalments, the insurance premiums, and the National Savings contributions.[58]

On 'filling up' financially

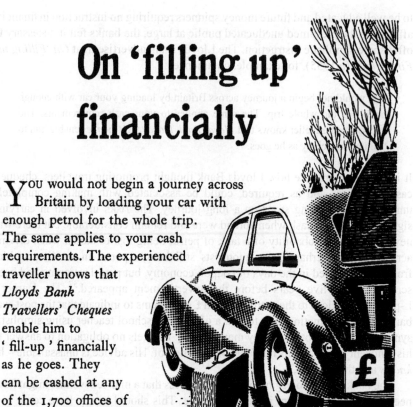

You would not begin a journey across Britain by loading your car with enough petrol for the whole trip. The same applies to your cash requirements. The experienced traveller knows that *Lloyds Bank Travellers' Cheques* enable him to ' fill-up ' financially as he goes. They can be cashed at any of the 1,700 offices of Lloyds Bank and, if need be, at the branches of almost all other British banks, and they are accepted by many hotels and stores.

    Lloyds Bank Travellers' Cheques can be obtained in units of £2, £5, £10 and £20, from any branch of the Bank and represent one of the most convenient ways of carrying travel money anywhere in the world.

✱ *Ask at any branch of Lloyds Bank for details of these facilities.*

LLOYDS BANK TRAVELLERS' CHEQUES

Figure 7.1   On 'filling up' financially
Note: Reproduced with kind permission of Lloyds Banking Group Archives.

Yet if a working-class or indeed middle-class wife contributed her own earnings to the household budget it remained a humiliation to her husband. His reputation as a provider was a revered social asset and, if pressed, he would deny that his wife went out to work or dismiss her job as an insignificant pastime. Men remained unenthusiastic about their wives working for money for more than another two decades, although usually for more practical reasons. Social researcher Marilyn Porter published her detailed recordings of the views of twenty-five working-class couples on a broad variety of aspects of life in Britain in the early 1970s, which demonstrate remarkably little change from the 1950s. Still the most common attitude to a wife's job was encapsulated in the blunt response: 'I don't like the idea'. Of the husbands just one actively encouraged his wife to stay in her paid job, while others commented:

> She's enough to do at home: It's all right provided what goes on in the home doesn't suffer: She's doing a part time job for her own pleasure: If she needs the money, it's OK – if she's bored, well it's greedy.[59]

A middle-class husband too believed it his duty to both generate the income and control its disbursement to support his family in the manner he considered appropriate. He was a professional or business executive and his wife was not. He had a bank account and his wife did not. He settled the household bills by cheque and despatched them by post without his wife's participation. He added to or withdrew the family savings or investments and fulfilled his legal obligation to enter his wife's income on his tax return. He saw no reason to involve her in such matters. None of this had changed since almost half the middle-class housewives interviewed in 1949 claimed to have been aware only of the cost of things they paid for themselves in cash. Then, the majority 'could give no estimate of their annual household expenditure on heating and lighting' because as one responded, evidently considering the question superfluous, 'My husband looks after that sort of thing'.[60]

When the banks decided to actively encourage married women to open accounts of their own, they instinctively took financial illiteracy for granted, as exemplified by the Lloyds Bank advertisement, *Then you won't require my husband's signature?* The hand-drawn illustration shows a well-dressed lady finding it most revealing and reassuring to be informed across the counter by a clerk (the manager would have seen a *valued* prospective customer in his office) that 'the day has gone when husbands regarded their wives as chattels' and that 'of course' her transactions will be 'treated with inviolable confidence'.[61]

*Then you won't require
my husband's signature?*

The day has gone when husbands regarded their wives as chattels. Among the customers of Lloyds Bank are many married women who have their private accounts and manage their own monetary affairs in complete independence. They enjoy all the facilities the bank offers ; and, of course, their transactions with the bank are treated with inviolable confidence.

Let LLOYDS BANK
look after *your* interests

Figure 7.2   Then you won't require my husband's signature?
Note: Reproduced with kind permission of Lloyds Banking Group Archives.

Even more patronising was the banks' view of the ability of the working-class man to responsibly conduct his own financial affairs. Fully aware that the income of many wage earners was approaching and in some cases exceeding that of their traditional customers, the 'Business Development Committee' of the Midland Bank set up a sub-committee in 1956 'with best brains' to research methods of capturing the emergent market. Having concluded in effect that a pound spent on advertising for working-class business was a pound wasted, the 'best brains' reported back:

> We have discussed the possibilities of a campaign to attract the wage-earning market. With present wage levels this might offer possibilities, as in the USA, but there seems little doubt that it would need to be launched with definite tangible inducements. At present we are under an inter-bank (non-competition) agreement not to offer widespread free terms, even if we were satisfied that this would be worthwhile and that it was otherwise good policy.[62]

It would be at least another twenty years before it was common to find a British wage earner with a cheque book of his own.

The Midland Bank, reputedly the most conservative of the 'big five', was also by far the most prolific advertiser.[vii] Observing that its own 'early booklets were severely factual in tone and no attempt was made to make them attractive in themselves' the Midland was the first to experiment with full-colour promotional literature.[63] Peppered with severely factual information about currency exchange rates and addresses of convenient branches, the illustrated London tourist guides it distributed free were, nonetheless, symptomatic of a change in attitude to customer service. In similar spirit, the Midland achieved another first in the 1950s when it cosmetically transformed touring caravans into 'mobile branches' and literally took the bank to its customers to promote an approachable image. This innovation was quickly copied by all the bank's competitors and was soon to become an indispensible service at agricultural or trade shows, race meetings, and other sports and open-air entertainment venues. The mobile branch proved more than simply a marketing tool: it brought home to both customers and bankers that the marble and mahogany clad banking halls had become redundant monuments to past glories. In recognition the Midland instructed its staff to try to make its sombre mausoleums look more welcoming, explaining that 'every branch office is an advertisement'.[64] Colourful posters, display cards and brochures soon began to herald the distinctive qualities of its services – identical to those available in the similarly bedecked premises of all its competitors.

Among the more curious of the colourful heralds of the identical qualities of banking services was the 'gift cheque', a fruitless novelty, according to sociologist Viviana Zelizer, rooted in American family tradition:

[vii]   The Midland Bank's 1956 publicity budget of £156,000 compared to National Provincial's £76,000 and Barclays' £74,000 (HSBCG: 0200/102, February 1957).

> Women's magazines describe with remarkable originality and skill the many and
> time-consuming and often elaborate strategies for converting legal tender into
> gift money; gold coins hidden in cookies, concealed by Christmas seals, dollar
> bills in belt buckles or encased within a picture frame – the better the disguise,
> the more acceptable the gift.[65]

Presuming their customers to be similarly coy about giving money to friends
and relations, British bankers began to distribute books of cheques individually
decorated with chocolate-box illustrations. These least subtle of gift vouchers,
symbolic of the spirit of 'elegant economy', retained their extraordinary appeal
for many years before fading away with the gaudy pictures that defaced, rather
than disguised, the sum manually written over them – possibly the true determiner
of how acceptable the gift.

Apart from such peripheral endeavours to present a human face, the banks
remained resolute in their long tried and trusted business model. It was a simple
enough formula. An established relationship of mutual respect between customer
and manager sanctioned an ongoing and versatile dialogue which enabled services,
and when necessary credit, to be provided with minimal formality. Full and frank
investment and business advice, counselling and assistance were uninhibited by
external supervisory bodies or statutory restraint. A customer never so much as
contemplated, let alone instigated, legal action: no one was so rich that they could
afford to lose the trust of their bank manager. In the late 1970s a retiring 'old-
school' manager of a large central London NatWest branch proudly confided to me
that never once in his lifelong career had he resorted to dishonouring a cheque. He
had been my own valued adviser for many years and I am certain that he spoke the
truth and that his record was far from unique.

The personal customer–manager relationship was another phenomenon that
had survived the war unscathed, and evidently unexploited. For all the allegations
of abject consumerism, in the late 1950s bank lending ratios remained well short
of their pre-war peak. In part this can be explained as a legacy of post-war the
credit squeeze but was probably more due to the British aversion to debt, which
too had survived the war unscathed. William Deacon's Bank branch returns (see
Chapter 3) are possibly unrepresentative of the industry as a whole and their
post-war patterns appear increasingly inconsistent, but they do underscore the
continuance of a widespread cautionary attitude to borrowing. In 1960 the
Blackburn branch was lending only 16.6 per cent of its deposits compared to
49 per cent in 1939 and at Blackpool Church Street, lending was a mere 8.3 per
cent against 68 per cent immediately before the war. Not until well into the 1970s
is there clear evidence of substantial sustained growth in branch lending ratios
and profitability.[66]

Neither William Deacon nor any other bank openly promoted its desire to
lend. Eased credit restrictions and profitable income from advances were no
reasons to abandon the first rule of banking, so saliently worded by satirical poet
Ogden Nash: 'Never lend money to anyone unless they don't need it'.[67] In accord

with this infallible commercial wisdom the appraisal of loan security remained a blunt instrument, with decisions based on judgement of the individual rather than substantiated proof of his wealth. The son of a 'prominent banker' wrote to *The Times* in 1958 that his father 'deprecated the *modern system* by which practically any customer who could deposit the necessary security was able to secure a loan without regard to *personal considerations*' (my italics).[68] Where 'personal considerations' induced enduring confidence the 'necessary security' would be relegated to a formality or even waived. Should it be considered expedient to charge an asset, all bankers adhered to a rough scale of acceptability, often at odds with their customers' values. The most favoured securities were of course readily realisable investments such as National Savings certificates, fixed-interest government bonds and high-equity endowment policies. Regardless of possible price fluctuation, bankers held gilt-edged and selected blue-chip stocks in similarly high esteem. Other marketable stocks and shares were acceptable, though always slightly frowned upon for their high risk. Personal guarantees of friends or relations might be taken, dependent on 'personal consideration' of the parties involved, often with only cursory investigation. However substantial, the equity value of freehold or leasehold property investments was always regarded as circumspect and an owner-occupied house charged only as a last resort. Banks, like building societies, feared nothing more than detrimental publicity ensuing from repossession of a customer's home, and were generally successful in ensuring that it was the rarest of events.

With similar detachment from their customers' values bank never advertised or fully clarified their methods of calculating charges. If formal guidelines were drawn up for managers (which is improbable), they were for their eyes only. It was widely believed that the periodic deduction that appeared without forewarning on a customer's bank statement was based on the type and volume of transactions but such calculations might have involved hours of laborious and uneconomical manual counting and computation. Before 15th February 1971, when Britain achieved the dubious distinction of being the last country in the world to decimalise its currency, no machine (including early computers) had been devised capable of multiplication, division or compound-interest calculation in pounds, shillings and pence. Overdraft interest on an active business account could thus seldom have been other than a 'guesstimate', while on a private account charges more often than not reflected the manager's arbitrary, and sometimes moral, judgement of how the account had been conducted. Through my five years (1957–1962) as an articled clerk and subsequently as a practising chartered accountant I never once saw a bank charge convincingly reconciled to the number or type of deposits and payments. Interest and chargescould be, and often were, challenged and renegotiated behind the closed doors. Mass-Observation's accountant diarist recorded his satisfaction at winning 'quite an argument' in a bank manager's office over excessive charges. That was in 1947, but he and his successors, including myself, continued to champion clients in such diplomatic arguments for almost another three decades.[69] On the other hand, it was exceptional for an arithmetical error to creep in among the disordered ciphers printed out by the loose black and red ink ribbons of primitive accounting machines.[viii] At the end of each day branch transactions were agreed to the last penny with the money (predominately cash) in the tills, even if it required tellers and clerks to work on into the small hours.

Meticulous as they were at counting the pennies, when it came to lending the pounds, bankers' values were often less professional than their customers might have wished. Avoidance of risk was their foremost reason to deposit money in the bank, yet their bankers gave small credence to the audited accounts of applicants for business loans and brushed aside records of past performance.[ix] All that mattered was confidence in the manager-customer relationship and no change to the system was considered necessary or desirable. Indeed, change would be a slow and reluctant process.[x] Francis Holford, a leading City commercial accountant, interviewed by Paul Thompson, recalls that as late as 1967:

> The bank manager didn't see the firm's accounts. They [the firm's partners] were in business as individuals, unlimited liability, and they thought that was good enough for anybody who wanted to assess the creditworthiness of the company.[70]

Building societies similarly attached secondary importance to documentary proof of financial substance. After 'personal considerations', mortgage providers (as they still do) put their faith in a so-called survey, an arbitrary valuation based on prices achieved in recent sales of comparable properties carried out by a local estate agent whose physical inspection, if any, might have involved no more than a glance from his car window. The prospective purchaser never saw the result but still paid for the pretence, and if wise, paid again for an independent survey, as wartime and post-war neglect often caused deterioration not externally apparent, which could distort the agent's valuation. In America, where the precise equivalent of the British building society did not exist, rather than a survey, loan providers relied on an evaluation of the mortgager's 'net worth' supported by formal evidence of his financial situation. This alone determined a maximum mortgage offer and in theory ensured that the buyer spent no more than he could afford. Sadly, the exacting standards once applied to this system seem to have slipped over the years causing American loan providers to pay dearly for granting mortgages to applicants of 'sub-prime' net worth. In Britain too, despite the imposition of supervisory

---

[viii] Small branches continued to write out bank statements by hand until the late 1950s – usually more legibly than the early machines.

[ix] At a lecture entitled 'A Banker Looks at Accounts' (c.1959) a senior banking executive left a lasting impression on me by tactlessly telling his audience of aspirant accountants that business accounts, which he hardly seemed to understand at all, were all but irrelevant and generally ignored in loan-making decisions.

[x] Attempts are currently (2011) being made to again make banking more personal, but due to the excessive developments in standardisation since the advent of the computer, it seems highly improbable that there could be a return to true 'relationship banking'.

bodies, many unaffordable mortgages have been granted with similarly disastrous consequences.

In 1951, as Addison writes, 'When the Conservatives came to office they gave full rein to private enterprise and encouraged building not only by the local authorities but by private builders as well ... and the production of houses ... did increase'.[71] Private purchasers encouraged by this generally improving situation were well advised to transfer their savings to a building society. Not only would they have received marginally better interest than from a savings bank but now would have been afforded a more realistic chance of a favourable response to a mortgage application. They were told that loyalty would be taken into account, but it was never the key factor. A non-member introduced by a known and trusted source, such as a helpful accountant or solicitor, often need do no more than go through the motions of opening an account, depositing a nominal sum (possibly for a matter of days), submitting an application and accepting an offer ahead of the queue. The less well-favoured, having loyally saved for months or years, found the building society manager under no obligation to clarify his reasons for refusal. Wage-earners were particularly handicapped by the inability to provide acceptable references, and might also encounter difficulties in meeting the requirements of a lengthy record of secure employment, an unblemished character, and clean legal record. Divorce, job dismissal, a County Court judgment or a criminal conviction however minor, were all certain disqualifiers.

This inflexible and often brutal code stood the building societies in good stead. A mortgage foreclosure was as rare as a completion without a snag or setback. As property developer and private banker Charles Gordon explains: 'the journey leading to the final destination, the purchase of a house, was a formidable pilgrim's progress of almost overwhelming obstacles'.[72] On top of the legal niceties of proof of title and conveyance, securing mortgage finance was indeed seldom other than an elaborate masquerade. A building society manager had no choice but to be pragmatic in his judgement of an applicant or survey valuation, since neither was the true arbiter of his decision. At the end of the day, applicants were at the mercy of his society's available cash or the periodic quota allocated by his head office, which then had no access to central funds or wholesale money markets. Frustrating as it all was, the British homebuyer refused to succumb and his perseverance was rewarded with increasing frequency.

Almost two and a half million new homes were built between the end of the war and 1960, and owner-occupation rose to a record high of over 42 per cent.[73] The rewards for surmounting the obstacles of the 'formidable pilgrim's progress' were greater than simply the purchase of a house. Apart from the permanent roof over the buyer's head, the most valuable was relief from income tax and surtax on every penny he paid in mortgage interest. The premiums on a life assurance plan paid to settle the mortgage at the end of its term or earlier death also qualified for partial relief. Together with every type, mortgage interest remained allowable without cap or condition until April 1975. Thereafter, the relief was reduced to interest on the first £25,000 borrowed (increased to £30,000 from 1983/84) and from 1990/91 withdrawn from higher-rate income tax until completely abolished on 5th April 2000. Every post-war government had given a prize, and in some cases a very large prize, to every competitor in the obstacle race and by so doing had enhanced their personal financial position through capital appreciation. Homeowners were, however, expected to make a small annual contribution to the prize fund. The Treasury regarded a house as a taxable benefit and until 1963 assessed its rateable value (or notional rental income) to income tax under 'Schedule A', but since there had been no post-war rating revaluation the imposition had long ceased to be onerous.

Immediately after the 1951 election, having briefed Butler to end austerity, Churchill next summoned Harold Macmillan and commanded him to 'build houses for the people'.[74] It required no great powers of foresight for *The Economist* to predict that Britain's first Minister of Housing and Local Government, in every way the antithesis of his Health Minister predecessor, Nye Bevan, would build those houses concerned more with quantity than quality. It reminded its readers: 'Dr Dalton [after Bevan resigned] at length shouldered the unpopularity of seeming to lower standards and Mr Macmillan can take advantage of the change without the opprobrium of having initiated it'.[75]

It was not from a standing start that in his four years of office Macmillan built more homes than in any comparable period before or since; but it would not have been in his nature to openly acknowledge the legacy of work-in-progress that the outgoing Labour government had bequeathed. Obsessed with the numerical expansion of its programme and converting his achievements into political capital, Macmillan showed scant interest in the practical concerns of the inhabitants of his 'houses for the people'. The deterioration in size and quality of council housing warrants no mention in his private diary, where at least twenty four entries record a childlike delight as the returns creep toward and eventually surpass his magic target – 300,000 per annum.[76] But there is nothing childlike about the intense competitive spirit behind the numbers which he reveals in his description of a vicious debate with his rival, the Chancellor of the Exchequer, in July 1952:

> Butler wants to cut the housing programme ... first he says 130,000, not 260,000 next year. When the Cabinet supports me on this ... he turns and says 'I'll cut your timber and steel'. When I say 'All right I'll build with less timber and steel', then he takes another twist and says, 'All right I'll cut your money'.[77]

At the end of 1953 Macmillan crowed over his success: '319,779, even *The Times* calls it "the Minister of Housing's triumph"'.[78] Somehow the future Prime Minister had procured the timber, the steel and the money, but his cheap and not very cheerful council estates were a far cry from the contented classless village communities of Aneurin Bevan's dreams. Within a decade they were dilapidating fast and evolving into the soulless class-segregated ghettos which would contribute to a host of urban social problems for the rest of the twentieth century.

For any of Macmillan's council tenants who aspired to owner occupation buying their rented homes was a lost cause. According to Martin Daunton: 'Councils were not compelled to sell and there was no right to purchase: by 1956 only 5,825 had been sold mainly because tenants were reluctant to buy rather than that councils were hesitant to sell'.[79] Given the continuing high levels of employment, generally affordable prices, and increasing friction between landlord and tenant, surely many more might have taken advantage of any opportunity to acquire their freehold – if it were true that councils were not hesitant to sell. It was not true. It was much easier for the councils to manage an entire estate without the inconvenience of dissenting private owners. Tenants were deterred not by lack of desire to own their homes but by the cost of maintaining cheaply-built houses and the near impossibility of raising finance. Neither a building society nor any other lender welcomed a council-house buyer even with a substantial deposit, more than adequate proven income, and the ability demonstrate that he was among the most secure of mortgagers when a modest price ensured high equity growth. The Housing Act 1957, which clarified the legal position, failed to appreciably reduce either the councils' hesitancy to sell or the tenants' reluctance to buy. Neither protested unduly when, as Daunton explains, Harold Wilson's 'Labour government expressed concern, stressing that councils should not sell while there was still an unsatisfied demand for rented houses, and urging that the encouragement of home ownership was a matter for the private sector'.[80] Not until Margaret Thatcher's Housing Act 1980 granted council tenants the unequivocal right to buy at a substantial discount and eased the raising of finance did a large number revise their attitude to investment in their freehold interests, and then to restoration and improvement.

Among Macmillan's early moves as Minister of Housing had been the abolition of the restrictive private sector building licence and an announcement of his intention to pursue an owner-occupation policy with 'common sense and moderation'. With regard to council tenants he said: 'Whenever it suits them better or satisfies some deep desire in their hearts, we mean to see that as many as possible get a chance to own their own houses'.[81] Translated into practice, this ambivalent statement meant that in building as many rent-subsidised properties as he possibly could Macmillan effectually prolonged the post-war recovery of both the private-sector construction industry and the housing market in general. Between 1951 and 1957 the average house price hovered at just above £2,000, before commencing an erratic fifteen-year climb culminating in the property boom of the early 1970s.

By the time Macmillan became Prime Minister in January 1957 wage levels had risen in real terms, interest rates remained modest, and near full employment endured.[xi] As he was to so memorably observe a few months later, most people had become appreciative of their rising prosperity and confident about investing in the enhancement of their lifestyle through material acquisition. In particular, British

---

[xi]   Unemployment at 0.9 per cent in 1948 had only risen to 1.2 per cent in 1957 (Williamson, 1990, 99).

consumers prioritised the purchase of a motor car, the quintessential symbol of conspicuous consumption, capable of advertising their social status to the widest possible audience. Their annual expenditure on new private vehicles grew from £94 million in 1950 to £325 million but they did not all buy British. The surge in sales since Butler made motor cars more affordable in 1953 had temporarily helped Britain to stay top of the European leagues of manufacturers and exporters but now it was struggling to keep pace. The French, Germans and Italians were edging ahead in production and racing ahead in technology and design.[82] Continental marques began to carry greater prestige value for British owners. Manufacturers selling to a market no longer receptive to the reputed superiority of their design and technology, in evident desperation, made an extraordinary appeal to patriotic brand loyalty. The merged giant British Motor Corporation (BMC) launched a series of almost identical new Morris, Austin, MG, Riley and Wolseley models, outwardly distinguishable from one another only by their trademarks, with prices ascending with conjectured, though to their buyers certainly real, prestige value. Marketing nostalgic emotion with an uninspired contemporary design (rather less flattering descriptions of the strategy circulated at the time) remarkably enjoyed a sustained period of success, and helped stave off continental, and then Japanese competitors for a few years.

Car buyers of course expected more for their money than a status symbol. Of equal importance to them was the ability to drive at will, in private, to and from precise locations, uninhibited by timetables, queues, tickets, delays, or 'standing room only'. Freedom and convenience would prove the most powerful emotive consumer expectancies in the evolution of post-war attitudes to personal borrowing. The Hire Purchase Act 1952, incorporating the overdue repeal of wartime credit restrictions marked the beginning of the end for motoring as a luxury for the rich alone. It was no coincidence that almost every manufacturer simultaneously brought out a range of models at prices ordinary people could afford – provided they paid by instalment.

New car buyers did not at first rub the Aladdin's lamp as eagerly as might be imagined. They signed hire-purchase agreements on only 14,048 (7.9 per cent) of the 180,000 new private vehicles registered in 1952. The following year they signed 26,486, almost twice as many, but no more than 9.1 per cent of the registrations.[83] In 1954, there was a large boost in production for the home market and new car sales jumped to 386,000. Still only 52,800 (13.7 per cent) were subject to hire purchase.[84] That year access to credit was eased for second-hand vehicles too and hire-purchase sales leapt from 90,587 (in 1952) to 253,463.[85]

The rapid growth in demand for both new and second-hand motor cars, in parallel with the revival of hire purchase, began a subsidence in working-class aversion to debt. For younger people, the daring act of scrawling their autograph at the foot of a binding contract, acquired a prestige value in its own right. Motor dealers established their own finance companies and promoted their ethereal product as keenly as the material models in their showrooms. Their salesmen waxed as lyrical of the powers of the genie of the lamp as they did of the joys of the open road. Inevitably, their emboldened clients, designated by C.K. Allen 'the more and more [drawn] into the alluring but unhealthy Never-Never Land', found themselves victims of his and other moral censure. The prolific *Times'* correspondent cites former Master of the Rolls, Lord Greene, complaining that 'a great deal of his time on the bench was occupied by people 'who are persuaded by persons whom they do not know to enter into contracts they do not understand to purchase goods they do not want with money they have not got".[86] Allen's uncharacteristically ill-considered discourse does not say when the judge's instructive *obiter dictum* was uttered but it was certainly before the 1938 Hire Purchase Act. Thereafter legislation had progressively strengthened consumer protection and, apart from in a handful of extreme cases, the judge's 'testimony', as Allen calls it, was inapplicable and outmoded on all counts by the time he wrote.

Had Allen not been such a respected figure *The Times* might have declined to publish his letter at all, given the wave of indignation provoked a year earlier by another denouncement of the evils of credit beneath the caption 'The Borrowing Attitude: Doubts on Loans for Marriage'. This diatribe from a Mr Brian Duckworth must surely rank among the least persuasive to have ever graced the august correspondence column. Its content defies commentary:

> Present joys are indeed more to flesh and blood than the dim prospect of a distant good, and a young couple whose combined incomes when single amounts to about £20 a week can hardly be blamed for rushing into marriage on the assumption that their income, if invested in hire-purchase agreements, will provide them with a house and comforts. How dangerous this can be. They have no secure foundations for their marriage, and have not learnt the need to save and work for their life together. They have purchased their marriage cheaply; it is a shoddy cut price job and may – as so often happens – fail to withstand the stresses of matrimonial life'.[87]

Unfounded invective of this kind, together with a spate of farfetched cautionary tales epitomised by Jack Trevor Story's *Live Now Pay Later*, left an impression of a Britain infested with fast-talking swindlers luring the gullible into ineradicable debt. Putting the situation into better perspective, Ralph Harris points out that 'in 1954 one of the more sensational newspapers threatened to launch a campaign to expose the 'great scandal' of hire purchase. For days it incited readers to provide evidence ... [but] after a fruitless week nothing more was heard of the matter'.[88] It seems readers were happy enough to provide evidence of their experiences of hire purchase – good experiences.

Again championing consumer protection, in 1956 *The Times* alerted its readers to the perils of 'Hire Without Purchase':

> If legal restrictions are put on hire purchase terms, people will naturally turn if they can to other forms of consumer credit. Much ingenuity has been lavished on finding substitutes for the conventional HP system. The simplest and most

obvious alternative plan is hire without the purchase. The government set out in February to close this *major loophole* [my italics] by bringing hire agreements under control ... Notably, it [a new hire contract restriction] was not applied to motor vehicles, and it is not surprising that arrangements for hiring of motor vehicles have been developed with enthusiasm.[89]

This suggests that unscrupulous traders or financiers were exceeding the legal hire-purchase time limit and accepting lower deposits than permitted by passing off contracts effectually for hire purchase as simple hire, and presumably managing to persuade buyers to gratuitously forfeit their legal right to ultimate possession. *The Times* calls for 'relatively mild' credit controls and argues that greater restriction would encourage greater abuse. Its forebodings proved of small avail, since credit controls, though sometimes relatively mild, were more often bewildering and a deterrent to trade than they were abused. Between February 1952 and June 1962 the minimum deposit and the maximum period for motor vehicle hire-purchase agreements were revised as many as twelve times, each revision being mirrored by a rise or fall in volume of sales. When the restrictions were abolished completely in July 1954 such frenetic demand was precipitated that they had to be reinstated at their prior levels within seven months.[90] By December 1960 these mercurial and seemingly quite pointless regulations had disrupted the motor-car industry to such an extent that the heads of rival leading manufacturers united to make representations to the government. Warning of dire consequences for the economy, they told the Board of Trade that foreign markets had become so intrusive that 'a relaxation of hire-purchase restrictions would be little more than a palliative'.[91] Within a month the Board extended the maximum hire-purchase repayment period to three years and permanently repealed the restrictions soon after.

As its economic and social benefits became widely more appreciated, its accessibility greater, and its desirability accepted, hire purchase steadily regained its pre-war popularity through the 1950s. Lord Mackintosh did no harm to his reputation for financial prudence by explaining to a delegate advocating its discouragement at the annual National Savings Assembly that 'Hire purchase has come to stay and a lot of our industry is geared to it. Without it we would have an unemployment problem which might surprise you'.[92]

The 'big five' banks proved more cautious in protecting their reputations for financial prudence. Selling hire-purchase products across their polished counters was, they evidently thought, unseemly. Nonetheless keen to exploit its commercial potential, in 1957 they each merged or strengthened their associations with the five leading hire-purchase houses: Barclays with UDT, Westminster with Mercantile Credit, Lloyds with Bowmaker, National Provincial with North Central Finance, while the Midland and its associate Clydesdale Bank acquired full control of Forward Trust in 1958.[93] A subsequent 'war between the big banks' added to the prodigious regeneration of the hire-purchase market. Amidst the fierce competition, by June of that year Britain's hire-purchase debt reached £293 million;[94]

915,000 contracts were registered on private vehicles in 1959 alone.[95] Thereafter, in ever more ingenious guises, hire purchase continued its ascent until restrained by the omnipotence of the plastic card.

The 1950s also witnessed a significant revival of a less promulgated style of personal credit which excited no indignant letters to *The Times* and to which no stigma was ever attached. On the contrary, to have an account with one of London's grand houses of retail commerce such as Harrods, Maples, Selfridges, Marshall and Snelgrove or the more reputable of their provincial imitators was a prized symbol of respectability. It was the post-war successor to the proud British tradition of unreasonably delaying payment to the forelock-tugging private grocer, tailor, joiner and silversmith, now displaced by purveyors of an illusion of gracious living with the recourses to dispense credit on their own terms. A store account thus carried no financial benefit: it was maintained for its prestige alone. To the moneyed being seen to sign the bill rather than handle vulgar cash or even write a cheque held a cachet of inestimable value. Perhaps a privileged few gloried in the highest social accolade of all – to be in debt to London's most illustrious grocer, Fortnum and Mason.

The many lacking the means to qualify for a department store account, a bank loan, or even hire purchase were not to be denied access to respectable credit. Literally on their doorstep they could find a catalogue-bearing representative only too willing to simultaneously furnish both their financial needs and their homes. The mail-order catalogue club was a unique commercial phenomenon. It alone could provide unsecured credit to the poor and working classes and avoid all admonition from Smilesian moralists. Like the 'big five' banks, the 'big five' mail-order houses: Empire Stores, Freemans, Grattan Warehouses, Great Universal Stores (Kays) and Littlewoods purveyed virtually identical products and services. Unlike the 'big five' banks they adapted quickly to evolving post-war attitudes to personal finance.

Of the founding fathers of these five fortuitous businesses, the brothers John and Cecil Moores of Littlewoods had displayed the most astute appreciation of the pre-war British working-class mindset. As young men from the humblest of origins, they were among the first to recognise the permanency of the nation's addiction to football and the disposition to bet on match results. By 1932, Littlewoods was already Britain's most successful football pool serving by far the largest number of regular 'investors'. This was not enough for elder brother John who, although 'against all ostentation ... wanted to prove he could be a "conventional millionaire"'. Inspired by the spectacular achievements of the American catalogue houses Sears Roebuck and Montgomery Ward, the brothers employed the same business consultant, Max Ritson, to advise on opening a Littlewoods mail-order division. Under his guidance they took advantage of their enormous mailing list to enclose questionnaires with betting coupons and research the British market.[96] The response was initially disappointing but membership grew rapidly after local organisers were recruited and trained to explain the benefits in people's homes. To a large extent attributable to being seen as a trustworthy preference to the purveyors of dubious credit and shoddy goods (see Chapter 2) Littlewoods and its competitors expanded dramatically between the wars. In the Second World War, factory and warehouse requisitioning, import limitations and manufacturing controls caused all mail-order business to be suspended. Thereafter recovery proved spasmodic, hampered principally by rationing and the restrictions on production for the home market. In the 1950s, however, easing of austerity regulations and changing attitudes to personal expenditure revived demand. By 1958 Littlewoods' mail-order division alone was turning over more than £50 million, employing ten thousand people, and represented throughout the land.[97]

Like football pools, the mail-order houses thrived on emotional consumer expectancy but only they could ensure its satisfaction. Club members' attitudes to money spending were quite distinct from those of the conventional working-class retail consumer. The catalogues did not sell on low or discounted prices. They followed the standard middle-class business method of promoting product quality first, service and delivery second, and price *last*. The mail-order club was thus the first (and probably the only) retailer to successfully convince the working-class consumer that there is no exception to the rule that this order of priority dominates every purchase of every kind.

In 1936 *Credit World* described Littlewoods as 'a wonderful business actuated by the highest ideals of philanthropy – except, of course to the retail trader, who pays local rates but whose customers are being urged to set up shop "without capital" and to make profits "without risk"'.[98] The mail-order houses had more advantages over retail traders than simply the avoidance of local rates and the capacity to set up shops without capital or risk. The overheads (including rates) of a central warehouse were proportionately lower than most shops; buying to order reduced stockholding investment; manufacturers paying for featuring their products in the catalogues brought in additional revenue; no expenditure on physical display or window dressing was necessary. These far outweighed the costs of catalogue design, print, distribution, order processing and commissions the traditional retailer did not have to pay, but mail-order even at its peak would never exceed 4 per cent of the national retail turnover.

In Dilwyn Porter's words, mail-order was 'especially attractive to the upwardly-mobile working class who had turned their backs on the tallyman'.[99] The clubs did indeed provide a form of credit trading tailored to fit the lowly pretender to the acquisitive society and cause the retreat of the tallyman and check trader. They demanded no security, required no evidence of status, ostensibly charged no interest, and best of all, employed no cold besuited bank managers. 'Home shopping' or 'picture shopping' offered a practical solution when a six-day working week diminished the opportunities for working-class families to bargain hunt or make major purchases together. Until the Sunday Trading Act 1994 permitted employment on the Sabbath, Britain's shops closed their doors on their customers on their only free day of the week. Buying through a mail-order club eliminated the inconveniences of opening hours, travelling time and expenses, and transporting purchases home. In the comfort of their own living room, under no obligation to buy, members could compare photographs, specifications and prices of eleven to twelve thousand catalogued objects of desire.[100] Members were able to peruse product information at their leisure and raise queries with their club agent, who at least in theory would not bamboozle them with sales talk, and place their orders confident of honest and efficient delivery. Their agent personally delivered smaller purchases, took them away if unsatisfactory and called to collect the weekly instalments, all invaluable services to inhabitants of remote rural areas and peripheral urban council estates long bus rides from the nearest shopping centre.

Zealous agents are known to have encouraged members to place new orders before settling the last, but there is no evidence that abuse of privilege was widely practised or the cause of financial difficulties. Apart from a small number of professionals, some employing teams of sub-agents, local mail-order agents were neither competitive nor seriously out to make money. Most were women, more interested in social visits to friends and neighbours than the average of four to seven shillings per week they earned for an inordinate amount of physical and paper work.[101] Peter Fattorini, the grandson of the founder of Empire Stores, recalls his father saying:

> It was amazing how the mail-order business carried on when basically a group
> of people who had no formal business education, a lot of them with not much
> education anyway, took credit decisions, collected the money, filled in the
> paperwork for you and the whole thing carried on – based on them.[102]

This group of poorly educated people were also the most effective of debt collectors. As Richard Coopey explains, 'Only the toughest of customers would delay payments to an agent whom they were likely to encounter every day'.[103] Like all other contemporary purveyors of credit, club agents trusted only their personal knowledge of the individual member in assessing his or her creditworthiness and were seldom mistaken.

According to *The Economist*, between 1950 and 1959 mail-order revenue expanded by about 15 per cent or at twice the rate of national retail trade.[104] Sustained growth seemed assured, yet within a decade home shopping had begun to lose its lustre. Not only was it being overtaken by more professional and competitive retailing and the general easing of credit, but social factors, including the decline of the nuclear family and the break-up of close-knit working-class communities, were changing British attitudes to money spending.

The mail-order club was not for the nation's new conspicuous consumers nurturing high expectancies of quality, personal service and social cachet. *Where* they bought was as important, possibly more important, as what they bought, why they bought it, and what they paid. They spent their money on the designer fashions, prestigious labels and conversation pieces which reflected their literally paid-up membership of the age of affluence. The age of austerity, when they had spent their money on stark practicalities, was the stuff of history. Conspicuous

consumption was the stuff of human nature, predating history itself, but still
denigrated by the many clinging to their belief in the rectitude of the wartime
and post-war 'elegant economy' mindset. The political left in particular vented its
moral spleen on those it stereotyped as ostentatious wasters (that is, Conservative
voters). In Lawrence Black's words:

> What also animated socialism's inanimate ethical instincts were the contrary
> values it saw promoted in the 'affluent society'. In its acquisitiveness, cultural
> choices and lifestyles, affluence chafed with socialism. Socialists were hostile to
> hire purchase, consumerism, commercial television, advertising and American
> mass culture, since their values were so far from those on which they anticipated
> socialism might be built.[105]

Socialists could not even break the habit of summarily passing judgement on
violators of their 'inanimate ethical instincts' who squandered their wages on
luxuries inappropriate to the working classes. They could not stomach the thought
that socialism itself might be rendered redundant by too great a spread of affluence.
In 1955 Hugh Gaitskell, now Labour leader, condemned 'the growing ownership
of cars, televisions, and washing-machines [as a] growing Americanisation of
outlook', while making small secret of his wealthy upper-middle-class background
and frequent indulgence in the pleasures of high society.[xii] Even Aneurin Bevan
would eventually pursue the life of an English country gentleman. Past the
pinnacle of his political career, in 1954 he paid £9,000 (over four times the average
house price) for the fifty acre Buckinghamshire farm he and his wife Jenny Lee
improved at great expense and inhabited until his premature death.[106] Both Bevan
and Gaitskell dismissed modern labour-saving domestic appliances as 'gadgets'
and like all good contemporary socialists lost no opportunity to blacken the name
of 'materialism'. Some forms of ethereal consumerism, such as modest savings
and investment, did, however, manage to escape their wrath and they positively
praised personal expenditure on the cultural activities they themselves judged
appropriate to the working classes.

Bevan can have expressed the socialist attitude to personal finance no better
than writing of 'Virtual affluence – based not on economic achievement but
'on the never-never', on homes mortgaged to the hilt and buying domestic equipment
and gadgets of all sorts on the hire-purchase system … a brash materialism shot
through with fear'.[107] Preceding Gaitskell, Bevan accused the British people of
becoming 'thoroughly Americanised',[108] denigrating modernity in the post-war
spirit of Cranfordian sour-grapeism and gratuitous self-righteousness. Not only
socialists but patriots, nationalists, satirists and bigots of every political persuasion
mindlessly poured scorn on this imaginary Americanised lifestyle. Still in the
late 1950s British people were prepared to deny the hygienic properties of the

---

[xii] Gaitskell had a long and well-documented affair with socialite Ann, Viscountess
Rothermere, wife of James Bond author Ian Fleming.

refrigerator, pronounce it an American indulgence, and refuse to buy one although they could well afford to do so. Still they were convinced that the reputed American habit of taking a daily shower was not only wasteful but bad for the skin, or the health, or ... . In Britain the ritual of the weekly bath endured even longer than the open coal fire. Still central heating was considered an uneconomical and unhealthy affectation that a decent British home could 'well do without, thank you'.

Of all Americanisations the most despised was the radio and television commercial. On 22nd September 1955 the BBC's hitherto unassailable monopoly as guardian of the nation's financial morals found itself challenged by a brash newcomer professing a very different mission. The mission of independent television was the promotion of consumption – material and ethereal, conspicuous and inconspicuous. In the House of Lords in March 1954 Reith had described the 'moral hurt' of the Commercial Television Bill[xiii] as the intrusion of a 'maggot ... into the body of England', and compared it to the 'introduction of smallpox, the Black Death and bubonic plague'.[109] 'Lord Hailsham likened ITV to "a Caliban emerging from his slimy cavern"'.[110] These and many other similar weakly camouflaged anti-Americanisation sentiments had no sustainable basis. Hard as it was for traditionalist Britons to accept, America now not only led the world in economic achievement, but in almost every branch of culture, science, industry, and pre-eminently, in building a materially richer and more fulfilled lifestyle for its people.

In America broadcasting had always been funded by sponsors and advertisers who were now many years ahead in the development of the techniques and arts of television marketing. With the advent of the independent channel British advertisers had to catch up and learn quickly that their only chance of keeping the viewer from going to make a cup of tea or to the lavatory during the commercial breaks was to create romantic, humorous or intriguing scenarios. They also had to learn, in some cases the hard way, that however creative, absorbing or enticing, the televised advertisement was indistinguishable from any other form of marketing in its impotence to generate a single sale in the absence of pre-created expectancy. The dramatic scripts, the polished performances launching the career of actor Terrance Brook, the music enjoying success in the charts, and the intense drama of the 1959 *Never Alone with a Strand* campaign ignominiously failed to popularise the brand. Smokers simply refused to buy cigarettes that did not satisfy their emotive expectancy. This exceptionally creative campaign remains the classic demonstration of the impossibility of thrusting a product onto an unreceptive market.[111]

The immutable rule of pre-created expectancy has no bearing on competition for a greater share of proven markets. Hence to maximise revenues, independent television had to do whatever was necessary to lure the largest possible audience from the BBC. The surest way to achieve this was to throw out as many pre-war

---

[xiii] A 'bitter debate' ensued in the Commons over substituting 'Independent' for 'Commercial' in which Gilbert Mitchison MP (Lab) commented: 'A skunk would still smell extremely nasty even if it were known as an independent raccoon' (Henry, 1986, 29).

Reithian edicts and outdated taboos as possible. ITV's most effective affront to broadcasting convention was the exploitation of monetary voyeurism, which like sexual voyeurism, has since biblical times had its private adherents and public dissenters – often the same people. On television even sex itself could hardly match the sales appeal of monetary voyeurism. When in 1955 the cosmetic company Revlon sponsored *The $64,000 Question* in America, its sales skyrocketed from the first broadcast. The show itself did not mention any of the products yet some sold out in a single day. So vast and so fixated was the audience that Revlon's turnover rose that year from $28 million to $86 million. David Halberstam eloquently describes *The $64,000 Question* phenomenon as:

> Emblematic of the American dream … It reflected a 'white Christmas' view of America, in which the immediate descendants of the immigrants caught up in their optimism about a new world and the nobility of the American experiment romanticised America and saw it as they wanted it to be.[112]

This or something similar could have been said with equal sincerity of Britain but contemporary British commentators found no nobility or romanticism in commercial television's so-called 'giveaway' shows, and invariably portrayed them as abhorrent. They constantly claimed that the abject depravity of the childish games was the breeder of nationwide gambling and greed. Such criticism ignored the fact that any element of chance was eliminated with the selection of the handful of participating 'gamblers' who had not a penny at stake, and that, however 'greedy' even the most mindless viewer could understand that he or she had not a penny to gain. In long-running giveaway shows like *Take Your Pick* and *Double Your Money*, smiling quizmasters spelled out answers to inane questions for a rehearsed studio audience to lead the viewers in a gasp at the award of an unmerited glittering prize or sum of money. In Britain direct sponsorship was unknown and these programmes did not intentionally promote specific material or ethereal products. They crowded the schedules of the independent channels because the audiences found them entertaining and relaxing and for no other reason. And if they helped create romantic expectancy thentheir effect on personal behaviour could have been no more negative than nursery rhymes, fairy tales or classical literature.

Nor is there any evidence that the romanticism of 'easy money' had any negative effect on personal behaviour. The effortless successes of James Bond in his larger-than-life adventures mocked the ice-cool celluloid British war hero whose exaggerated derring-do enjoyed similar popularity in the 1940s and 1950s, but neither caused anyone in their right mind to emulate them. Fifty years on such programmes as *Who Wants to be a Millionaire* retain their audience fascination, as indeed do the fictitious war hero and James Bond, because they stimulate the imagination to the expectancies and aspirations upon which both commerce and culture thrive. In 1994 Peter Hennessy accused Hughie Green, the presenter of *Double Your Money* from 1955 to 1968, of being a 'debaucher of popular culture' and found him 'understandably touchy' and unrepentant. Hennessy also cites Richard Hoggart being appalled at ITV 'going for the audience as fast as it could because that means more advertising revenue'.[113] Yet Hoggart himself, nothing if not a defender of working-class culture, forwards the most erudite case for the cultural merit of monetary voyeurism when writing:

> We come then to the nature of the interest in money itself, a strange interest because it is not avaricious, not concerned to amass it. It may be like figures and counting, but is less interested in the sums of money than in what that money can buy (not necessarily for you) and so in what those purchases can signify … Virginia Woolf was mistaken to think [Arnold] Bennett's love of all the thisness of things and their prices indicated a lack of spirituality, of response to an inner being. Bennett's love of objects and their value expressed itself in some extravagant personal ways (the expensive shirts and all that). But these things were poetic to him, luminous, vibrating with suggestions of luxury, of a glamour and a freedom the *Five Towns* never knew and which were not merely ostentatious or vulgar.[114]

Hennessy illustrates his commentary on the money obsession of commercial television with a graph headed 'The Impact of Television' which, among other data, indicates that between 1954 and 1962 books issued at public libraries rose in almost exact parallel with expenditure on television advertising.[115] Little, if any, of that expenditure was for the promotion of literature but had the graph been extended to the 1980s and beyond, usage of free public libraries would have shown a significant downswing and the line indicating book buying would have soared above the page. The number, size and quality of booksellers, supplemented in recent years by the phenomenal volume of internet sales, would have been inconceivable in the 1950s. As the mass media, including commercial television, became ever more informative and creative it inspired expenditure on literature and every form of culture. Pop music has of course enjoyed the most consistent commercial success but in smaller proportion expenditure on jazz, classical and serious music recordings, as well as live cultural performance too have increased to a level similarly inconceivable in the 1950s. Cultural consumption has arguably made a more significant contribution to the rise of the affluent society than material consumption.

When in July 1957 Harold Macmillan persuaded the crowd gathered at Bedford football ground they had 'never had it so good' the term 'affluent society' had yet to enter either his or their vocabulary. The UK edition of Galbraith's best seller would not be published until the following year, but those British people prepared to face reality needed neither a foreign economist nor an ambitious Prime Minister to spell out the evolution of post-war social culture. Their children were being taught the Second World War, make-do-and-mend, fair shares and ration books in their history classes at school. The lost pleasures and benefits of a pre-war era had been found and were set out on Britain's post-war stalls alongside post-war modernity for all to see and buy.

People of all classes were feeling comfortable about realising or borrowing against their savings, investments, endowment policies and property equity, to employ the proceeds in the quest for a better lifestyle. While, as ever, the growing numbers simultaneously burdening themselves with personal debt were subjected to moral censure and prophecies of doom, legal insolvencies remained few and far between. The *Annual Report(s) by the Inspector-General in Bankruptcy to the Board of Trade* confirm that the universal solvency of the war years prevailed for almost two decades. Receiving orders under the Bankruptcy and Deeds of Arrangement Acts had come off their wartime lows by 1949, but still totalled just 1,693, against 4,708 in 1938. The liabilities of this unfortunate few were £5.9 million compared to the £10.3 million a year before the war, but the average debt, higher by approximately 50 per cent, was of small significance when taking account of inflation in the intervening eleven years. The 1949 bankrupts had included one clergyman, seven barristers and solicitors, and just eight 'bookmakers and other persons engaged in betting':[116] the last, in particular, discredits the concurrent condemnation of the prevailing cult of gambling (see Chapter 4). Not until 1960 did bankruptcy debt return to its 1938 level and even then the 3,068 bankrupts were well outnumbered by their pre-war peers. As late as 1967 the 4,189 bankrupts remained over 500 fewer than in 1938, though now their liabilities exceeded £20 million. In 1957 only 2,061 receiving orders were instigated under the Bankruptcy Acts, with the net liabilities of bankrupt debtors totalling less than £4 million, while a mere 313 deeds of arrangement contrasted with 3,105 in 1938.[117]

While these figures add weight to Macmillan's assertion of a 'state of prosperity such as we have never had ... in the history of this country', they also indicate that war-born habits of financial prudence were yet to be fully eradicated. The Prime Minister's portrayal of the nation as a paradise found was intended to warn that it might soon be a paradise lost. His cautionary words fell mainly upon deaf ears, but they were heard clearly enough by the sizable minority who remained unconvinced that they had been sufficiently liberated from the impact of war to permit themselves to partake of the fruits of his flawed paradise. These stalwarts of 'elegant economy' saw every sign of private affluence countered by another indicating that in production, technological progress and standards of living, European countries, including wartime enemies, were striding ahead and challenging their nation's economy. The majority interpreted Macmillan's words to mean that liberation in their attitudes to personal finance would be a defence against these challenges and a contribution to economic progress. A personally conservative Conservative Prime Minister had brought conspicuous consumption into the public arena and pronounced it respectable. The swelling middle classes could feel free to wear with pride social status distinguished not by birthright, education or 'old' money but by respectable aspirations to new material consumption.

The decade which followed was not destined to be characterised by respectable aspirations of any kind, but by their antitheses: youth, sexual and consumer 'revolutions'. All were inevitable manifestations of a general progression of consumer expectancy but contemporary commentators attributed to them a profusion of destructive influences out of all proportion to reality. Then retrospective commentators attributed to them a wealth of cultural benefits out of all proportion to reality. Then, Sandbrook and other recent historians, in reasonable proportion to reality, exposed the popular image of the 'revolutions' of the 'swinging sixties' to have had little discernable effect on the daily life of the overwhelming majority. Between 1950 and 1957 the British people had experienced a passive evolution towards the wider and, arguably more constructive, employment of their personal finance. Many nonetheless had yet to exorcise attitudes formed by their experience of the war and its aftermath. The spreading shadow of 'conspicuous consumption' was clearly visible across the sphere of 'elegant economy' but still had some way to go to complete its total eclipse.

Endnotes

[1] Porter, Dilwyn, 'Never-Never Land!: Britain under the Conservatives, 1951–1964' in Tiratsoo, Nick (ed.), *From Blitz to Blair: A New History of Britain since 1939* (1997), 103.

[2] Black, Lawrence, *The Political Culture of the Left in Affluent Britain, 1951–1964: Old Labour, New Britain* (2003), citing Universities and the Left Review, 28.

[3] Sandbrook, Dominic, *Never Had It So Good: A History of Britain from Suez to the Beatles* (2005), xvii.

[4] MO: FR1037.

[5] Burnett (1993), 280.

[6] Todd (1966), 14.

[7] MO: FR 3161, 'The London Middle-class Housewife and her Housekeeping Expenditure', September 1949.

[8] Sandbrook (2005), 98.

[9] Black (2003), 15 et seq.

[10] Jenkins, Roy, *Churchill* (2001), 121, 208, 804.

[11] Howard, Anthony, *RAB: The Life of R A Butler* (1987), 179.

[12] Dell, Edmund, *The Chancellors: A History of the Chancellors of the Exchequer 1945–1990* (1997), 162.

[13] Pagnamenta, Peter and Overy, Richard, *All Our Working Lives* (1984), 253.

[14] *Manchester Guardian*, 1st January 1952.

[15] Ibid., 12th March 1952.

[16] *News Chronicle*, 12th March 1952.

[17] *Daily Telegraph*, 14th March 1952.

[18] Dell (1997), 182.

[19] *Daily Herald*, 12th March 1952.

[20] *Daily Mail*, 12th March 1952.

[21] *The Times*, 15th April 1953.
[22] *The Times* and *Daily Telegraph*, 15th April 1953.
[23] Pelling, Henry, *Churchill's Peacetime Ministry, 1951–1955* (1997), 31.
[24] *Daily Herald*, 15th March 1953.
[25] *News Chronicle*, 15th April 1953.
[26] *Glasgow Herald*, 15th April 1953.
[27] Howard (1987), 194.
[28] *Daily Mail*, 21st April 1953.
[29] *Financial Times*, 15th April 1953.
[30] Stacey (1970), 177.
[31] Ibid., 58, 72.
[32] MO: TC57; Madge (1943).
[33] Stacey (1970), 148–149.
[34] Marwick (2003), 79.
[35] MO: FR 3106: 'Mass-Observation Television Panel', April 1949.
[36] Black (2003), p. 38.
[37] Rubinstein, W.D., *Wealth and Inequality in Britain* (1986), 79.
[38] *Daily Mail*, 12th March 1952.
[39] Howard (1987), 203.
[40] *The Times*, 7th April 1954.
[41] Emmett (1956), Table 1, 286.
[42] Howard (1987), 214–215.
[43] *Manchester Guardian*, 21st April 1955.
[44] *Financial Times* and *Daily Sketch*, 21st April 1955.
[45] Dell (1997), 200.
[46] Howard (1987), 217.
[47] *The Times*, 5th October 1955.
[48] *Hansard*, HC, 26th October 1955, vol. 545, cc. 202–206.
[49] *The Times*, 18th April 1956, 10.
[50] *Hansard*, HCDeb. 18th April 1956, vol. 551, cc. 1014–1136.
[51] *The Times*, 19th, 21st April 1956.
[52] Ibid.
[53] Catterall, Peter, *The Macmillan Diaries: The Cabinet Years, 1950–1957* (2003), entry 26th April 1956, 554.
[54] *Financial Times*, letter from F.T. Salomon, 27th February 1957.
[55] *The Times, Financial Times*, 10th April 1957.
[56] *The Times*, 14th September 1956.
[57] LTSB: HO/GM/ADV/14, 1955.
[58] PGA: *Prudential Bulletin*, January 1948, 5.
[59] Porter, Marilyn, *Home, Work and Class Consciousness* (1983), 123–124.
[60] MO: FR 3161, September 1949.
[61] LTSB: HO/GM/ADV/6, 1947.
[62] HSBGC: 0200/102, 'First Report of the Business Development Committee', October 1956.
[63] HSBCG: 0200/040a, Booklet, 'Presenting the Midland Bank' (*c.*1958).

64 Ibid.
65 Zelizer, Viviana A., *The Social Meaning of Money, Pin Money, Paychecks, Poor Relief, and Other Currencies* (1994), 105.
66 RBSG: WD/377/3.
67 Ogden Nash, *Bankers are Just Like Anybody Else, Except Richer* (1938).
68 *The Times*, letter from H.C.C. Batten, 1st September 1958.
69 M0: Diary 5076, 25th September 1947.
70 Thompson (1997, part 1), 'Francis Holford', 300.
71 Addison (1985), 62.
72 Gordon, Charles, *The Cedar Story: The Night the City was Saved* (1993), 45.
73 Williamson, Bill, *The Temper of the Times: British Society since World War II* (1990), 99.
74 Catterall (2004), entry 28th October 1951, 113.
75 *The Economist*, 10th November 1951.
76 Catterall (2004), entries 15th December 1951 to 29th September 1954, 123–357.
77 Ibid., 23rd July 1952, 175.
78 Ibid., 6th February 1954, 290.
79 Daunton (1987), 79.
80 Ibid., 79.
81 Daunton (1987), 78.
82 Church, Roy, *The Rise and Decline of the British Motor Industry* (1994), 'Motor Vehicle Production by Country, 1945–77', Figure 5.1.
83 NA, PRO, BT/70/677; *Hire Purchase Journal*, February 1954, 12.
84 NA, PRO, BT/258/458: 'Ministry of Transport New Registrations of Private Cars and Percentage on Hire Purchase Agreements 1946–1954', 'Hire-Purchase Contracts Effected in the UK', Tables 1 and 1(A).
85 NA, PRO, BT/70/677, 'Supplement to Appendix A'.
86 *The Times*, 1st September 1958.
87 *The Times*, 8th July 1957.
88 Harris et al. (1961), 31.
89 *The Times*, 28th August 1956.
90 Harris et al. (1961), 299–300.
91 NA, PRO, BT/213/111, 'Changes and rates H.P. Restrictions' (National Advisory Committee of the Motor Manufacturing Industry, December 1960).
92 *Business Credit*, July 1954.
93 HSBCGA: 0200/301.
94 Maskell, R.E., *The HP and Instalment Habit* (1964), 23–24.
95 Harris et al. (1961), 295.
96 Wyatt, Woodrow, *Distinguished for Talent: Some Men of Influence and Enterprise* (1958), 223–224.
97 Coopey, Richard, O'Connell, Sean, and Porter, Dilwyn, *Mail Order Retailing in Britain: A Business and Social History* (2005), 95.
98 Ibid., citing *Credit World*, February 1936, 37.
99 Porter in Tiratsoo (1997), 119.

[100] Coopey, Richard, O'Connell, Sean, and Porter, Dilwyn, 'Mail Order in the United Kingdom c1880–1990: How Mail Order Competed with Other Forms of Retailing' in *The International Review of Retail Distribution and Consumer Research*, 9:3 July 1999, 267.

[101] Idem (2005), 120.

[102] Ibid., 119.

[103] Idem (1999), 270.

[104] *The Economist*, 27th February 1960.

[105] Black (2003), 13.

[106] Lysaght, C.E., *Brendan Bracken* (1979), 208; Lee, Jennie, *My Life With Nye* (1980), 245.

[107] *Tribune*, Aneurin Bevan, 'Whither Labour Now', 19th September 1952.

[108] Black (2003), 87.

[109] James (2006), 431.

[110] Henry, Brian, *British Television Advertising: The First 30 Years* (1986), 29–30; *Hansard*, 5th Series (House of Lords), 188, 250, 355–356.

[111] Henry (1986), 442–443.

[112] Halberstam, David, *The Fifties* (1993), 644.

[113] Hennessy, Peter, *Having It So Good: Britain in the Fifties* (2006), 536.

[114] Hoggart (1990), 190–191.

[115] Hennessy (2006), 537.

[116] HMSO/Board of Trade, *Report by the Inspector-General in Bankruptcy for the Years 1939–1953*, 4–5; *1966/67*, 9, 26–29.

[117] Ibid., 1960, Table, 8.

Chapter 8

Total Eclipse and Corona
(*1957 and Beyond*)

Indeed let us be frank about it. Most of our people have never had it so good ... Go around the country, go to the industrial towns, go to the farms and you will see a state of prosperity such as we have never had in my lifetime or indeed in the history of this country.

Harold Macmillan, Bedford, 20th July 1957

The eclipse of the sun by the moon is a fleeting moment. Both spheres are in perpetual motion. They move on and mankind is devoid of power to lure them back to admire the instant of total concealment and its bright corona. An eclipse is a natural phenomenon but self-denial and 'sour-grapeism' are not natural phenomena. Nature does not allow them to be practised in perpetuity. Mankind has always striven to make life as comfortable as circumstances allow: to build the safest shelter, to hunt and gather the most palatable food, to make the most practical clothing, and to seek the most attractive bodily adornment. Bertrand Russell reasoned that 'competition has been, ever since the origin of Man, the spur to most serious activities'.[1] Man is therefore not simply a social animal but a competitive animal and if competitiveness is a natural phenomenon then 'conspicuous consumption' is a natural phenomenon, while 'elegant economy' cannot be so.

Describing Britain in the late 1950s and early 1960s, Arthur Marwick claims:

It would be wrong to exaggerate the changes in everyday life ... But it would be fair to say there was a new hedonism abroad in the land; that life was lived with greater gusto than ever it had been since the evangelicals set their stamp upon the mores of the middle class.[2]

Marwick, like most commentators on this period, suggests that Elizabeth Gaskell's parsimonious sour grapeism had become entirely eclipsed by the vulgarities and ostentation of conspicuous consumption. 'Elegant economy', however, might have been out of sight but it was not out of mind. Unravelling the knots of austerity born culture and its institutions would be an unhurried and unending process. Yet Eric Hobsbawm describes an engendered 'social upheaval ... a profound and in many ways sudden, moral and cultural revolution; a dramatic transformation of the conventions of social and personal behaviour'.[3] Applied to the majority, this and similar overstated descriptions of social upheaval transpire on closer examination to be unsustainable hyperbole, often invented to mask anti-consumerist prejudice or to discredit the creativity of the mass-communicators who achieved so much more than tempt readers and audiences with the carrots of consumption. Selective self-denial was a convention too deeply rooted within the British psyche to be suddenly exorcised by social upheaval, however profound.

Attitudes to Britain's economic stability had evolved slowly yet significantly from those prevailing in October 1951 when the Conservatives resumed power amidst portentous rising inflation and an atmosphere of drab and dispiriting austerity. Then, only memories and mementos of the recently closed Festival of Britain survived to remind the nation's optimists that it harboured the resources to recreate the best of its pre-war past and to procreate a better post-war future. Now, in 1957, advancing technology, creative and competitive mass media and their publicists were breathing new life into commercial markets of every kind. Now, there were more reasons to be optimistic. Now, there were more optimists – but still the albeit fading spectre of a long and abhorrent world war hung over consumption, consumerism and consuming.

It is particularly destructive to Hobsbawm's exaggerated depiction of recklessness to observe the progression of personal savings as a percentage of disposable income. The National Savings movement, as we have seen, constantly goaded by the post-war Labour government to fund rearmament and reduction of national debt continued to vigorously promote thrift through the post-war era, yet by 1951 the savings ratio had fallen to just 1.6 per cent. In the first five years of Conservative rule it hesitantly rose to 5.5 per cent before falling back marginally in 1958 and 1959, conceivably influenced by Macmillan's speech. The following year, the first of the 'swinging sixties', Britons saved an average of 7.4 per cent of their income, while in 1961 the people Marwick supposed to be living life with 'greater gusto than ever' in a land with 'new hedonism abroad', cautiously put aside an optimum 8.9 per cent of their income for an uncertain future. Commenting on these figures in 1973, Sir Harry Page's National Savings Committee of Enquiry claimed that 'the observed fluctuations in the savings ratios are broadly consistent with the view that the ratio varies with the growth of income'.[4] The accuracy of this statement is open to question, but it supports the view that the people who Hobsbawm saw as experiencing 'a dramatic transformation of the conventions of social and personal behaviour' did not dramatically transform their overriding attitudes to personal finance in the 1960s.

Harold Macmillan's celebrated words cited at the head of this chapter also do not suggest that he had observed any transformation in conventional behaviour, yet were dramatic in their impact on emotional and romantic consumer expectancy. His intention to warn those who had *never had it so good* that inflation might soon eat into the bread on their affluent tables, was overwhelmed by his probably ill-considered choice of words and interpreted as a prime ministerial blessing upon material consumption. Ironically, the rate of inflation that had risen from 1.9 per cent to 4.7 per cent between 1954 and 1956, thereafter fell back to just 0.9 per cent at the end of the decade.

Little direct commentary on his visit to Bedford can be found among the musings in Macmillan's private diary, but a week thereafter he does enter a brief evident misjudgement: 'The speech was well reported in the Sunday press and I think it helped steady things a bit'.[5] Some days later he writes: 'The press is terrible – it gets worse every day' but in evident self-satisfied justification adds, 'This reflects the tremendously high standard of comfort and well-being of the people. When things are really difficult, even the press does not complain very much'.[6] His reaction to the terrible press, his faith in its tolerance when things are really difficult and his reference to the well-being of the people, all might suggest that he was contented with the encouragement of greater consumer expenditure. He might have even been saying that he was not entirely surprised by the humorists who pounced on the uncharacteristic phraseology from a man posing as the quintessential English gentleman, accustomed to giving careless thought to the costs of maintaining a grand country house and pursuing his considerable talent for blood sport. It is, however, improbable that at the time he appreciated the sexual innuendo at the root of the many popular jokes he provoked, which might have soon been forgotten had his words not so forcibly affirmed the innocence of self-indulgence and personal expenditure.

Macmillan's own brand of self-indulgence was indeed innocent and involved little personal expenditure, as most of his leisure time was devoted to devouring an abundance of classical literature, much of it published by his own company. It is thus not impossible that at Bedford he intentionally emulated *Cranford* by mocking 'elegant economy' to stimulate the conspicuous consumption widely thought to have contributed to his one hundred and seven seat victory in the general election of October 1959. While the benefits and pleasures of conspicuous consumption were said to be foreign to the Prime Minister himself ('he never owned a television set or had any taste for fine wine'),[7] he was pragmatic enough to appreciate that there was political capital in endorsing the fruitlessness of self-denial. Criticised for celebrating his selection victory in 1957 with oysters and champagne, he responded 'sardonically' that 'In Smith Square [Butler's home] there would have been plain living and high thinking', rather as if he disapproved of that lifestyle.[8]

In the wake of the Suez debacle, he had confidently declared: 'So do not let us have any more defeatist talk of second-class powers or of dreadful things to come. Britain has been great, is great and will stay great, provided we close our ranks and get on with the job'.[9] Such hollow rhetoric by no means convinced everyone, especially those who had survived the war and heard it so many times before, but there can be little doubt that this Prime Minister did make a difference and did generate optimism. Britain's consumers responded with alacrity to his signal that enjoyment of the financial spoils of war should be postponed no longer. In 1957 they spent £1,004 million on durable goods and in 1960 £1,465 million (over 45 per cent more), while the number of households with a refrigerator rose by 58 per cent and motor-car ownership by 25 per cent.[10] According to Dilwyn Porter: 'By June 1960 the 34 per cent who believed that their standard of living was going up clearly outnumbered the 13 per cent who thought things were getting worse, a trend that was enhanced in the course of the following eighteen months'.[11] Macmillan, as a recent Chancellor of the Exchequer, appreciated that a thriving economy and a rising standard of living had become interdependent. Defence saving had to be relegated to the museums and history books together with the rest of the negative memorabilia of the Second World War, while its positive legacies were employed for the common good. Britain was struggling for survival in export markets but incentive to greater productivity and greater earnings could buoy home markets and boost government revenues.

More and more people came to accept the pragmatism in the philosophy Bertrand Russell chose to expound when the editor of *National Savings*, it would seem ill-advisedly, had turned to him to help promote post-war thrift:

> It is pathetic to see an elderly rich businessman, who from work and worry
> in youth has become dyspeptic, so that he can only eat dry toast and drink
> only water, while his careless guests feast; the joys of wealth, which he had
> anticipated throughout long laborious years, elude him and his only pleasure is
> the use of financial power to compel his sons to submit in turn to similar futile
> drudgery.[12]

Macmillan, who in some ways would come to resemble Russell's pathetic portrait, now in part echoed his sentiments. He favoured hard work and accumulation of wealth and had demonstrated that frugality and procrastination were uneconomical in the face of inflation. He had caused the British people to ask themselves – why pay tomorrow's higher prices when the material trappings of modernity can be yours today for the completion of a hire-purchase form at the car showroom or department store? The reasons for cheering the ostensibly high-thinking-plain-living Attlees in 1945 as they drove to Buckingham Palace in their pre-war Standard 10 were moribund, but conspicuous consumption was nascent and propitious. A younger generation with money in its pockets had no interest in saving for the defence of the realm. It had no cause to display the wartime qualities of reserve to counter American servicemen flaunting dollar bills as a reminder of Britain's dependency on their government's generosity. The Americans had all gone home leaving behind nothing but a large bill at the Treasury. Britons with baby-boom children to support had no time to think about the nation's mortgage. They had their own mortgage to think about, their own house to furnish, and their own future to secure.

A younger generation with expectancies impervious to pre-war or wartime experience had emerged, and no one, not even a Prime Minister allegedly detached from the lives of ordinary people, could be blind to its presence. From about 1957 the world of commerce was galvanised by the re-emergence of what had been little more than a niche market before the war. Working-class teenage consumers had begun to voice new expectancies with unprecedented confidence. Job opportunities, higher wages and greater access to credit gave them the right to be discerning in their purchases. Fowler describes this post-war generation as having 'tastes in dress, in amusements and in many other things, widely different and more costly than any their [working-class] parents were able to entertain'.[13] They could afford to be less deferential to social status and less inhibited by the stigma of conspicuous consumption. They could demand that their longer leisure hours be filled with imaginative and innovative entertainment. Technological developers responded to their demands with improved radio and television sets, gramophones, records, and tape recorders, while entrepreneurs, artists and their promoters exploited them, made popular culture ever more accessible and, with economy of scale, ever more affordable.

The strongest contender for the most celebrated example of the fusion of technology, commerce and popular culture was arguably Achille Gaggia's Heath-Robinson-like apparatus for painfully slowly squeezing a hint of coffee into a small cup and covering it with white froth. First installed in Soho in 1952, this much derided machine and its product acquired an inexplicable cult status. The coffee bars that had appeared across the country by the end of the 1950s were unique in catering exclusively for young people – at prices their working-class parents were unable to entertain.[14] Never rationed but unobtainable during the war and for some time thereafter, coffee remained a preserve of the middle-class home. Teenagers often experienced its taste for the first time in one of the crowded, subterranean glorified cafes that arguably played a more significant role in changing social attitudes than has been attributed to them. If nothing else, they provided an audience for the new conspicuous consumer. The intimate ambience of these temples to youth culture inspired personal emotional and romantic expectancies of music, fashion, furnishing, décor, and perhaps even coffee. Their influence in softening class inhibition and the encouragement of consumerism is comparable to that of the mass media itself.

Young musicians and singers with revolutionary performing styles and precocious appearances, added to gratuitous media and word-of-mouth publicity in provoking the desires of young people to personally experience the mushrooming pop concerts, discothèques, youth-orientated films, theatre, and 'new-wave' literature. New breeds of author, playwright, journalist, designer, composer, musician, satirist, impresario, sport promoter, film and radio and television director all strained their talents to the limit to simultaneously create and exploit ubiquitous romantic and emotional expectancies. Never before had there been so many professional practitioners of the arts; never before had the arts produced such impressive results; never before had the arts been so widely influential; never before had the arts been so lucrative; and never before had the arts been so disparaged on all these counts. In serving the nation's youth, commerce and its offspring, advertising and publicity, patronised not only the arts but science, technology and culture – and still they provoked their conservative adversaries.

The younger generation of the late 1950s and 1960s was, in fact, distinguished from its predecessors by nothing other than its spending power and its willingness to spend to conspicuously affront the rigid conventions of the past by conforming to the only slightly more malleable conventions of the present. The older generation (and some non-conforming younger people accepting the rectitude of their parents' pre-war nostalgia), could not easily come to terms with this social evolution and opposed it with zeal. No one fought harder to repel the magnetic appeal of modernity than the adherents to the ethics of socialism. As Lawrence Black puts it: '[For socialists] never having so much did not necessarily mean never having had it so good'. This was certainly the stance of the more disgruntled left wingers but Black subsequently cites American academic Chris Waters: 'Ethical and puritan objections disabled the Left in the face of the commercialisation of popular culture and distanced it from many workers'. Voters who put greater faith in commerce than politics had little sympathy for socialist theories deeply mourning the passing of austerity culture. At the 1959 Labour Party Conference, a year before he died, Aneurin Bevan exerted all his oratorical genius in a final appeal for a renaissance of his vision of the pure and simple pre-war working-class life. His legendary judgement on materialism preached only to the converted: 'This so-called affluent society is an ugly society still. It is a vulgar society. It is a meretricious society. It is a society in which priorities have gone all wrong'.[15]

Socialists concurring with Bevan's view would have included J.B. Priestley, who until the day he died, 14th August 1984, never ceased to denounce the menace of his contrived bête noire, 'admass' (see Chapter 5).[16] His offensive argument that the British would 'cheerfully exchange their last glimpse of freedom for a new car, a refrigerator or a fourteen inch television screen' was outdated by 1957.[17] Priestley and those of similar mind could never accept that by exploiting negative factors such as prejudice, superstition, envy, fear, guilt and hate, the political demagogue and firebrand preacher can sway or indoctrinate his audience or readers, while the commercial advertiser can persuade only with positive and truthful imagery.

Romanticists like Bevan and Priestley had become anachronisms in their lifetime. Their beloved island race no longer had reason to fruitlessly yearn a fictitious pre-war classless paradise. Attitudes to patriotism itself had changed. The ubiquitous hoardings, first erected by the Empire Marketing Board (1926–1933), that continued to implore patriots to 'Buy British' had become as redundant as the Empire itself. In the world of commerce, the adjective 'British' held no connotation of patriotism. Whether a product was made in Britain, the remnant of its Empire or elsewhere was irrelevant to the British consumer: if it met his or her expectancy it was British enough.

This changed attitude proved an opportunity to be exploited by immigrant entrepreneurs. By the late 1950s Indian, Italian and Chinese restaurants had begun to appear in every town and village. America too perceived changes in British tastes and exported its products in abundance. Not all were well received. Among the many rejected was Hershey, its most popular chocolate. In the war and its aftermath, British children deprived by rationing of sweets and chocolate had been more than grateful to any US serviceman who gave them a Hersey bar or two, but in no other circumstances could Hershey please the British (or European) palate. Coca-Cola's fizzy drink and MacDonald's hamburgers, on the other hand, unmercifully exploited an unfathomable universal taste. Of all the spurned American imports, the most conspicuous were the monster chromium emblazoned motor cars that added to the congestion of Britain's neglected roads for a few years in the 1960s and 1970s, attracting more interest from cartoonists and comedians than buyers, before being returned unwanted and unsuitable. Britons bought only products that satisfied British expectancy: country of origin was irrelevant.

The consumer boom of the 1960s was not, as might be imagined, accompanied by a credit boom of equal magnitude but living life with 'hedonism and gusto' did engender increasing confidence in borrowing. Britain's banks ceased to feign distaste for hire purchase. Its most improbable of champions, the Church of Scotland, had preached that: '[Hire purchase was] not veiled moneylending but beneficial to society; not only was it superior to gambling but regular payments encouraged planning of domestic economy'.[18] Unorthodox doctrines of this kind undoubtedly inspired more faith in credit than in God, and with the rise of secularism conservative religious factions refocused their attacks on debt and again damned it as the root of poverty, depravity and crime. Baseless as such accusations were, constant media attention and calls for greater moral restraint forced the debate into the public arena. In 1968 the government, probably reluctantly since an inconclusive outcome was inevitable, appointed a Committee on Consumer Credit under the chairmanship of journalist and businessman Lord Geoffrey Crowther to investigate the cultural effects of personal credit. Predictably, it reported: 'On balance, consumer credit is beneficial since it makes a useful contribution to the living standards and the economic and social well-being of the majority of the British people'.[19] Crowther himself added: 'It is too difficult to devise administrative and legal measures for protecting the few who borrow unwisely without depriving the much larger numbers of consumers, who do use credit wisely, of its considerable benefits'.[20]

Even by the end of the 1950s, consumers in all walks of life had accepted the reality of Crowther's statement but British banks were yet to be persuaded of its universal application and remained generally averse to the wage-earning customer. In 1958 the chairman of the Midland Bank, Lord Monckton, openly admitted that 'social changes have brought many a working-man's income to where he ought to have a bank account'.[21] While this was unquestionably the case, Monckton, his fellow bankers and the working man all seemed incapable of envisaging how such a bank account might be beneficially employed.

Although sections of the Truck Acts dating from 1831 banning payment of wages other than in notes and coin would not be repealed until 1991, in January 1960 payment by cheque was permitted with the formal consent of the employee. Shortly prior to this long overdue relaxation in the law consultants for the Midland Bank, evidently without regard for the view of wage earners, produced a report once again opposing blue-collar custom. Unconvinced in the light of the proposed legislation, the bank's directors convened another high-level internal investigation, which similarly reported back that encouraging wage-earner accounts would be fruitless because 'many [working men] would not willingly have their pay credited to an account which their wife might see, [and] might cash a cheque at a shop and disclose to the shopkeeper how much they were earning'.[22] This lengthy and, it must be presumed, carefully considered document goes on to explain that among the main difficulties would be the inability of branches to cope with the rush of workers demanding to cash their cheques during the lunch hour on pay days. This problem, it suggests, could be alleviated by setting up sub-offices on the premises of larger employers or dispatching mobile branches specifically for the purpose. Seemingly, it was believed that no worker would ever use a bank account other than to cash his pay cheque in full immediately on receipt. The report takes no account of the many wage earners who for decades had been savings-bank and building-society depositors, homeowners with mortgages, security investors, borrowers, and involved in financial transactions of every kind.

A subsequent memorandum proposes a practical solution: 'Large employers might also be persuaded to maintain at their factories a cash float out of which they would be prepared to cash [wage] cheques at agreed times'.[23] The author of this inspired footnote fails to clarify to what end an employer might draw money from the bank simply to cash cheques drawn on the same account, or how this practice might alleviate the work of pay days for the employer, employee or indeed the bank.

Not until May 1964 did Lloyds Bank's 'Publicity Council' produce a memorandum informing the 'General Manager Administration' that 'Midland and Barclays use media which we have not yet tried ... film'.[i] This intelligence is apparently given no further consideration for two years and even then the bank claims that it is improbable that an annual budget of £25,000 '*could*' (not would) be spent on commercial film production.[24] A further two years pass before, in April 1968, the Council is reminded: 'We still have in mind the production of a film either for exhibition in commercial cinemas or for private distribution to institutes, societies and so on, but so far we have not found an acceptable script'. Fifteen months later a further memorandum states: 'A sixty-second advertising film for showing at cinemas is nearing completion, with a second in course of preparation ... designed to appeal to young audiences'. In July 1970, the bank's directors learn that the first two Lloyds Bank commercials have been shown in two hundred cinemas.[25] This surely should have encouraged some enthusiasm for cinema publicity but in June 1971 the Publicity Council seems barely concerned by the slow progress when noting: 'We have, now, in course of preparation a film dealing with money in relation to the lives of a variety of individuals. The aim is to produce an interesting documentary film with a booklet as the selling medium'.[26] The minutes record no further reference to the progress of this or any other film that year.

Bankers, who considered themselves the equal of doctors, lawyers, accountants and similar professionals, whose governing bodies strictly prohibited any form of advertising, were particularly sceptical of venturing into the trade polluted

---

[i]   The Midland Bank had first produced commercial films in 1947 (see Chapter 4).

waters of commercial television. It would take years of soul searching for them to be persuaded that there could be merit in targeting the individual customer at home. In 1960 Britain's clearing banks together spent no more than £800,000 on press and television advertising and even in 1980 less than half their combined £17.8 million budget was spent on air time and production of commercials.[27] By then the National Provincial and Westminster Banks had merged (in 1968) to form the National Westminster leaving a 'big four' to contend for the viewer's attention. Until the break-up of their agreement on non-competitive advertising in the early 1970s, a naïve joint campaign had centred on the 'Bank Manager in the Cupboard'. The precise function of this solitarily confined individual was never appreciated by viewers or customers, or indeed by managers themselves, who in general held the commercials in utter contempt. They bore not even a metaphorical resemblance to anyone's experience of the services of a bank. Once freed to advertise individually and instruct their own professional agents, the banks soon learned how to adapt their approach to the modern customer. In the words of economist David Stafford: 'No longer could the banks rely on providing what they could produce: now they would have to produce what they could sell'.[28]

A seldom remembered event in accordance with this change of heart had occurred in August 1958, when the Midland Bank advertised an apparently innocuous offer: 'Loans of up to £500, without security, at an interest rate of 5 per cent'. According to Australian writer, R.E. Maskell, the intention of this marketing ploy was '"to attract mainly England's middle class" which tends to abhor hire purchase as such'.[29] The other leading banks, as always, immediately followed with similar offers, but things did not quite turn out as intended. A 'war between the big banks and the hire-purchase houses' developed after the seven hundred branch United Drapery Stores (UDS), reduced its hire-purchase interest rate from 5 to 3½ per cent.[30] Before long, UDS and other hire-purchase providers were complaining that they had approached the banks 'for a reference on an intended hire purchaser only to find that the bank manager went direct to the customer and invited him to take a personal loan, or alternatively to deal with the finance house associated with the bank'.[31]

The unsecured small loan scheme, abused as it was, arguably marked the start of one of the most significant post-war developments in post-war banking. Before the war, apart from business overdraft facilities, a bank loan meant just that: a sum of money advanced at interest. A formal contract was usually drawn up only where security was to be charged and although a final settlement date was agreed, capital could be wholly or partially repaid as and when convenient to the borrower. If a balance remained outstanding, the term might be extended or a new loan granted rather than resort to legal enforcement. By the early 1960s the traditional personal bank loan had vanished and been replaced by the pre-designed 'financial product', subject to a standard contract and fixed terms, invariably including repayment by regular instalment and usually penalties for early settlement.

The 1960s also saw the start of a profound change in attitudes to owner-occupation. Mortgage providers tentatively began to dismantle the barriers to wage earners, while buyers and owners of all classes increasingly acknowledged their appreciation of the financial benefits of property investment. As Michael Heseltine would later put it: 'There is in this country a deeply ingrained desire for home ownership ... It reflects the wishes of the people, ensures the wide spread of wealth through society [and] enables people to accrue wealth for their children'.[32] Despite this ingrained desire and the general enhancement of personal prosperity, the average house price (£2,330 in 1957) would rise by no more than two to three hundred pounds per annum, or roughly in line with inflation, for over thirteen years. Then, a year after the 1970 election of Edward Heath's Conservative government, Britain experienced an unprecedented explosion in the housing market. Buyers, sometimes literally, raced one another to any estate agent with just one house offered for sale. Others queued through the night at building sites to sign unread and unquestioned binding contracts to buy at prices that had risen while they waited. Surprised house builders were swamped by demand. At times no residential property in the south of England and in all but the most depressed areas of the north, stayed on the market for more than a few hours before being snapped up at the asking price or above. The average house price that had taken the ten years until 1970 to double to £4,975 reached £7,374 in 1972 and then jumped almost 35 per cent to £9,942 in 1973.[33] At the height of the boom, former Labour MP Alan Brown was reported to have committed suicide after discovering that the buyer of the presumably palatial home he had let go for £107,000, had sold it on for £215,000 in less than three months.[34]

There is no simple explanation for the upsurge in private house buying. Heath's administration is remembered for little else than economic gloom and pessimism, hardly conducive to the confidence required to commit to an exorbitant mortgage. By 1971 inflation had risen to 8.6 per cent, the highest since the early war years (apart from a short period in 1951) and the bank rate was exceptionally high, rising to an untenable 13 per cent in November 1973. Gerald Ely, *The Times*' property correspondent, suggested that the boom was caused by a combination of factors: disillusionment with stock market investment, more readily obtainable mortgages, the 'traditional allure of bricks and mortar' and pressure on those not owning a house to acquire a freehold stake 'before it is too late'.[35] Buyers were certainly taking advantage of the government's inability to stem house-price inflation but it is surprising that Ely omits mention of the role of capital gains tax, the introduction of which in 1965 had ended Britain's tenure as a haven for successful speculators. The tax was in its formative years and the boundless opportunities to realise large unanticipated gains on sale, literally brought home the true value of the owner-occupier exemption. Also more people than ever were paying higher-rate income tax and reaping the benefits of full mortgage interest relief.[ii] Owner-occupiers new and old, 'professional house movers' and amateur property investors all watched

---

[ii]   Taxable capital gains were treated as additional income and charged at the payer's highest rate. Surtax was abolished and replaced from 6th April 1972 by unified higher rates of income tax. Full mortgage interest relief continued until 5th April 1975.

their equity growing and their mortgage debt fading before their eyes – and the final curtain falling on the culture of post-war austerity.

At the end of the war almost every Briton, including many subscribing to socialism and even to communism, had become a minor capitalist. Some did not remain so for long but that a majority did and retained the freedom to spend or to save for the lifestyle of their choice, helps explain why Britain remained relatively politically stable. Its people had fought hard, on and off the battlefields, for that cherished freedom and would never relinquish it for political conviction. Successive governments constantly struggling with economic stability possibly remained minded of the words of Sir Harold Bellman, the founder of the Building Society Association: 'The thrifty man is seldom or never an extremist agitator. To him revolution is an anathema'.[36] Similar views had been aired by commentators of every political persuasion, but from the 1960s it was no longer the thrifty man but the indebted man to whom revolution was an anathema, and the British economy had become dependent upon him for its stability.

Thrift lost its predominance over the national lifestyle. The significance of its unsolved 'Paradox' abated. Luxury was no longer quite so odious. Acquiescence to the manifest virtue of 'elegant economy' diminished. Sour-grapeism no longer offered personal solace against the privations of austerity. Conspicuous consumption, if still not invariably respectable, was no longer invariably condemned. Constant attention to personal financial affairs was no longer only for the rich and avaricious. Income tax and national insurance were no longer irrelevant to daily life. For the working classes cash was no longer the only type of money. For them, and almost everyone else, credit was continually becoming more intrusive and perplexing.

Among the prime objects of this book has been to demonstrate that attitudes to personal finance are of greater significance to modern economic and social history than has hitherto been acknowledged. The impact of the Second World War and its aftermath was to cause long entrenched attitudes to be discarded or displaced. In particular, the futile struggle against 'conspicuous consumption' to stem the rise of affluence was surrendered on recognition that its sole alternative was the still more futile struggle to maintain the affectations of 'elegant economy'.

It has been shown that the terms 'consumption', 'consumerism' and 'consumerist' defy precise definition and that only by comprising within their bounds every form of personal expenditure, including the consumption of money itself, can their historical significance be fully expounded. Expenditure on the 'ethereal' has always been a greater stimulant to change than expenditure on the 'material' to which so many commentators attach great significance. With the ending of austerity, they claim, Britain evolved into an affluent society whose lifeblood was circulated by material consumption. The true lifeblood of affluence was circulated by ethereal consumption, and while not everyone enjoyed all its benefits and pleasures, to no one was it wholly irrelevant. It caused conscious appreciation of the emotional, conventional or romantic expectancy inherent to every financial transaction, experienced by every individual, and which affected every aspect of life.

The quest for ethereal benefit and pleasure grew out of all proportion to conspicuous consumption. Expensive material possessions became sufficiently commonplace to lose some but not, of course, all their potency as symbols of social status or financial success. The ethereal product of modernity proved the more capable of satisfying ordinary people's expectancy of a more secure and fulfilled lifestyle. The pre-war instinctive dread of debt diminished in the face of such powerful incentive. And if all of this can be interpreted as the total eclipse of 'elegant economy', with a corona signalling the start of an eclipse of 'conspicuous consumption' itself by more rational attitudes to personal finance, then it was surely an evolution to the good.

Endnotes

[1] Bertrand Russell, *Authority and the Individual: The Reith Lectures 1948–49*.
[2] Marwick (2003), 122.
[3] Hobsbawm (1994), 319.
[4] NSI: Page Report (1973), Table 7: 'The Personal Savings Ratio'.
[5] Catterall, Peter, *Macmillan Diaries, Prime Minister and After 1957–1966* (2011), entry 26th July 1957, 50–51.
[6] Ibid., 9th August 1957, 54.
[7] Idem (2003), xvii.
[8] Horne, Alistair, *Macmillan 1957–1986: vol. II of the Official l Biography* (1989), 5; Sandbrook (2005), 71.
[9] Ibid., 72.
[10] Porter in Tiratsoo (1997), 119.
[11] Ibid., 121.
[12] NSI, *National Savings*, vol. 6, No. 12 (1949).
[13] Fowler (1995), 1.
[14] Sandbrook (2005), 132.
[15] Black (2003), 8, 111, 125.
[16] Priestley, J.B., *The English* (1973), 217–220; Priestley and Jacquetta Hawkes, *Journey Down a Rainbow* (1955), 51.
[17] Priestley, J.B., 'Our new Society' in *Thoughts in the Wilderness* (1957), 122.
[18] Harris et al. (1961), 28.
[19] Sir Gordon Borrie, Eleanor Rathbone Lecture, *The Credit Society – Its Benefits and Burdens*, 6th March 1986, citing the Crowther 'Report of the Committee on Consumer Credit' (1968–1971), Cmnd. 4596, 1971, 3.
[20] Ibid.
[21] Hopkins (1964), 420.
[22] HSBCGA: 0200/148, 'Report to the Chief General Manager', 5th June 1959.
[23] Ibid., memorandum 11th February 1960.
[24] LTSB: HO/GM/Adv/2, 4th May 1964, 17th June 1966.

25 LTSB: 1678, Advertising 1931–72, 'Memoranda from Advertising Committee to Board', 19th April 1968, 18th July 1969, 31st July 1970.
26 Ibid., 18th June 1971.
27 Stafford, David C., *Bank Competition and Advertising* (1982), 13, 17, 22.
28 Ibid., 66.
29 Maskell (1964), 23.
30 Ibid., 24.
31 Harris et al. (1961), citing *Financial Times*, 13th February 1959, 120; *Hire Trading*, Summer 1960.
32 Michael Heseltine, *Hansard*, 15th January 1980, col. 1445, 70.
33 Office of the Deputy Prime Minister: 'Housing Market: Prices from 1930'.
34 *Daily Mail*, 11th January 1972.
35 *The Times*, 31st December 1971.
36 Daunton (1987), 70; Ritchie, Berry, *A Key to the Door: The Abbey National Story* (1989), 96.

Selected Bibliography

Addison, Paul, *Now the War is Over: A Social History of Britain 1945–51* (London, BBC Publications, 1985).

Aldridge, Alan, *Consumption* (Cambridge, Cambridge University Press, 2003).

Barnett, Correlli, *The Audit of War: The Illusion and Reality of Britain as a Great Nation* (London, Macmillan, 1986).

Barnett, Correlli, *The Verdict of Peace: Britain Between Her Yesterday and the Future* (London, Macmillan, 2001).

Benson, John, *Affluence and Authority: A Social History of 20th Century Britain* (London, Hodder Arnold, 2005).

Berry, Christopher J., *The Idea of Luxury: A Conceptual and Historical Investigation* (Cambridge, Cambridge University Press, 1994).

Black, Lawrence, *The Political Culture of the Left in Affluent Britain, 1951–64 – Old Labour, New Britain* (Basingstoke and New York, Palgrave Macmillan, 2003).

Black, Lawrence and Pemberton, Hugh (eds), *An Affluent Society? Britain's Post-War 'Golden Age'* (Aldershot, Ashgate Publishing, 2004).

Blake, David, *Pension Schemes and Pension Funds in the United Kingdom* (Oxford, Oxford University Press, 2003).

Bonner, Arnold, *British Co-operation: The History, Principles and Organisation of the British Co-operative Movement* (Manchester, Co-operative Union, 1961).

Brendon, Piers, *Thomas Cook: 150 Years of Popular Tourism* (London, Secker and Warburg, 1991).

Brown, Callum G., *The Death of Christian Britain: Understanding Secularisation 1800–2000* (London and New York, Routledge, 2001).

Burnett, John, *A Social History of Housing 1815–1985* (London and New York, Routledge, 1993).

Cairncross, Alec, *The British Economy since 1945*, 1992 (Oxford, Blackwell, 1995).

Cassell, Michael, *Inside Nationwide: One Hundred Years of Co-operation* (Nationwide Building Society, 1984).

Catterall, Peter, *The Macmillan Diaries: The Cabinet Years, 1950–1957* (Basingstoke and Oxford, Macmillan, 2003).

Catterall, Peter, *Macmillan Diaries, Prime Minister and After 1957–66* (Basingstoke and Oxford, Macmillan, 2011).

Catterall, Peter, Seymour-Ure, Colin and Smith, Adrian (eds), *Northcliffe's Legacy: Aspects of the Popular Press*, Basingstoke (Basingstoke, Macmillan, 2000).

Clapson, Mark, *A Bit of a Flutter: Popular Gambling and English Society, c.1823–1961* (Manchester, Manchester University Press, 1992).

Clarke, Peter, *The Cripps Version: The Life of Sir Stafford Cripps, 1889–1952* (London, Allen Lane, 2002).

Clarke, Peter, *Hope and Glory: Britain 1900–2000*, 1996 (London, Penguin, 2004).

Coopey, Richard, O'Connell, Sean and Porter, Dilwyn, *Mail Order Retailing in Britain: A Business and Social History* (Oxford, Oxford University Press, 2005).

Cordery, Simon, *British Friendly Societies 1750–1914* (Basingstoke, Palgrave Macmillan, 2003).

Crisell, Andrew, *An Introductory History of British Broadcasting* (London and New York, Routledge, 1997).

Daunton, Martin J., *A Property Owning Democracy? Housing in Britain* (London, Faber and Faber, 1987).

Daunton, Martin J., *Just Taxes: The Politics of Taxation in Britain: 1914–1979* (Cambridge, Cambridge University Press, 2002).

Dell, Edmund, *The Chancellors: A History of the Chancellors of the Exchequer 1945–1990* (London, HarperCollins, 1997).

Fowler, David, *The First Teenagers: The Lifestyle of Young Wage-earners in Interwar Britain* (London, Woburn Press, 1995).

Galbraith, John Kenneth, *The Affluent Society*, 1958 (London, Penguin, 1999).

Gardiner, Juliet, *Over Here: The GIs in Wartime Britain* (London, Collins and Brown, 1992).

Gardiner, Juliet, *Wartime: Britain 1939–1945* (London, Headline Book Publishing, 2004).

Garnet, R.G., *A Century of Co-operative Insurance* (Manchester, George Allen and Unwin, 1968).

Goldthorpe, John H., *Social Mobility and Class Structure in Modern Britain*, 1980 (Oxford, Clarendon Press, 1987).

Goldthorpe, John H., Lockwood, David, Bechhofer, Frank and Platt, Jennifer, *The Affluent Worker in the Class Structure* (Cambridge, Cambridge University Press, 1969).

Hardyment, Christina, *From Mangle to Microwave: The Mechanisation of Household Work*, 1988 (Oxford, Basil Blackwell, 1990).

Harris, Ralph, Naylor, Margo and Seldon, Arthur, *Hire Purchase in Free Society* (London, Hutchinson, 1961).

Hennessy, Peter, *Never Again: Britain 1945–51* (London, Jonathan Cape, 1992).

Hennessy, Peter, *Having It So Good: Britain in the Fifties* (London, Allen Lane, Penguin, 2006).

Hilton, Matthew, *Consumerism in 20th Century Britain: The Search for a Historical Movement* (Cambridge, Cambridge University Press, 2003).

Himmelfarb, Gertrude, *The De-moralization of Society: From Victorian Virtues to Modern Values* (New York, Alfred A. Knopf, 1995).

Hobsbawm, Eric, *The Age of Extremes: The Short 20th Century 1914–1991* (London, Abacus, 2003).

Hoggart, Richard, *A Sort of Clowning: Life and Times, vol. II, 1940–1959* (London, Chatto and Windus, 1990).

Hoggart, Richard, *The Uses of Literacy: Aspects of Working-Class Life, With Special Reference to Publications and Entertainments*, 1957 (London, Penguin, 1992).

Hopkins, Harry, *The New Look: A Social History of the Forties and Fifties in Britain* (London, Secker and Warburg, 1964).

Johnson, Paul, *Saving and Spending: The Working-class Economy in Britain 1870–1939*, 1995 (Oxford, Clarendon Press, 1991).

Longmate, Norman, *How We Lived Then: A History of Everyday Life during the Second World War* (London, Hutchinson, 1971).

McKibbin, Ross, *Classes and Cultures: 1918–1951* (Oxford, Oxford University Press, 1998).

McKibbin, Ross, *The Ideologies of Class: Social Relations in Britain 1880–1950* (Oxford, Clarendon Press, 1990).

Madge, Charles, *Wartime Patterns of Saving and Spending* (Cambridge, National Institute of Economic and Social Research, 1943).

Marwick, Arthur, *British Society since 1945*, 1982 (London, Penguin Books, 2003).

Michie, Ranald, *The London Stock Exchange: A History* (Oxford, Oxford University Press, 1999).

Monod, Paul K., *The Murder of Mr Grebel: Madness and Civility in an English Town* (New Haven and London, Yale University Press, 2003).

Morgan, Kenneth O., *The People's Peace: British History 1945–1990* (Oxford, Oxford University Press, 1992).

Nightingale, Benedict, *Charities* (London, Allen Lane, 1973).

Pimlott, J.A.R., *The Englishman's Holiday: A Social History*, 1976 (Sussex, Harvester, 1976).

Porter, Marilyn, *Home, Work and Class Consciousness* (Manchester, Manchester University Press, 1983).

Prochaska, Frank, *The Voluntary Impulse: Philanthropy in Modern Britain* (London, Faber, 1988).

Prochaska, Frank, *Royal Bounty: The Making of Welfare Monarchy* (New Haven and London, Yale University Press, 1995).

Richards, Jeffrey, *Happiest Days: The Public Schools in English Fiction* (Manchester, Manchester University Press, 1988).

Richards, Jeffrey, *Films and British National Identity: From Dickens to Dad's Army* (Manchester, Manchester University Press, 1997).

Richardson, Sir William, *The CWS in War and Peace 1938–1976* (Manchester, CWS, 1977).

Rivett, Geoffrey, *From Cradle to Grave: 50 Year of NHS* (London, King's Fund Publishing, 1998).

Rubinstein, W.D., *Wealth and Inequality in Britain* (London and Boston, Faber and Faber, 1986).

Sandbrook, Dominic, *Never Had it So Good: A History of Britain from Suez to the Beatles* (London, Little Brown, 2005).

Sissons, Michael and French, Philip (eds), *Age of Austerity, 1945–51* (London, Hodder and Stoughton, 1963).

Stacey, Margaret, *Tradition and Change: A Study of Banbury*, 1960 (London, Oxford University Press, 1970).

Stearns, Peter N., *Consumerism in World History: The Global Transformation of Desire* (London and New York, Routledge, 2001).

Tebbutt, Melanie, *Making Ends Meet: Pawnbroking and Working Class Credit* (Leicester, Leicester University Press, 1983).

Thane, Pat, *Foundations of the Welfare State* (London and New York, Longman, 1982).

Thomas, Donald, *An Underworld at War: Spivs, Deserters, Racketeers and Civilians in the Second World War* (London, John Murray, 2004).

Thompson, Paul and Courtney, Cathy, *City Lives: The Changing Voice of British Finance* (London, Methuen, 1996).

Tiratsoo, Nick (ed.), *From Blitz to Blair: A New History of Britain since 1939* (London, Weidenfeld and Nicolson, 1997).

Veblen, Thorstein, *The Theory of the Leisure Class: An Economic Study in Institutions*, 1899 (London, George Allen and Unwin, 1924).

Williamson, Bill, *The Temper of the Times: British Society since World War II* (Oxford, Basil Blackwell Ltd, 1990).

Zelizer, Viviana, A., *The Social Meaning of Money, Pin Money, Paychecks, Poor Relief, and Other Currencies* (New York, Harper and Collins, 1994).

Zweiniger-Bargielowska, Ina, *Austerity in Britain: Rationing, Controls and Consumption 1939–1955*, 2000 (Oxford, Oxford University Press, 2004).

Index

Modern Economic and Social History Series

General Editor
Derek H. Aldcroft, University Fellow, Department of Economic and Social
History,
University of Leicester, UK

Patrick Duffy
The Skilled Compositor, 1850–1914
An Aristocrat Among Working Men
0 7546 0255 9 (2000)

Robert Conlon and John Perkins
Wheels and Deals
The Automotive Industry in Twentieth-Century Australia
0 7546 0405 5 (2001)

Geoffrey Channon
Railways in Britain and the United States, 1830–1940
Studies in Economic and Business History
1 84014 253 7 (2001)

Sam Mustafa
Merchants and Migrations
Germans and Americans in Connection, 1776–1835
0 7546 0590 6 (2001)

Bernard Cronin
Technology, Industrial Conflict and the Development of Technical Education in
19th-Century England
0 7546 0313 X (2001)

Andrew Popp
Business Structure, Business Culture and the Industrial District
The Potteries, c. 1850–1914
0 7546 0176 5 (2001)

Scott Kelly
The Myth of Mr Butskell
The Politics of British Economic Policy, 1950–55
0 7546 0604 X (2002)

Michael Ferguson
The Rise of Management Consulting in Britain
0 7546 0561 2 (2002)

Alan Fowler
Lancashire Cotton Operatives and Work, 1900–1950
A Social History of Lancashire Cotton Operatives in the Twentieth Century
0 7546 0116 1 (2003)

John F. Wilson and Andrew Popp (eds)
Industrial Clusters and Regional Business Networks in England, 1750–1970
0 7546 0761 5 (2003)

John Hassan
The Seaside, Health and the Environment in England and Wales since 1800
1 84014 265 0 (2003)
Marshall J. Bastable

Arms and the State
Sir William Armstrong and the Remaking of British Naval Power, 1854–1914
0 7546 3404 3 (2004)

Robin Pearson
Insuring the Industrial Revolution
Fire Insurance in Great Britain, 1700–1850
0 7546 3363 2 (2004)

Andrew Dawson
Lives of the Philadelphia Engineers
Capital, Class and Revolution, 1830–1890
0 7546 3396 9 (2004)

Lawrence Black and Hugh Pemberton (eds)
An Affluent Society?
Britain's Post-War 'Golden Age' Revisited
0 7546 3528 7 (2004)

Joseph Harrison and David Corkill
Spain
A Modern European Economy
0 7546 0145 5 (2004)

Ross E. Catterall and Derek H. Aldcroft (eds)
Exchange Rates and Economic Policy in the 20th Century
1 84014 264 2 (2004)

Armin Grünbacher
Reconstruction and Cold War in Germany
The Kreditanstalt für Wiederaufbau (1948–1961)
0 7546 3806 5 (2004)

Till Geiger
Britain and the Economic Problem of the Cold War
The Political Economy and the Economic Impact
of the British Defence Effort, 1945–1955
0 7546 0287 7 (2004)

Anne Clendinning
Demons of Domesticity
Women and the English Gas Industry, 1889–1939
0 7546 0692 9 (2004)

Timothy Cuff
The Hidden Cost of Economic Development
The Biological Standard of Living in Antebellum Pennsylvania
0 7546 4119 8 (2005)

Julian Greaves
Industrial Reorganization and Government Policy in Interwar Britain
0 7546 0355 5 (2005)

Derek H. Aldcroft
Europe's Third World
The European Periphery in the Interwar Years
0 7546 0599 X (2006)

James P. Huzel
The Popularization of Malthus in Early Nineteenth-Century England
Martineau, Cobbett and the Pauper Press
0 7546 5427 3 (2006)

Richard Perren
Taste, Trade and Technology
The Development of the International Meat Industry since 1840
978 0 7546 3648 9 (2006)

Roger Lloyd-Jones and M.J. Lewis
Alfred Herbert Ltd and the British Machine Tool Industry, 1887–1983
978 0 7546 0523 2 (2006)

Anthony Howe and Simon Morgan (eds)
Rethinking Nineteenth-Century Liberalism
Richard Cobden Bicentenary Essays
978 0 7546 5572 5 (2006)

Espen Moe
Governance, Growth and Global Leadership
The Role of the State in Technological Progress, 1750–2000
978 0 7546 5743 9 (2007)

Peter Scott
Triumph of the South
A Regional Economic History of Early Twentieth Century Britain
978 1 84014 613 4 (2007)

David Turnock
Aspects of Independent Romania's Economic History with Particular Reference
to Transition for EU Accession
978 0 7546 5892 4 (2007)

David Oldroyd
Estates, Enterprise and Investment at the Dawn of the Industrial Revolution
Estate Management and Accounting in the North-East of England, c.1700–1780
978 0 7546 3455 3 (2007)

Ralf Roth and Günter Dinhobl (eds)
Across the Borders
Financing the World's Railways in the Nineteenth and Twentieth Centuries
978 0 7546 6029 3 (2008)

Vincent Barnett and Joachim Zweynert (eds)
Economics in Russia
Studies in Intellectual History
978 0 7546 6149 8 (2008)

Raymond E. Dumett (ed.)
Mining Tycoons in the Age of Empire, 1870–1945
Entrepreneurship, High Finance, Politics and Territorial Expansion
978 0 7546 6303 4 (2009)

Peter Dorey
British Conservatism and Trade Unionism, 1945–1964
978 0 7546 6659 2 (2009)

Shigeru Akita and Nicholas J. White (eds)
The International Order of Asia in the 1930s and 1950s
978 0 7546 5341 7 (2010)

Myrddin John Lewis, Roger Lloyd-Jones, Josephine Maltby
and Mark David Matthews
Personal Capitalism and Corporate Governance
British Manufacturing in the First Half of the Twentieth Century
978 0 7546 5587 9 (2010)

John Murphy
A Decent Provision
Australian Welfare Policy, 1870 to 1949
978 1 4094 0759 1 (2011)

Robert Lee (ed.)
Commerce and Culture
Nineteenth-Century Business Elites
978 0 7546 6398 0 (2011)